PRAISE FOR
SPIN MASTERS

"*Spin Masters* shows just how far to the left the news media have lurched. There are other ways to study media bias, but Freddoso's book is a lot more fun than poring through the first forty-two Gail Collins columns in the *New York Times* about Mitt Romney driving with a dog on the roof of his car. (The dog liked it!)"

—**Ann Coulter,**
New York Times bestselling author of *Mugged*

"David Freddoso's terrific new book *Spin Masters* documents more than routine media bias—though he has plenty of outrageous examples of that. It's about how the media ignored or buried the big stories—like how Obama has hollowed out our economy or openly trampled on the Constitution—in favor of Democratic Party press releases. Freddoso reports the news you didn't hear during the election—and also shows how we can avoid falling prey to the hypocritical and absurdly partisan liberal media again."

—**David Limbaugh,**
New York Times bestselling author of *The Great Destroyer*

"If you had a scintilla of respect left for the mainstream media, David Freddoso's excellent new book *Spin Masters* will shred it. He reports on the big stories the mainstream media didn't and shows how if you relied on the mainstream media, you would have been less well informed than if you turned off your radio and television and cancelled your newspaper subscription."

—**David Harsanyi,**
author of *Obama's Four Horsemen*

"Media bias mostly takes the form of omission. In 2012, the media mostly omitted mention of Obama's many offenses against ethics, good-government, and the truth. In *Spin Masters*, David Freddoso deftly tells the stories that most of the mainstream media missed because a dog on the roof of a car was more interesting than, say, an illegal military intervention in Libya or serial abuse of presidential power. I challenge anyone to read this book and then honestly deny that Obama's reelection was aided by a media that didn't do its job right."

—**Timothy P. Carney,**
senior political columnist, *Washington Examiner*

"Conservatives need to know they are not just up against political activists on the left. They are also up against a media that leans left, regurgitates left-wing talking points, and transitions back and forth between left-wing institutions and the mainstream media. David Freddoso does an excellent job shedding light on just what conservatives are up against and what they must do to fight back."

—**Erick Erickson,**
editor of RedState.com

"Freddoso not only shows how deeply in the Obama tank many journalists were in 2012. He also serves as an alternate-universe assignment desk for the stories unbiased reporters might have written."

—**Byron York,**
chief political correspondent, *Washington Examiner*

SPIN MASTERS

SPIN
MASTERS

HOW THE MEDIA IGNORED THE REAL NEWS
AND HELPED REELECT BARACK OBAMA

DAVID FREDDOSO

New York Times bestselling author of *The Case Against Barack Obama*

Since 1947
**REGNERY
PUBLISHING, INC.**
An Eagle Publishing Company • Washington, DC

Cataloging-in-Publication data on file with the Library of Congress

ISBN 978-1-62157-080-6

Published in the United States by
Regnery Publishing, Inc.
One Massachusetts Avenue NW
Washington, DC 20001
www.Regnery.com

Manufactured in the United States of America
10 9 8 7 6 5 4 3 2 1
Books are available in quantity for promotional or premium use. Write to Director of Special Sales, Regnery Publishing, Inc., One Massachusetts Avenue NW, Washington, DC 20001, for information on discounts and terms, or call (202) 216-0600.

Distributed to the trade by
Perseus Distribution
250 West 57th Street
New York, NY 10107

To my children.
"Et cognoscetis veritatem et veritas liberabit vos."
Jn 8:32

CONTENTS

CHAPTER ONE

A GREAT, SLOBBERING LOVE AFFAIR CONTINUED

S *late*, the online magazine, has a laudable quadrennial tradition. Before each presidential election, its staffers disclose to the public how they intend to vote.

The first year they did this, in 2000, Democrat Al Gore won 78.4 percent of their support, and Republican George W. Bush won 10.8 percent.[1] In 2004, John Kerry had the backing of 84.9 percent of *Slate*'s staff.[2]

In 2008, Barack Obama was backed by fifty-five staffers out of fifty-eight, and John McCain by just one. (Another respondent answered merely, "Not McCain.")[3] As you may recall, Obama got a bit less than 94.8 percent from the general population in that election. In 2012, Obama again received a much smaller share of the popular vote than the 83.8 percent that *Slate's* staff gave him.[4]

I admire *Slate* for disclosing how its writers vote, providing a look inside the minds of political journalists whose work I enjoy. But obviously, what stands out here is their degree of ideological uniformity.

It isn't just *Slate*. In 1981, academics S. Robert Lichter and Stanley Rothman, who later wrote *The Media Elite*, surveyed 240 journalists at some of the nation's most prestigious national media organizations. They found that four in five, 80 percent, had voted Democratic in *all four* of the presidential elections between 1964 and 1976, including the Nixon landslide of 1972.[5] Rothman followed up with a similar survey in 1995 and found that 91 percent of journalists had voted for Bill Clinton in 1992—a year when he received just 43 percent of the popular vote.[6]

When it comes to their political giving, journalists are even more slanted. In 2008, William Tate of *Investor's Business Daily* found that twenty journalists gave to Obama for every one who gave to John McCain.[7] *Political Moneyline* (now *CQ Moneyline*) found in July 2004 that ninety-three journalists gave to John Kerry for every one who gave to George W. Bush.[8]

It would be too much to expect newsrooms to look—politically speaking—like America does. But 90 percent voting Democrat? It's difficult to get that many people in a poll to say they like apple pie.

Journalism is one of the most influential professions, and also one of the most thoroughly and consistently politically lopsided. The media have a political party, and they are far more loyal in their partisanship than many of the voter blocs that probably come to mind when you think of partisan loyalty: Evangelical Christians, union members, Mormons, atheists—all of those groups are bastions of independent thought compared to journalists when it comes to their political thinking and voting patterns.

It's More Than Bias

Conservatives often overdo it when they criticize media bias. They find it in every unfavorable story and sometimes in places where it doesn't matter. I'll say it: they whine too much. But that doesn't mean they're wrong. Former CBS News reporter Bernard Goldberg put it this way in *Bias* (2001), his seminal and bestselling book:

> Some right-wing ideologues do blame "the liberal news media" for everything from crime to cancer. But that doesn't detract from another truth: that, by and large, the media elites really are liberal. And Democrats, too. And both affect their news judgment.[9]

Bias was one of the first books I read after coming to Washington in 2001. There's a reason it made number one on the *New York Times* bestseller list and stayed on the list for nineteen weeks, seven of them in the top slot. It provided an insider's confirmation of a very real phenomenon—liberal media bias—that had irked conservatives for decades. *Bias* provided concrete examples of the subtle and overt ways that media bias affects coverage of the issues of the day.

Thanks to works like *The Media Elite* and *Bias*, and organizations like the Media Research Center, Americans aren't really surprised anymore when they hear, say, a story about a room full of reporters at a presidential debate cheering at a good Obama debate line, as they did on October 17, 2012.[10]

A participant in one of Frank Luntz's post-debate focus groups might have been a bit foul-mouthed but he was not alone when he complained about the media's role in creating, promoting, and propping up the Obama presidency:

> That's why I voted for him [in 2008]. I bought his bull. And he's lied about everything, he hasn't provided, he

hasn't come through on anything, and he's been bullsh--
ting the public with the media behind him.[11]

Most journalists claim that they report the news as it is, and that
they do not allow their personal political beliefs to influence how
they report it. Objectivity, every aspiring reporter is taught, is a first
principle of journalism. That is true even for opinion journalists and
commentators, who also have a responsibility to present facts in a
reasonable, honest way—and who, at their best, make a point of
confronting facts that are inconvenient to the positions they take.

But no one is without biases. Any journalist, liberal or conservative, can report facts fairly. Even so, any journalist who thinks he's
perfectly unbiased is only deceiving himself.

The political coverage in 2012 was very biased. This book will
explore many of the stories that bias prompted the media to ignore,
and others that it prompted the media to tell *ad nauseam* despite
their relative lack of importance.

Why does this happen? As Goldberg writes in both *Bias* and his
2009 book, *A Slobbering Love Affair*, it's not that the heads of the
media world are in some tall Manhattan building, consciously trying
to slant the news and help the political party they like. They are more
often prisoners to their own worldview, unable to recognize a good
story (or its significance) if it falls outside of it. And this organic,
institutional bias is further reinforced by their colleagues' ideological
uniformity. If they are exposed to any conservative arguments at all,
they are usually weak and poorly grounded ones. As Goldberg put it:

> The problem, in a word, is groupthink. There simply are
> too many like-minded people in America's most important
> newsrooms, and like-mindedness has a way of reinforcing
> biases....

...Yes, it is theoretically possible for journalists to be overwhelmingly liberal, and to overwhelmingly support Democratic candidates for president, and still be fair and objective in their journalism. But realistically, and in practice, there's no way. That liberal bias seeps into just about everything the media touch. The problem is that life inside the liberal media bubble is too comfortable. It dulls the senses. It turns even well-educated journalists into narrow-minded provincial rubes.... It lulls journalists into thinking that they really are fair and honest brokers of information.[12]

If Goldberg's talk of narrow-mindedness seems too strong, think back to the most spectacular journalistic failure of this century. Dan Rather's downfall in 2004 came as a result of his instinctual willingness to believe anything negative about George W. Bush—anything! When a document of dubious provenance fell into his lap (it purported to document a backroom political deal that won Bush special treatment during the Vietnam War), he put it on the air with hardly a second thought.[13] When you're certain enough about your conclusion, any proof will do.

One can certainly fail without failing as dramatically as Rather did. An instinctual *unwillingness to believe anything bad* about a president results in journalistic failures, too—failures that don't end careers, but that do result in important stories never being told, and in journalists bending over backwards to defend politicians they like in a way they never would for politicians they don't like.

The flashy meltdowns on national television—the moments when overt bias spills over into coverage—have a very high entertainment value. They can be ridiculous and embarrassing for all involved. The 2012 election saw its fair share, and many will be discussed in this book.

But this book is not just about the awkward Obama cheerleading that occurred in some segments of the leg-tingling media. The deeper problem is the more subtle one. At the highest levels of journalism, editorial judgments are made about what matters and what deserves coverage. And yes, facts are facts, but their significance may not be obvious to someone whose view of the world is sufficiently one-dimensional.

In the coverage of the 2012 presidential race, news judgments generally sided with fluff, often coming straight from President Obama's campaign, over substance. This made campaign coverage, in a word, stupider. It also made it a lot more helpful to Obama. The parade of bright shiny objects that distracts from the pain voters feel—of economic failure, of seeing their money wasted by a government that's taking away their freedoms and claiming new, unprecedented powers every day—is exactly what an incumbent with a shaky record needs most.

On his trip to Poland in late July 2012, GOP presidential nominee Mitt Romney visited the Tomb of the Unknown Soldier in Warsaw—a solemn site filled with more sorrowful and painful memories than Americans have at Arlington Cemetery. The American press, roped off at a distance, shouted out—or really, whined out—their profound questions after him. Here were three of the five:

> CNN: "Governor Romney are you concerned about some of the mishaps of your trip?"

> *Washington Post*: "What about your gaffes?"

> *New York Times*: "Governor Romney do you feel that your gaffes have overshadowed your foreign trip?"[14]

Ladies and gentlemen, that was your media during Campaign 2012. The CNN journalist then shouted out a fourth question, noting that Romney hadn't been taking many questions from the press during his trip to Europe. But if these were the kind of questions they were asking, it's hard to see this as a big loss. How would Romney have even answered? "I am quite concerned about my gaffes"? Or perhaps: "My gaffes are the best gaffes; that's what I like about them"?

Yes, there was good journalism done in 2012. There were keen insights and hard-hitting stories published. But on aggregate, the press let the public down. And the public noticed.

The Pew Center for Excellence in Journalism released its post-election scorecard poll on November 15. The press received a gentleman's C-minus—the lowest of any entity graded, and a lower grade than either campaign. But that wasn't the most significant finding. In 2008, 57 percent of respondents told Pew that there was "more discussion of the issues than usual" during the election. In 2012, only 38 percent thought so, and 51 percent thought that the issues were discussed "less than usual."[15] That was the political media's net contribution in 2012.

For example, the most important issue for many valuable days in the life of the Republic in 2012 was whether someone was going to ban birth control. No one had proposed any such thing, and no one running for president—no, not even Rick Santorum—supported it. But it became the burning issue anyway, and this was made possible when a Democratic operative-turned-television-journalist asked a question about it in a Republican presidential primary debate. In fact, George Stephanopoulos kept repeating the question until the debate audience booed him. From that moment on, the media provided a megaphone for the Obama campaign, so that it could carry this non-issue well into the late stages of the race. Months after that debate, NBC News Anchor Brian Williams would remark on air, "Who woke up in the Republican Party one day recently and said, 'I know what we'll go after, let's go after reproductive rights?' What was that about?"

For several days, the entire 2012 election seemed to hang on this purely academic question: In the event abortion was somehow made illegal nationwide (care to calculate the odds of this?), what would a Republican president do with respect to the 1 percent of abortions performed in cases of rape? It was not enough that one politician self-immolated by speaking of "legitimate rape" and asserting some utter nonsense about reproductive biology. The media helped Obama's campaign tease that out into countless news segments and stories, so that every Republican in America had to be asked about it. It became the most important topic in American politics for some time.

Then there was the war on Big Bird. Then there was the preoccupation with every Republican criticism of President Obama as a sign of latent, or overt, racism. There were endless charges of voter suppression, prompted by entirely reasonable attempts to have voters produce identification at the polls, as they must in nearly every other nation on earth where the people have a right to vote.

All of this came at the expense of coverage of the many serious issues that surrounded the 2012 election. Here are a few stories that ended up on the short end of that equation:

- A "recovery" was underway in which a wraith-like version of the job market was rising from the grave to replace what had been there before the financial crisis. Mid-career workers (age twenty-five to fifty-four) were in a persistent labor market depression that included no jobs recovery at all.
- More and more people who had lost full-time jobs were forced to settle for part-time ones (which helped keep the unemployment rate low), and unprecedented numbers had no choice but to go on government assistance.

- President Obama's policy of drone strikes—including on U.S. citizens—imposed a death penalty without trial on a sixteen-year-old boy, whose only apparent crime was being the son of a terrorist.
- The president unilaterally brought the United States into a war without seeking or receiving congressional approval.
- A U.S. ambassador was murdered on the anniversary of the 9/11 attacks, possibly because of official negligence. The president, the secretary of state, and other high-level administration officials all rushed to blame a YouTube video, despite that explanation's *prima facie* improbability and intelligence information to the contrary.
- The president's extensive foreign policy efforts at rapprochement with the Arab world utterly failed to win it over.
- Al Qaeda was making a comeback, despite the death of Osama bin Laden.
- The president circumvented constitutional restrictions on his office by making "recess" appointments when the Senate was not even in recess.
- With an executive privilege claim, the president of the United States officially involved himself in covering up a law enforcement scandal that had resulted in numerous deaths.
- President Obama and his administration stubbornly defended a failing policy of wasting billions in taxpayers' money on dodgy clean energy projects and green job training that hadn't created any jobs.
- The transformational president who promised to set pettiness aside and work across the aisle centered his

reelection campaign on wedge issues—especially social issues—to divide America and distract people from economic conditions.

These stories could have made a real difference in how people viewed the Obama presidency. They were suppressed. The media had more important things to cover, like Mitt Romney's gaffes, his dog, a fictitious "War on Women," and Big Bird.

In some cases, stories that did deserve coverage—like Romney's refusal to release his tax returns—were given such a ridiculously disproportionate airing that substantive stories about Obama's presidency were buried in heaps of straw. Obama's campaign team could not have possibly expected as much help from the media as it actually got.

It wasn't just the distractions or the suppression, but also the tone of the coverage that worked in Obama's favor. The Pew Center's study on coverage of the candidates tells an interesting story. Between August 27 and October 23, the heart of the campaign, the body of stories written and broadcast about Romney was only about 27 percent more negative and 21 percent less positive than the body of Obama coverage. Believe it or not, that's not bad by U.S. media standards—in 2008, Pew found that Obama got nearly 89 percent more positive coverage than Republican John McCain.

But Pew also broke out the numbers for the five weeks before the brightest moment of Romney's campaign—the first presidential debate on October 3. Romney won that debate so decisively that the media had to give him some good ink. Before that happened, the body of Obama coverage was indeed 100 percent more positive than Romney coverage (22 percent of stories on Obama were positive versus 11 percent for Romney). And coverage of Romney was also 63 percent more negative than Obama coverage (44 percent of stories versus 27 percent).[16]

It would be wrong to expect perfectly equal coverage—candidates earn negatives sometimes, and Romney certainly earned his share. But the media's collective judgment about what merits negative coverage, and how much of it, is rather arbitrary, and it's hard to avoid the conclusion that it mirrors journalists' documented groupthink in matters of political opinion. Somehow, for example, Romney's hasty reaction to the embassy protests on September 11 became a bigger story than the Benghazi attack, the murder of Ambassador Christopher Stevens, and a presidential administration's rush to blame it all on a YouTube video. It was as clear a case of horserace coverage trumping substance as there ever has been.

For all that, Romney did deserve negative coverage. Team Obama's efforts to portray him as a heartless plutocrat never did as much damage to Romney as he did to himself with his comments about the "47 percent." But you might not be surprised that Romney's "47 percent" got considerably more play than, say, Obama's comments during his first presidential campaign about the people who live in flyover country:

> It's not surprising then they get bitter, they cling to guns or religion or antipathy to people who aren't like them or anti-immigrant sentiment or anti-trade sentiment as a way to explain their frustrations.[17]

Don't forget: in a very similar, closed-door fundraising situation with committed supporters, Obama had written off the same percentage of Americans as Romney did. He was never subjected to nearly so much coverage as punishment, especially once the 2008 election began. Again, media groupthink. How can political journalists be expected to recognize Obama's comments as a story when so many of them share that condescending view of the average Republican voter in the heartland?

For conservatives to demand gentler coverage for Republicans would be to miss the point—and frankly, to ask for something bad for the country. The problem isn't that journalists are too hard on Republicans. The problem is that they often won't do journalism at all unless they are covering a Republican. My *Washington Examiner* colleague Tim Carney remarked jokingly during the 2012 campaign that he hoped Mitt Romney would win, so that America could go back to having an anti-war movement again. I'll go one further: a Romney win would have meant we could have had journalism again.

Did the media win the election for Obama? It's not an easy question to answer. Mitt Romney did many things wrong in the 2012 campaign, and he may have deserved to lose on those grounds alone. Obama did many things right, and on those grounds he may have deserved to win. There is no certain way to know whether Obama wouldn't have won anyway without getting so much help from the media.

But why should we ever have to ask such a question?

On June 14, 2012, President Obama was raising campaign cash at the Manhattan home of Sarah Jessica Parker—one of the dozens of celebrity fundraisers he held during the campaign (that's another story not often mentioned). He told the star-studded crowd, "You're the ultimate arbiter of which direction this country goes."[18]

Joseph Pulitzer had a different take. His most enduring quotation is enshrined in the lobby of Columbia's Graduate School of Journalism along with his statue:

> Our Republic and its press will rise or fall together. An able, disinterested, public-spirited press, with trained intelligence to know the right and courage to do it, can preserve that public virtue without which popular government is a sham and a mockery. A cynical, mercenary, demagogic

press will produce in time a people as base as itself. The power to mold the future of the Republic will be in the hands of the journalists of future generations.

The future is in the journalists' hands. How do you think they did in 2012?

CHAPTER TWO

THE MEDIA
MAKES
A PRESIDENT

*"It's one of the great political myths, about press bias.
Most reporters don't know whether they're Republican or
Democrat, and vote every which way."*

—CBS News Anchor Dan Rather, February 8, 1995[1]

During his quick ascent from an anonymous state senator to a U.S. senator, Barack Obama encountered what can only be described as an adoring media. Obama himself conceded in his biography *The Audacity of Hope* that during his political rise he was "the beneficiary of unusually—and at times undeservedly—positive press coverage."[2]

That's putting it mildly. As *Politico*'s John F. Harris told CNN's *Reliable Sources* in January 2008, "A couple years ago, you would send a reporter out with Obama, and it was like they needed to go through detox when they came back—'Oh, he's so impressive, he's so charismatic,' and we're kind of like, 'Down, boy.'"[3]

The media's adoration of Obama reached its crescendo during his 2008 presidential run. In *A Slobbering Love Affair*, Bernard

Goldberg contends that the media didn't "merely spin the news to help the Democrats; this time they *de facto* enlisted in the Obama campaign. And they didn't give a damn what you or anybody else thought about it."[4]

After Obama won the Iowa caucuses, an NBC News correspondent admitted that "it's almost hard to remain objective" when covering Obama.[5] He was right, except perhaps for the "almost." Obama was described by the Obama-adoring opinion columnist Mark Morford as a "Lightworker...who can actually help usher in *a new way of being on the planet.*"[6] Morford somehow avoided dying of embarrassment for putting that sentence on paper.

Obama's words provoked a physiological response in some journalists. MSNBC's Chris Matthews reacted in such a way that even fellow Obamaphile Keith Olbermann had to rein him in.

> Chris Matthews: "I have to tell you, you know, it's part of reporting this case, this election, the feeling most people get when they hear Barack Obama's speech. My—I felt this thrill going up my leg. I mean, I don't have that too often."
>
> Co-anchor Keith Olbermann: "Steady."
>
> Matthews: "No, seriously. It's a dramatic event. He speaks about America in a way that has nothing to do with politics. It has to do with the feeling we have about our country. And that is an objective assessment."[7]

Matthews' "thrill going up my leg" earned him a lot of derision, all of it deserved. But it was his claim to objectivity that was most absurd. As Goldberg noted, Matthews had essentially enlisted as a freelancer in the Obama campaign—and didn't give a damn who knew it.

"Obama deserved tougher scrutiny than he got," the *Washington Post*'s ombudsman reported days after the 2008 election. This was especially true of his "undergraduate years, his start in Chicago and his relationship with Antoin 'Tony' Rezko, who was convicted this year of influence-peddling in Chicago."[8]

ABC's Jake Tapper conceded that the media "tilt[ed]...the scales a little bit" for Obama in 2008.[9] *New York* magazine political reporter John Heilemann wrote that "No person with eyes in his head in 2008 could have failed to see the way that soft coverage helped to propel Obama first to the Democratic nomination and then into the White House."[10]

The Center for Media and Public Affairs at George Mason University found that of 585 network news stories during a crucial five-week stretch of the campaign, 65 percent of the coverage Obama received was favorable, while just 36 percent of the coverage McCain got was positive.[11]

A Pew Research Center Project for Excellence in Journalism study found that the media's coverage of the presidential campaign was skewed more than 2 to 1 in favor of Barack Obama.[12]

More important than *whether* a news outlet is biased is *how* that bias affects election outcomes. Leading up to the 2004 election, *Newsweek* assistant managing editor Evan Thomas said he felt the establishment media wanted John Kerry to win, and that the consequent bias was "worth maybe 15 points."[13]

Perhaps that's an exaggeration, but in 2008, Barack Obama told a reporter, "I am convinced that if there were no Fox News, I might be two or three points higher in the polls."[14]

The adoration continued through Obama's first term. *Newsweek*'s Evan Thomas said at one point that Obama's approach to world affairs made him "sort of God" who's "going to bring all different sides together."[15]

ABC *Nightline* co-anchor Terry Moran compared Obama to the nation's first president. "I like to say that, in some ways, Barack Obama is the first President since George Washington to be taking a step down into the Oval Office," he said.[16]

Former *Newsweek* editor Jon Meacham compared Obama to another founding father, telling an NBC *Today* audience after Obama's reelection, that Thomas Jefferson "was a tall, cool, cerebral president who won re-election, who was actually really good at politics even though he didn't want to act as though he was. So there's some similarities with President Obama."[17]

CNN host Piers Morgan revealed to Obama strategist David Axelrod what he loves about Obama.

> When you watch the President like that, I always feel he's got so many pluses, doesn't he? In a sense, he's personable, he's handsome, he can be funny. You know, abroad he has this great image for America. A lot of things are just perfect about Barack Obama.[18]

That's the easy part of love. The hard part comes when things go badly. And when things started to go south politically—when unemployment rose and Obama's approval ratings declined—the media proved themselves worthy lovers. They even chided the public for failing to appreciate the greatness of Obama's achievements.

"People don't appreciate some of the amazing legislative agenda that he's accomplished," was the rebuke from ABC's Christiane Amanpour.[19]

Journalist Andrew Sullivan became one of Obama's chief defenders during his first term. "Given the enormity of what he inherited, and given what he explicitly promised, it remains simply a fact that Obama has delivered in a way that the unhinged right and purist left have yet to understand or absorb," Sullivan wrote in a *Newsweek* cover story in early 2012.

> What I see in front of my nose is a President whose character, record, and promise remain as grotesquely underappreciated now as they were absurdly hyped in 2008. And I feel confident that sooner rather than later, the American people will come to see his first term from the same calm, sane perspective. And decide to finish what they started.[20]

Of course, nobody could top MSNBC's Chris Matthews in over-the-top Obama adoration. "This guy's done everything right," Matthews said one night on his show, *Hardball with Chris Matthews*.

> He's raised his family right, he's fought his way all the way to the top of the *Harvard Law Review*, in a blind test becomes head of the *Review*, the top editor there. Everything he's done is clean as a whistle. He's never not only broken any law, he's never done anything wrong. He's the perfect father, the perfect husband, the perfect American and all they do is trash the guy.[21]

The media strained for its metaphors as it touted Obama's few successes. Howard Fineman remarked that in his targeting of Osama bin Laden, Obama "proved himself—vividly, in almost Biblical terms—to be an effective commander-in-chief of the armed forces of the United States."[22]

On the first anniversary of the Navy SEAL raid that killed Osama bin Laden, NBC *Nightly News* anchor Brian Williams interviewed

Obama about his decision to authorize the raid, putting the stakes in overly dramatic terms:

> You had to go to Tuscaloosa. You had to go have fun at the Correspondents' Dinner. Seth Meyers makes a joke about Osama bin Laden. How do you keep an even keel? Even when we look back on the videotape of that night, there's no real depiction that there's something afoot.... If this had failed in spectacular fashion, it would have blown up your presidency, I think, by all estimates. It would have been your Waterloo, and, perhaps your Watergate, consumed with hearings and inquiries. How thick did the specter of Jimmy Carter, Desert One hang in the air here?[23]

Obama's Waterloo? His Watergate? I think it's safe to assume the media wouldn't have made such comparisons had the raid failed.

Even as Obama's first term failed to live up to the hype, the media refused to abandon him. They were too invested. In fact, when they weren't praising him to the skies, journalists and other employees within the bubble of media companies were also opening their wallets for him.

An August 2012 piece in the *New York Times* found that "Donations by Media Companies Tilt Heavily to Obama" and that "all the major media companies...have made larger contributions to President Obama than to his rival, former Gov. Mitt Romney."[24]

The *Times* noted that even "conservative" news outlets such as Rupert Murdoch's News Corporation, which owns Fox News, the *Wall Street Journal* and the *New York Post*, among other media outlets, gave significantly more money to Obama than to Romney.

The numbers are staggering. Among News Corporation employees, eight of the top ten donation recipients were Democrats. In 2008

News Corp. employees contributed more than $10 to Obama for every $1 they gave to John McCain.[25]

According to the non-partisan Center for Responsive Politics, employees at Time Warner, which owns CNN and *Time* magazine, gave nearly $200,000 to Obama and just $10,750 to Romney. At the Walt Disney Company, which owns ESPN and ABC and controls a fair share of America's entertainment content as well, employees contributed $125,856 to Obama and $9,950 to Romney. Similar contrasts were evident in the contributions of employees from NBC and other top media companies.[26]

Revolving Door

Sometimes, it isn't enough for members of the media to act as if they're on the Obama administration's payroll. Many of them have gone the whole hog, as Obama has hired a curiously large number of former journalists.

After Obama was elected, many journalists who covered candidate Obama couldn't wait to start working for their new president. The *New York Times* commented days after Obama's inauguration in January 2009, "An unusual number of journalists from prominent, mainstream organizations started new government jobs in January, providing new kindling to the debate over whether Obama is receiving unusually favorable treatment in the news media."[27] The *Times* reported:

> These are not opinionated talkers in the vein of Chris Matthews.... Rather, they are, for the most part, more traditional journalists from organizations that strive to approach the news with objectivity.[28]

By my colleague Paul Bedard's tally, by early 2012, nineteen journalists and media executives had gone on to jobs in the Obama administration or center-left groups supporting him and his agenda. Bedard counted five from the *Washington Post*, three from ABC, and three from CNN.[29]

The chart below shows a partial list of journalists who have entered the Obama administration.

Name	Media Organization	Obama Administration Position
Jay Carney	*Time*	White House Press Secretary
Shailagh Murray	*Washington Post*	Vice President Joe Biden's Communications Director
Stephen Barr	*Washington Post*	Senior Managing Director of the Office of Public Affairs, Labor Department
Warren Bass	*Washington Post*	Speech writer for U.N Ambassador Susan Rice
Linda Douglass	ABC/*National Journal*	Spokeswoman, Department of Health and Human Services
Sasha Johnson	CNN	Press Secretary, Department of Transportation
Peter Gosselin	*Los Angeles Times*	Speechwriter for Treasury Secretary Timothy Geithner
Jill Zuckman	*Chicago Tribune*	Director of Public Affairs, Department of Transportation

There used to be a stigma attached to reporters who crossed over to work for those they once covered. With Obama, it's become more commonplace.

Battered Journalist Syndrome

But for all the love they give him, Barack Obama seems to loathe the media. Not just the conservative media, but also most of the mainstream political press that sings his praises.

Obama's abuse of the media has intensified throughout his presidency, yet most journalists still treat him with an adoration and deference that isn't really healthy for democracy. One could almost say they suffer from battered journalist syndrome.

Though a writer himself, Obama has long felt animosity toward the Fourth Estate. In the prologue to *The Audacity of Hope*, Obama groups the media in with other bad guys (money, interest groups, the legislative process) as examples of "institutional forces...that stifle even the best-intentioned politician."[30]

He writes that political journalism on television and the Internet "coarsens the political culture," "makes tempers flare," and "helps breed distrust.... And whether we politicians like to admit it or not, the constant vitriol can wear on the spirit."[31]

Obama became a harsh critic of the media during his first term. That's because as president, Amy Chozick wrote in the *New York Times*, "[Obama] has come to believe the news media have had a role in frustrating his ambitions to change the terms of the country's political discussion."[32]

Chozick dubbed Obama the "news media critic in chief," asserting that Obama has "developed a detailed critique of modern news coverage that he regularly expresses to those around him."[33]

In her book *The Obamas*, journalist Jodi Kantor wrote that Obama "took his frustration out on the media, which he largely viewed with condescension bordering on contempt."[34] A White House aide told Kantor that "the president was perversely fascinated by cable news—he liked to see 'what the idiots are paying attention to [aide's words, not Obama's].'"[35]

Obama once told a sports radio station, "It also turns out that political reporters are a lot like sports reporters. They've all got opinions, even if they didn't play."[36]

According to the *Times*' Chozick, "Mr. Obama has articulated what he sees as two overarching problems: coverage that focuses on political winners and losers rather than substance; and a 'false balance,' in which two opposing sides are given equal weight regardless of the facts."[37]

Yet Obama's behavior toward the media does not always line up very well with his criticism. When it comes to "the facts," the Obama administration has shown a marked reluctance to cooperate in helping the media obtain even the "facts" to which they are legally entitled.

While running for president in 2008, and in his first year in the Oval Office, Obama pledged to increase transparency throughout his administration. He promised to release documents and set up an agency to declassify more than 370 million pages of archived material. One minute after Obama took office, the White House website proclaimed that his administration would be "the most open and transparent in history."[38] Obama issued a memo to his administration, stating, "The Freedom of Information Act should be administered with a clear presumption: In the face of doubt, openness prevails."[39]

None of that happened. As the *Washington Post* reported in 2012, "[B]y some measures the government is keeping more secrets than before."[40]

A 2009 government workshop on government openness was closed to the public.[41] In 2009 the Associated Press reported, "As Obama's first year in office ends, the government's actions when the public and press seek information are not yet matching up with the president's words."[42]

And the administration only became less transparent over time. Media organizations and others seeking government documents under the Freedom of Information Act (FOIA) in 2011 were less likely to receive the material than in 2010 at ten of the fifteen cabinet-level departments, according to a *Washington Post* analysis of government agencies' annual reports.[43]

The FOIA went into effect in 1967 to give the public access to undisclosed, unclassified federal government information.

In many cases the administration has produced information only after journalists pressed them for weeks or months, and sometimes only after being sued. Transparency watch-dogs have accused the administration of refusing to turn over important records, of constantly fighting FOIA requests, and of prosecuting whistleblowers.

As Katherine Meyer, a Washington attorney who's been filing FOIA cases since 1978, put it to *Politico* in 2012,

> Obama is the sixth administration that's been in office since I've been doing Freedom of Information Act work.... It's kind of shocking to me to say this, but of the six, this administration is the worst on FOIA issues. The worst. There's just no question about it. This administration is raising one barrier after another.... It's gotten to the point where I'm stunned—I'm really stunned.[44]

One reporter, Bloomberg News' Mark Pittman, died in 2009 while waiting for the Federal Reserve to release documents related to its more than $2 trillion in assistance to financial firms.[45]

In the Fast and Furious scandal—addressed elsewhere herein—Obama went so far as to block all disclosure. He made a claim of executive privilege over what his administration had maintained all along was just a low-level law enforcement mistake. Even liberal reporters, when pressed, often concede that the Obama administration is less "transparent" than previous administrations and less interested in making the president available to the press.

All of which raises the question: How does Obama expect reporters to delve into "substance" and "facts" when he himself is keeping the information from them?

Even when he's not avoiding reporters' questions or refusing to grant information to the press, Obama can be rather petty with journalists, especially the ones from news outlets he doesn't like. In the final days of his first presidential run, Obama barred three journalists from his campaign plane, supposedly to make room for reporters from his hometown newspapers.[46] As Bernard Goldberg noted, "I'm sure it is nothing more than an odd coincidence that the three papers that got booted—the *Washington Times*, the *New York Post*, and the *Dallas Morning News*—all endorsed McCain for president."[47]

Early in his presidency, Obama made it clear he would not tolerate much criticism. *Time* magazine suggested that the White House's strategy was to "become a player, issuing biting attacks on those pundits, politicians and outlets that make what the White House believes to be misleading or simply false claims."[48]

Obama was one of a group of Democratic presidential candidates who refused to attend a debate co-sponsored by Fox News in 2007.[49] Early in his term, Obama told congressional Republicans to stop listening to Rush Limbaugh.[50]

As president, Obama has tried to isolate Fox News, which he and his advisors urged other journalists to shun as illegitimate. Obama senior advisor David Axelrod once told ABC's George Stephanopoulos that Fox News is "not really a news station." He said:

> It's really not news—it's pushing a point of view. And the bigger thing is that other news organizations like yours ought not to treat them that way, and we're not going to treat them that way. We're going to appear on their shows. We're going to participate but understanding that they represent a point of view.[51]

Don't forget—he was saying this on air to a former Clinton administration communications director.

Former White House Chief of Staff Rahm Emanuel once told CNN that "[Fox News is] not a news organization so much as it has a perspective"—as if other cable news channels are any different.[52]

One-time White House Communications Director Anita Dunn once told CNN that Fox News was a "wing of the Republican Party"[53] and the *New York Times* that it was "undertaking a war against Barack Obama and the White House," and that the White House was "going to treat them the way we would treat an opponent."[54]

The Obama administration once even tried to bar a Fox News White House correspondent from the press pool.[55] Other journalists, to their credit, rebelled.

But it's not just Fox News that Obama has tried to manipulate. The Obama White House has on numerous occasions announced draconian ground rules for local interviews of the president. Obama has also shunned the White House press corps, holding few press conferences and taking few questions.

The frequency with which Obama excludes the media from conferences and summits prompted liberal *Washington Post* opinion columnist Dana Milbank to accuse Obama of "putting on a clinic for some of the world's greatest dictators in how to circumvent a free press."[56]

And despite all the abuse, the media just can't quit Obama. They're battered and bruised and treated with contempt, yet, as Mark Halperin said in 2012, "the media is very susceptible to doing what the Obama campaign wants...."[57]

In April 2012, *New York Times* public editor Arthur Brisbane criticized his paper's pro-Obama bias. Now that the Republican primaries were winding down, Brisbane wrote, "the general election season is on, and *The Times* needs to offer an aggressive look at the president's record, policy promises and campaign operation to answer the question: Who is the real Barack Obama?"[58]

Admitting that his paper "basked a bit in the warm glow of Mr. Obama's election in 2008," Brisbane went on, "Many critics view *The Times* as constitutionally unable to address the election in an unbiased fashion."[59]

The *Huffington Post*'s Howard Fineman has said that the media bias toward Obama is so strong that he campaigned "without having to seriously and substantively defend his first-term failed promises and shortcomings."[60]

> Obama was such a cool and uplifting story to so many in the media in 2008 that they essentially ceded ground to him that they have yet to reclaim. He ran a tightly controlled message campaign then, and has run an even more tightly controlled White House, with few press conferences and deep access only to those most likely to write positive stories.[61]

Obama compared political reporters to sports reporters. But former Jimmy Carter pollster Patrick Caddell offered a different sports analogy. "We have a political campaign where, to put the best metaphor I can on it, the referees on the field are sacking the quarterback of one team, tripping up their runners, throwing their bodies in front of blockers, and nobody says anything."[62]

At least a few of them said something. But nobody stopped it from happening.

The ESPN President

Like other presidents before him, Barack Obama enjoys playing, watching, and talking about sports. Look at photos taken in the Oval Office and you can often spy a football or basketball in the background (or in Obama's hands).[63]

But Obama also attracts more attention from the sports media than any president before him. It helps that Obama usually knows what he's talking about. He can sit down with ESPN's Bill "the sports guy" Simmons for a multi-part interview and talk about how he knew how good basketball player Jeremy Lin was before the rest of the country, and then brag that he once fooled all-star NBA guard Chris Paul with a crossover dribble during a pickup game.[64]

New York Times columnist David Brooks labeled Obama "The ESPN Man" because he "has displayed a kind of ESPN masculinity: postfeminist in his values, but also thoroughly traditional in style— hypercompetitive, restrained, not given to self-doubt, rarely self-indulgent."[65]

Whatever the reason, the sports media can't get enough of Barack Obama. It's not just that every game Obama attends is discussed on the sports networks, as when he hosted British Prime Minister David Cameron at the 2012 NCAA basketball tournament.[66] Even his opinions on sports are broadcast and dissected by sports journalists at every level. When Obama gave an interview to a sports radio station in Columbus, Ohio, he offered his opinion on the New York Jets' signing of Tim Tebow and ESPN's Skip Bayless just ate it up. "I loved what he said on a Columbus radio station…I loved what Obama said. It was smart! It was insightful! It was interesting to me," Bayless gushed. "His Regular-Guy stock goes way up with me, 'cause he can really talk sports. He can talk it in depth…."[67]

Check out this sample of Obama-related headlines from ESPN. com:

"President Obama Picks Dream Team"
"Obama Questions Tim Tebow Trade"
"Obama Wants Michael Vick to Slide"
"Obama: Disputed game means NFL needs regular refs"

"President Obama Kids David Beckham"
"President Obama Watching Jeremy Lin"
"Obama's Women's Pick? Baylor"
"Secret Golfing Life of Barack Obama"

Obama's tradition of making yearly NCAA tournament picks has even spawned a new word, "Baracketology," which describes the event (often televised) of Obama unveiling his NCAA men's and women's basketball picks.

ESPN reporter John Clayton even credited Obama with ending the NFL referee lockout. Clayton wrote:

> With President Obama expressing his disappointment with the replacement officiating and poor officiating being the lead story of network news coverage, NFL commissioner Roger Goodell had to act—and he did.[68]

What did the president do to deserve all the credit? He tweeted, "NFL fans on both sides of the aisle hope the refs' lockout is settled soon."[69]

Obama knows the sports world loves him. In the 2008 and 2012 elections, the Obama campaign even advertised on popular sports video games like Madden NFL.[70]

After Obama's reelection, *Sports Illustrated* columnist Ian Thomsen wrote, "Barack Obama's re-election is a victory for basketball."[71]

Well, it's certainly a victory for all of the sports journalists who can't get enough of him.

Measuring the Slant

Think of the most liberal city in America—San Francisco, say, or Cambridge, Massachusetts. In 2008, both of those cities voted for Barack Obama over John McCain by margins of 86 percent to 14 percent.[72]

Those margins probably don't surprise you, but here's something that might: the residents of those cities are actually more conservative, on aggregate, than the Washington press corps—the people who report the political news.

In fact, according to UCLA political scientist Tim Groseclose, San Francisco and Cambridge are roughly twice as conservative as Washington correspondents.[73]

Conservatives have long complained that the media are too liberal. They refer derisively to "Big Media," "the drive by media," and the "lamestream media" whenever they want to signal their skepticism about something they hear in the mainstream press.

Liberals usually respond in one of two ways. They argue that the media only seem liberal because conservatives and their favorite media outlets are so far to the right. Alternatively, they insist that although most reporters hold liberal views and vote for Democrats consistently, they are still professionals who would never even dream of injecting their personal views into their craft.

Multiple studies refute these claims—and so does any objective reading of the newspapers and viewing of newscasts.

As I noted in the first chapter, journalists have voted disproportionately for Democratic presidential candidates in every election for at least two generations, and the imbalance is actually getting worse. In the lead-up to the 2004 election, *New York Times* columnist John Tierney conducted an unscientific poll of 153 journalists. When asked who would make a better president, the journalists from outside the beltway chose Democrat John Kerry 3 to 1. But those based in Washington, D.C., preferred Kerry *12 to 1*.[74]

Journalists are also much more likely to embrace the liberal label than are average Americans. Among the American population at large, 41 percent self-identify as conservative and 23 percent as liberal.[75] According to a 2008 survey of more than 200 journalists by the Pew Research Center for the People and the Press, self-described liberals outnumbered conservatives 4 to 1.[76]

In his 2011 book *Left Turn: How Liberal Media Bias Distorts the American Mind*, Groseclose set out to calculate media bias mathematically. Using sophisticated statistical analysis, Groseclose concluded that "every mainstream national news outlet in the United States has a liberal bias."[77]

Groseclose found that eighteen of twenty news sources he studied were left of center. The only two to the right were the *Washington Times* and the Fox News *Special Report with Brit Hume.*[78]

Groseclose's conclusions generated an avalanche of negative media attention from liberal news outlets, as well as a lot of personal hate mail. But they were rooted in statistical analysis that had been designed to measure the ideological positions of members of Congress, and based on a paper he co-authored that appeared in the peer-reviewed *Quarterly Journal of Economics.*

Groseclose calculated that the *New York Times'* ideological slant is roughly on par with that of Senator Joe Lieberman, the Connecticut Democrat.[79] Groseclose also writes:

> According to my analysis, the Drudge Report is approximately the most fair, balanced, and centrist news outlet in the United States. Yet, the overwhelming majority of media commentators claim that it has a conservative bias. The problem, I believe, is that such commentators mistake relative bias for absolute bias. Yes, the Drudge Report is more conservative than the average U.S. news outlet. But it is a logical mistake to use that to infer that it is biased on an absolute scale.[80]

There are some surprises for conservatives in Groseclose's findings. For instance, two shows that he described as straight down the middle are ABC's *Good Morning America* and PBS's *The News Hour with Jim Lehrer*. Also, he found that while National Public Radio was liberal, it was no more so than the *Washington Post* or *Time*, and in fact less liberal than the *New York Times*.[81]

In an email interview, Groseclose asserted, "Without media bias, America would vote about like Texas or Kentucky." That's a pretty bold claim, but it certainly isn't crazy to think that the media have some effect on how people vote—an effect helpful to Democrats.

The Honeymoon Continues

The public was very aware of the media's liberal bias in the 2012 election. According to an August 2012 Rasmussen Reports public opinion poll, 59 percent of likely voters believed Obama had received the most favorable treatment from the media during the campaign.[82] Just 18 percent thought that of Romney. Rasmussen also found that 51 percent of likely voters expected the media to help Obama, while only 9 percent expected the media to help Romney.[83]

This followed 2008, when 70 percent of respondents in a Pew poll felt the media wanted Obama to win. Only 9 percent believed they wanted McCain to win.[84]

And Obama's reelection didn't stop the favorable news stories about him; it multiplied them. Obama's victory had journalists searching for comparisons to other beleaguered presidents who secured second terms.

George W. Bush or Bill Clinton might come readily to your mind. But MSNBC's Chris Jansing aimed a bit higher when she compared Obama's reelection to that of America's sixteenth president, Abraham Lincoln.

Having just watched Steven Spielberg's film *Lincoln*, Jansing said, "You have a president who is newly elected, who faces a divided Congress and a divided country." Introducing guest Gloria Reuben, an actress in *Lincoln*, Jansing asked, "You're a social activist. You've been very big in [the] pro-choice [cause]. You've been a supporter of Barack Obama and the AIDS movement.... You must find these parallels fascinating."[85]

Indeed.

Obama's post-election press conference on November 14, 2012, was his first full press conference in eight months. Ahead of it, *Politico* published an interesting piece, predicting the types of tough questions Obama would be asked.[86] Among their suggested queries:

- "Do you believe the FBI should have told you and Congress sooner about the investigation that led Gen. Petraeus to resign?"
- "On the fiscal cliff, is your bottom line rates or revenue? Is it enough to close tax loopholes and deductions on the wealthy, or must tax rates also go up in order for you to sign a deal?"
- "Why was the U.S. Consulate in Benghazi so lightly guarded, despite complaints about deteriorating security conditions in Libya?"

And do you suppose journalists asked these? A few tough questions were asked, but there was also a lot of fluff. Here were some of the questions the Washington correspondents asked the president of the United States after he had been under wraps for eight months:

- "What lessons, if any, did Democrats learn from this last election and the Latino vote?"

- "Mr. President, on election night you said that you were looking forward to speaking with Governor Romney, sitting down in the coming weeks to discuss ways that you could work together on this nation's problems. Have you extended that invitation? Has he accepted? And in what ways do you think you can work together?"[87]

One reporter even offered her congratulations to the newly reelected president. With such a cooperative media, it's a wonder why Obama doesn't hold more press conferences. It's always important for a politician to keep in touch with his base.

CHAPTER THREE

WHAT
RECOVERY?

In poll after poll after poll, Americans identified jobs and the economy as the most important issues of the 2012 election. Economic recovery was the big thing on everyone's mind—and there were a lot of stories that should have been written about it but were not.

As he frequently reminds the public, President Obama was not responsible for the financial crisis of 2008 or the recession that came with it. Nor was he ever really in danger of being blamed. According to exit polling, even the voters who turned out in the 2010 midterm election—the ones who gave his party what Obama described as a "shellacking" at the polls—didn't hold him responsible for the recession.[1]

But Obama does bear responsibility—as much as one can fairly attribute to a president—for the recovery over which he has presided, especially since the recession ended in June 2009. He asked for this by making so many enormous promises about how quickly the job market would come back, about how many jobs and how much growth the recovery would create, and about what it would look like.

Immediately upon entering office, Obama made the case in Congress for his $800 billion stimulus package, using very specific projections. If it passed, he had the unemployment rate falling to just above 5 percent by the time this book is published—and unless a miracle occurs soon, that's not going to happen.[2] In retrospect, his projections seem wildly optimistic. But just as important was the *kind* of recovery Obama promised—the kind that would bring the "jobs of the future"[3] in the "industries of the future."[4]

In Elkhart, Indiana, just weeks after his inauguration in 2009, Obama promised that his stimulus package would "save or create 3 to 4 million jobs over the next two years." And he went on:

> But not just any jobs—jobs that meet the needs we've neglected for far too long, jobs that lay the groundwork for long-term economic growth; jobs fixing our schools; computerizing medical records to save costs and save lives; jobs repairing our roads and our bridges and our levees; jobs investing in renewable energy to help us move towards energy independence.... [O]ur economy will be stronger for generations to come if we commit ourselves to the work that needs to be done.[5]

On his hundredth day in office, Obama used similar language:

> Even as we clear away the wreckage of this recession, I have also said that we cannot go back to an economy that

is built on a pile of sand.... We must lay a new foundation for growth—a foundation that will strengthen our
economy and help us compete in the 21st century.[6]

Americans didn't need much help from the media to realize during the 2012 campaign that the stimulus hadn't been a big success,
or that the recovery was not proceeding along the lines Obama
promised. The press were slow even to pick up on the fact that
nearly all of the improvement in the unemployment rate from its
peak (at 10 percent) was the result of people leaving the work force,
not of job creation keeping up with population growth. But most
Americans probably still aren't aware of the many ways in which
the American job market is fundamentally changing during the
Obama recovery—nearly all of them for the worse. Those stories
weren't really told.

Good-paying manufacturing jobs, firm foundations for growth,
industries of the future, *et cetera*—those things have not materialized.
The Labor Department's numbers tell the story of an ever-weaker
foundation for future growth. The young cannot find work, the old
hang on longer to what jobs they have, and low-wage and part-time
jobs are replacing the high-wage, full-time jobs that disappeared in
the recession. In the Obama recovery, workers make less money and
more of them are forced to rely on government assistance.

Meanwhile, the economy is getting life-support not from a stimulus package, and not from a clean energy revolution, but from an
unexpected oil and gas boom that is happening on private land. And
the employers that dare set up shop are doing so in the safe haven
of states that have right-to-work laws, reducing their exposure to a
White House labor policy that is chiefly focused on rewarding
political allies.

This is the real recovery—the one that was rarely, if ever, reported
in the news.

Story Idea: Obama's "Gray Jobs" Recovery

We think of people between the ages of twenty-five and fifty-four as being in the heart of their careers. It's the period when you take your first job in the field that interests you, then begin moving up the ranks and up the pay scale. You start a family and you buy your first home. You establish your complete independence from your parents and build the foundations of your own life.

In the Obama recovery, those days are over.

During the forty months between the recession's end (June 2009) and the election, the absolute number of people with jobs in the 25 to 54 age group actually shrank by 800,000. How big a deal is this? The last time employment levels were this low among 25- to 54-year-olds, Hong Kong was still a British colony and the Dow Jones Industrial Average had yet to close above 8,000. Jobs for mid-career workers have actually receded to mid-1997 levels.

There has been no rebound in jobs for people age twenty-five to fifty-four, even after they lost 5.4 million jobs between January 2007 and June 2009. People in this age group are experiencing an ongoing depression. You'd think the media would notice a story like this one, but they were too busy transcribing the Obama administration's claims, dating back as early as summer 2010, that the whole economy was just a few days from turning around. Recovery Summer, remember?

In the Obama recovery, nearly all job growth has occurred among those older than fifty-five. There were 3.8 million more people over age fifty-five working in October 2012 than there were in June 2009. Part of this is the aging of the population, but older workers are also deferring retirement, and some retirees have re-entered the work force in low-wage, part-time jobs.

Meanwhile, younger people who lost their jobs and their careers in the crash have seen their economic lives put on hold. They are not gaining experience or skills or earning power. Given that older, experienced workers can't keep going forever, this will only exacerbate

America's problems as it tries to remain globally competitive in future decades.

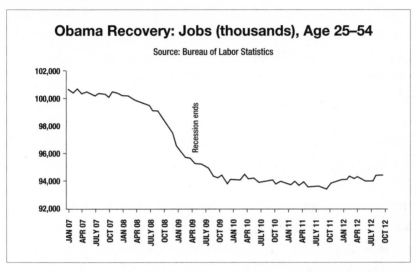

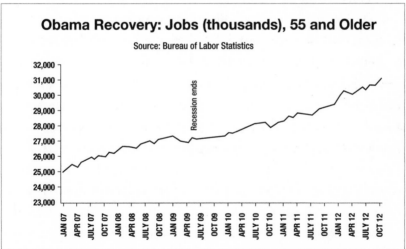

Story Idea: Obama's Low-Wage Jobs Recovery

What sort of jobs disappeared in the financial crisis, and what sort are being created in the recovery? The National Employment Law Project (NELP), a left-wing non-profit, conducted a study that provides a rough idea.[7] It found that:

- Lower-wage occupations (paying less than $13.83 per hour) made up 21 percent of recessionary job losses, but 58 percent of the jobs created in the recovery.
- Mid-wage occupations (between $13.84 and $21.13 per hour) made up 60 percent of job losses in the recession, but only 22 percent of the jobs created in the recovery.

The Labor Department data on wages confirm this trend: Adjusted for inflation, private-sector workers in October 2012 were making about 1.5 percent less than they had been when the recession ended in June 2009.[8] An August 2012 report by Sentier research suggested even bigger losses, finding that the average household was making $3,000 less than when the recovery began.[9]

The NELP study reported that the jobs lost in better-paying areas, such as manufacturing, trucking, data entry, carpentry, real estate, and office management, were being replaced in low-wage fields such as food preparation, retail sales, and waiting tables.

Remember "McJobs?" That's what the press trots out when there's a Republican in the White House. Well, here's what $800 billion plus in stimulus spending (and a trillion dollars a year in deficit spending) has done for America's economy: it has supersized McJobs and downsized nearly everything else. Isn't that a story?

Story Idea: Obama's Part-Time Jobs Recovery

Speaking of waiting tables, here's another troubling trend that very few noticed. The American work force is going part-time.

Yes, this tends to happen when a recession hits—it also happened in the early 1980s and the early 1990s, for example. But this time, during the recovery, the trend isn't reversing—in fact, it appears to be getting worse.

Three and a half years after the recession's end in June 2009, Labor Department data show that part-time work hasn't come back down—neither in absolute numbers (27.9 million as of October

2012) nor as a percentage of those employed. The number of workers at the margin, who work part-time because they cannot find full-time work, is not only more than twice what it was before the recession, but also up 25 percent since the recovery began.

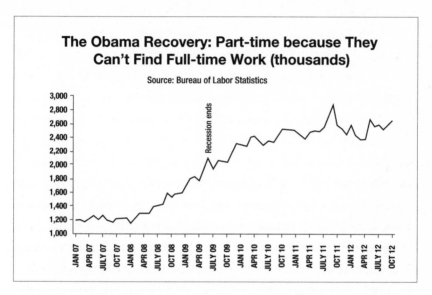

By election time, Obama's forty-month recovery had replaced only 2.7 million of the 8.8 million full-time jobs lost in the crash. Nearly one in five American jobs is part time. It makes the topline unemployment numbers look better than they would be otherwise, but it isn't healing the economy. And there are good reasons to expect that this trend will continue.

Another story: companies planning for Obamacare's implementation may have already played a large role in the ongoing "part-timing" of the workforce. In the final days of the 2012 election campaign, a few businesses did begin discussing the matter openly. Especially in the hotel and restaurant industry, employers are reducing hours among their workers, citing Obamacare as the reason.

Take Darden, the large, publicly traded company that owns the Olive Garden and Red Lobster restaurant chains. It announced that it was beginning an experiment of shifting more of its workforce below thirty hours a week. The goal is to avoid paying the fines and costs associated with Obamacare.[10]

Before you chalk this up to employer greed, first understand that Darden already offers health insurance to all 185,000 of its employees. But for the 75 percent of them working what's traditionally considered "part-time"—thirty-five hours or less—Darden provides an affordable health insurance plan of the sort that Obamacare forbids. So-called "mini-med" plans have long been a favorite with many organizations—especially restaurant chains, but also labor unions and others. Depending on the precise terms, premiums for such plans can run as cheap as $1,000 to $6,000 per year, as opposed to traditional family insurance plans, which averaged $15,745 in 2012.[11]

Mini-meds are more affordable because they have low limits on annual benefits. For example, the SEIU Local 1199 has long provided its New Jersey nursing home workers with a plan that capped coverage at $50,000 per year. Only 1 percent of the local's members ever exceeded the cap, and in those cases the union simply provided extra help.[12] (You may remember from 2010 the controversy over waivers that the Obama administration provided to several businesses and unions. This is what they were for. Those waivers allowed Local 1199 and other entities to keep their mini-med plans an extra year or two before they are finally outlawed by Obamacare.)

Darden, CKE Restaurants (which owns Carl's Jr. and Hardee's), and many other businesses and unions that currently offer mini-meds to their employees now face a choice. They can either dramatically increase their health care costs; they can drop employee insurance and pay large fines under the law ($2,000 for each full-time employee after the first thirty); or they can get creative. In this case, the businesses are getting creative, reducing workers' hours and limiting new hires to part-time—which, under Obamacare's new definition, is just thirty hours per week.

Among the other employers in the process of or considering "part-timing" their staff are White Castle, McDonald's, Anna's Linens, and

Pillar Hotels and Resorts. So are franchisees of major chains like Denny's, Papa John's, Applebee's, and Jimmy John's. The restaurant business has small profit margins as it is—it can't just absorb massive new fines or health care costs, nor can it raise prices to pay for them without losing business.

And these industries are a huge part of the Obama economy. Between June 2009 and October 2012, the retail, leisure, and hospitality industries accounted for one quarter of all private-sector jobs created in the United States.

In some instances, full-time workers will be "part-timed," but the workers most likely to be hurt are already "part-time" under the traditional federal definition of thirty-five hours per week. In 2011, there were 10.7 million people—8 percent of all American workers—working between thirty and thirty-four hours per week, according to the Bureau of Labor Statistics. There's no telling how many of them will see their hours reduced to twenty-nine per week or less because of Obamacare. As for companies that hire in the future, Obamacare provides a perverse incentive for them to avoid creating full-time positions, especially for low-skill jobs, in favor of part-time ones. That, in turn, might make the unemployment figures look better, as businesses take on more part-time workers, but only at the expense of workers who otherwise might have had a living.

As much as Americans laughed at the French policy of the 35-hour limit on the work week, Obama has probably just imposed a backdoor 30-hour work week for millions—and unfortunately restaurants are not alone in this trend. The Community College of Allegheny County in Pittsburgh recently announced it will drop four hundred of its employees—half of them teaching adjuncts—down to twenty-five hours, citing Obamacare as the reason.[13] The public college is facing budget cuts, and the cost of putting those employees on Obamacare-compliant health insurance plans would be $6 million—more than a quarter of its annual budget.

Adam Davis, an adjunct biology professor affected by the change, told the *Pittsburgh Post-Gazette*, "It's kind of a double whammy for us because we are facing a legal requirement [under the new law] to get health care and if the college is reducing our hours, we don't have the money to pay for it." Jeff Cech, a Steelworkers' union operative who is trying to unionize adjuncts at nearby Duquesne University, said that every adjunct in town is chattering fearfully about the community college's decision. "If they are doing it at CCAC," he said, "it can't be long before they do it other places."[14]

And if they're doing it at colleges and universities in Pittsburgh, it may not be long before they're doing it everywhere.

At least teaching adjuncts obtain an education and have (in theory) decent prospects. Most of the workers affected by this change—low-wage workers with few skills—have only one consolation. They will gain the ability, under Obamacare, to buy a more comprehensive health insurance plan with a subsidy. But in exchange for that, they will be paid less because they will work fewer hours. They will see their standard of living deteriorate. Unfortunately, you can't pay the rent or the cable bill with a health insurance subsidy, nor can you buy your kid a Christmas present.

Aside from the obvious story about a negative, unintended consequence of Obamacare, this is also a story about where the labor market is going long-term—and about why, and about who is to blame. It turns out that when Obama talked about the "jobs of the future," he was talking about part-time work.

Story Idea: Obama Doesn't Learn from Mistakes

President Obama travelled to Holland, Michigan, on July 15, 2010, to give a speech on the $151 million stimulus grant that his administration had made to build the LG Chem electric car battery factory. He declared that the plant "is a symbol of where Michigan is going, this is a symbol of where Holland is going, this is a symbol of where America is going."[15]

In a way, he was right, because the factory was a perfect example of Obamanomics in action.

As of late 2012, the factory had not shipped a single battery. The plant's workers had "so little work to do that they spend hours playing cards and board games, reading magazines or watching movies."[16] Why? Because in deciding to fund this factory, Obama and the other central planners wildly overestimated consumer demand for electric cars. As a result, the workers are idle. They had to beg management to let them do charitable work on company time, just so they could feel useful.

Unless you read one of a handful of conservative opinion writers, you've probably never even heard this story. That's because the only television outlet to run with it was WOOD, the NBC affiliate in western Michigan, whose local investigative team put it together. They did some great journalism, but NBC News didn't even bother to pick up their work. Nor did they follow up on it, nor did CBS, nor ABC, nor Fox News, nor CNN, nor MSNBC. The only national television network even to mention the LG Chem plant in Holland before the election, according to a search of LexisNexis, was Fox Business. And we mentioned it in an editorial in the *Washington Examiner*, but outside of that, no major newspaper outside Michigan wrote anything.

It boggles the mind that this remained just a local story, given that it was a presidential election year. Here was a trend story on one of Obama's most touted programs. The failure of Obama's green energy initiatives received appropriate attention in connection with only one company—Solyndra. But in fact, the story was a lot bigger than that.

The most optimistic and forward-looking part of Obama's agenda was the green energy future that he described in countless speeches. It was a future in which workers received high wages manufacturing and installing environmentally friendly technologies. During his first run for the presidency, Obama had promised to create 5 million "green" jobs over ten years, and to spend $150 billion on the effort. And once in office, he at least kept the second part of that promise.

In one of Obama's Saturday radio addresses in 2010, he announced $2 billion for two new clean energy projects (one of them has since gone bankrupt). He pledged:

> [W]e're going to keep competing aggressively to make sure the jobs and industries of the future are taking root right here in America. That's one of the reasons why we're accelerating the transition to a clean energy economy and doubling our use of renewable energy sources like wind and solar power—steps that have the potential to create whole new industries and hundreds of thousands of new jobs in America.[17]

Obama did, in fact, increase the amount of renewable electricity generated. Solar and wind went from generating 1.4 percent of all U.S. electricity in 2008 to 2.9 percent in the first eight months of 2012. But aside from this gain, which came at great cost to taxpayers and ratepayers, all this business about a future filled with clean energy jobs was already a total bust by the end of Obama's first term.

It's not just that there were major failures. It's that there weren't even any bright spots to point to—no evidence that any of the billions of dollars dedicated to this effort were creating anything substantial that would outlast his presidency.

Green energy money went to things like *de minimis* worker training that led to $26,000-a-year jobs. It was used to prop up dozens of bad companies like Solyndra (at least for a little while) that were already well along the path to insolvency.

Five million is a lot of jobs. And of the 5 million Obama promised by 2019, how many were created in his first term? It's hard to say, since there's no clear definition of what a "green" job really is. The most generous definitions merely reclassify millions of existing employees. Bus drivers and garbage men, for example, become "green" if their buses and trucks use clean fuels, and plumbers become "green" if they install low-flow toilets.

The more realistic math on green job creation goes something like this:

> The American Recovery and Reinvestment Act of 2009 set aside $90 billion in renewable energy grants and loans for a grab bag of thousands of projects—wind farms, solar installations, natural gas fueling stations, biofuel research, and a $5 billion weatherization project for low-income homes. Digging into the public records of the $21 billion spent so far through 19 U.S. Department of Energy programs reveals 3,960 projects that employ 28,854 people. That's not 5 million.[18]

In fact, it's not even 1 percent of 5 million.

The green jobs training program was a small line-item in Obama's stimulus package, but it was a big part of his pitch. In October 2012, the Labor Department's Inspector General released a report on it, showing that the program was on pace to fall far, far short of its goal of placing 71,000 workers in long-term "green" jobs.[19]

Taxpayers had spent $329 million dollars (up to that point) on a program that trained 81,354 workers. The Inspector General found that:

- 21 percent of all trainees (17,374) received only one day of training.
- 47 percent of all trainees (38,366) received five days of training or less.
- Only 25,396 of the trainees took new jobs after training that could be classified as related to the training. This includes not only workers who started "green" jobs with new companies, but also workers who already had jobs and took new positions at their companies after getting the training.
- Of the 59,205 trainees who had finished training as of December 31, 2011, only 11,613 had taken new jobs and retained them for six months—about 16 percent of the program's target.
- The average wage for the new jobs that trainees got was $25,926.

There was another interesting finding. Forty-nine percent of the people who entered into these programs already had jobs when they started, and were simply looking for new skills. The Inspector General interviewed a sample of eighty-one such trainees, and reported: "[O]ur audit found no evidence that any of the 81 incumbent workers we identified in our sample needed green job training to secure a new job or retain their current jobs." Note that these job-holders accounted for several thousand of the trainees who got new jobs related to the training.

If the green jobs program was a small and quiet failure, the energy start-up loans were far too big for the media to ignore completely. And they did not completely ignore Solyndra. But the bigger picture was never explained. Obama's green energy push was as clear a demonstration as could be offered that he was in way over his head with this business of creating "new industries." New industries? Jobs of the future? It was a campaign slogan, not an economic plan. None of it was coming true. Conservatives had predicted this, based on simple laws of economics. Government cannot trick markets.

The Energy Department's stimulus loan program for green energy companies—the program Solyndra made famous—committed $16 billion to 27 loans. Twenty-three of these were rated "junk" by the rating agencies at the time they were made, thanks to the poor financial condition and business prospects of the companies involved.[20] Unsurprisingly, many of these companies are now in deep financial trouble or have already declared bankruptcy. The fact that many of these companies had ties to Obama administration officials and campaign fundraisers—another story that didn't really have its day—isn't even necessary to make this newsworthy.[21]

Obama's vision for creating green jobs included loans, loan guarantees, and grants to green companies, and they seem to have been awarded without much regard for their prospects of success. In late October 2012, Ashe Schow of the Heritage Foundation's Foundry blog provided a complete list of the wreckage—thirty-three floundering or dead companies that had been offered or given federal money.[22] Along this proverbial road to hell lay nineteen bankrupt corpses, including Solyndra, A123 Systems, Beacon Power, Azure Dynamics, Thompson River Power, and Stirling Systems. Another fourteen companies faced serious financial woes, with many laying off workers or canceling projects.

The most important thing is that President Obama did not appear to learn from any of the failures. As the election approached, he kept calling for still more subsidies. At times, he chided those who criticized these programs as "flat-earthers."[23] Amusingly, even after Solyndra shut its doors and laid off its workers, Energy Department press secretary Damien LaVera insisted that infamous "investment" had been a success: "The project that we supported succeeded," he told the *New York Times*. "The facility was producing the product it said it would produce, and consumers were buying the product."[24]

This is the story of Obama's entire green energy vision—again, arguably the most optimistic part of his agenda, one of his biggest failures, and a case study in how he didn't intend to correct course no matter how wrong he was proven.

If you rely on the mainstream media for news, you would have gotten the impression that this centerpiece of Obama's economic plan—the waste of billions of dollars creating a vanity industry with no jobs to speak of—was a minor matter, of far less significance than say, Mitt Romney's tax returns or his dog Seamus.

Story Idea: The Disappearing Workers

The mainstream media certainly reported on the topline numbers in the employment market. They told the story of an unemployment rate that had gradually slipped from its 2010 high down to 7.9 percent by Election Day. It was a good two and a half points above the prediction that had been used to sell Obama's stimulus package, but at least it seemed to be going in the right direction.[25]

But of course, this appearance was slightly deceptive. Some of the reporting gave a hint as to why the unemployment rate was really falling. Americans, in large numbers, were giving up on finding jobs and leaving the workforce. They were no longer counted as "unemployed." Practically none of the mainstream media identified this as an ongoing feature of the Obama recovery—a part of the new normal and the "new foundation" for the economy that Obama surely didn't intend.

As a result, most Americans are probably unaware that labor force participation—the measure of how many people are either employed or seeking jobs—has collapsed throughout the Obama recovery. It fell as the stimulus money was spent, through the

"Recovery Summer" of 2010, and in fact kept plumbing new depths even as Election Day approached.

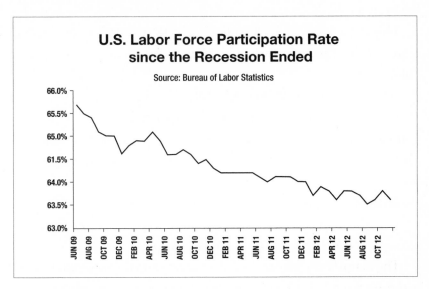

Aside from a few conservative writers and bloggers, there wasn't anyone trying to give context to this—to put it in terms people could understand.

The American Enterprise Institute's Jim Pethokoukis tried at times to illustrate the point by asking what the unemployment rate would look like if so many people hadn't given up on finding jobs. He found that, according to the Congressional Budget Office's labor force projections from before the recession (which takes things like the aging population into account), the unemployment rate would have been 10.4 percent in November 2012—not 7.7 percent.[26] If workforce participation had just stayed level with where it had been a year earlier, the unemployment rate would have been 8.3 percent.

To be sure, the contraction of the labor force began before President Obama took office. But four years into his presidency, it continued—and continues—to be a story. The "new foundation" of the Obama recovery involved a smaller share of Americans working or seeking work than at any time since 1981, when the number of women in the workforce was still experiencing its historic rise.

For the most part, readers looked in vain to the mainstream media for any help in understanding what the unemployment reports were saying. And this worked in Obama's favor.

Story Idea: Amid "Recovery," a Rush on Public Assistance

Where do workers go when times get so tough that they stop looking for jobs? There's no one answer, but some of them go to the government.

In hard times, more people claim government benefits. And when there's a rush on benefits, it's a story—not just a story about entitlements and welfare, but also about the economy.

Economists sometimes look to Social Security Disability claims as a barometer of economic health. When the job market gets tough, applications for Social Security Disability benefits (not to be confused with retirement and survivors' benefits) jump. The 2008 crisis was no exception.

Most disability claims are denied for one reason or another, and there are fakers, but that's not the issue. Many people who genuinely think they are eligible for disability (whether they are or not) would rather work as long as they can.[27] But when economic conditions no longer allow them to work, they apply for benefits instead.

Applications for disability stood at 577,000 in the fourth quarter of 2008. By the time the recession ended two quarters later, the number had jumped 26 percent, to 727,000. Three years into the recovery, one might expect that number to edge downward, but that just hasn't happened. In the third quarter of 2012, 726,000 people applied for disability. Even though the rate of rejected applications increased, the number of added to the program kept rising. In 2011, the ratio of workers receiving disability to workers with jobs topped 6 percent, a first in the program's history.[28]

Provided they live long enough, most people who leave the disability rolls do so when they start collecting Social Security retirement benefits. That much larger entitlement, though earned through years of payroll taxes, is very expensive to the Treasury and the subject of some political controversy. When the economy gets bad enough, fewer workers find jobs each month, and more people already near the retirement age take the plunge into Social Security.

In the third quarter of 2012—long after the recession was over and well into the Obama recovery—this produced a rather dramatic effect. On net, about seven workers were added to Social Security's disability and retirement rolls for every ten workers who found jobs.[29] The current ratio is just above three retirees for every ten workers. This does not bode well for the Social Security program's health.

And then there are programs for the poor. Social Security, like unemployment insurance, is a benefit for which you and your employer pay. But when times are very difficult, the taxpayer steps in to assist those most in need through what are known as "means-tested" programs.

In an era when there seems to be a new corporate welfare giveaway every week, means-tested programs are not the worst use of American taxpayers' money. But when the number of people on public assistance spikes, it's not something to celebrate—it's a sign that things are going horribly wrong in the economy.

The food stamp issue was never given the treatment it deserved during the 2012 cycle. That's primarily because, in certain corners of the media, charges of racism were routinely leveled at anyone who dared mention it. This was a fool-proof method for suppressing this big story—not about the people who go on food stamps, but about the economic conditions that forced them to go there by taking away their self-sufficiency.

Obviously, one expects to see a rise in public assistance when a recession is on. But more than three years after the recession's end, dependence on government for basic needs continued to grow rapidly. In June 2009, when the recession ended, there were 35 million participants in the food stamp program nationwide. By August 2012, there were 47 million—an increase of 34 percent.[30] Not only have those who enrolled in the program not left it, but new people are being added each month. The food stamp rolls are setting new records month after month.

The program's modest benefit surely helped a lot of needy people feed their families. One need not object to this to realize that such a handout is not the same thing as an economic recovery that helps people stand on their own two feet—an economic recovery that hasn't happened under President Obama's policies. And that's a story.

People who have the manufacturing jobs with good pay that Obama promised to deliver generally aren't eligible for food stamps.

Story Idea: Dirty Fuels Drive the "Obama Recovery"

You can't blame Barack Obama for being president during an unexpected oil and gas boom any more than you can blame him for inheriting a financial crisis.

Obama has tried to take some credit for the gas part of this fossil fuel bonanza—the more environmentally friendly part. But he spends a lot more time demonizing the oil companies that are currently building America's economic future—the ones that are hiring people to wages well above the national average and making the Obama recovery look a lot better than it otherwise would.

"Unlike my opponent," Obama said in his speech at the Democratic National Convention, "I will not let oil companies write this country's energy plan, or endanger our coastlines, or collect another $4 billion in corporate welfare from our taxpayers."[31] This was typical fare for Obama throughout the campaign. At times, he promised to end the industry's tax breaks ("I'm not worried about the big oil companies," he explained) as part of a plan to lower gas prices for American families.[32] And yes, that makes no sense, but … global warming. So there.

When the news media report that 100,000 jobs are created in a month, that's a net number. It really means that millions of workers lost jobs, millions found jobs, and 100,000 was the difference between the two. Economic surges in some industries and in some states cancel out the grim and depressing stories of layoffs from others. High-wages in one field cancel out declining wages in another.

So to the extent that there were good jobs being created in the Obama recovery, where were they coming from? What if the only major source of good-paying, full-time sustainable jobs is the industry Obama routinely denounces and threatens, and whose "clean energy" competitors he is constantly subsidizing?

Obama did his part to tamp down oil and gas exploration on federal land during his first term, but he can only do so much. The Interior Department clamped down—despite a lack of scientific justification—on federal production after the BP oil spill, with the result that oil production on federal lands and waters fell by 14 percent between 2010 and 2011 and is now below 2003 levels. Production in the Gulf of Mexico, where most federal oil is produced, was projected to fall even further in 2012.[33]

Natural gas production on federal lands also fell by about 14 percent in Obama's first two fiscal years in office. In September 2012, offshore natural gas production in the Gulf of Mexico—which again accounts for most federal offshore production—was down 44 percent from the month Obama took office.[34]

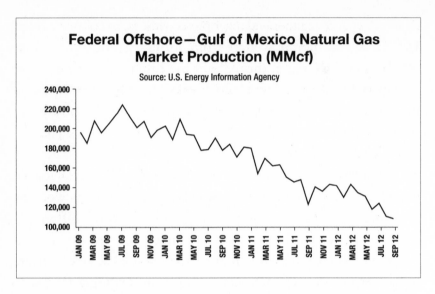

But private lands have more than made up the difference. Despite Obama's best efforts, gas production overall still increased by more than 11 percent over the same period.

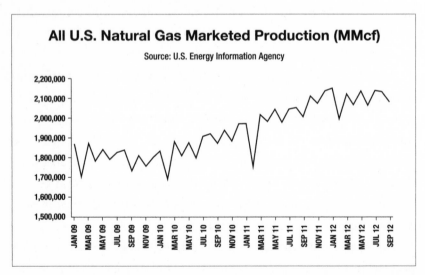

Part of the reason for the decline in federal production is that in 2012, it took 307 days on average to get a permit to drill on federal land—nearly twice the time it took in 2005.[35] But in little North Dakota, it takes just ten days to get a permit to drill on private land. And they're drilling, all right.

North Dakota is setting new records in oil production every month, and has passed up traditional oil powerhouse states like Alaska and California. Over a six-year period, the state increased its oil production six-fold, to 730,000 barrels per day. Energy policy wonks now jokingly refer to "Saudi Dakota," and indeed, the state's production will soon reach 10 percent that of the Middle Eastern kingdom everyone immediately associates with oil.

Then there's natural gas. The amount produced and sold in North Dakota tripled between June 2009 and September 2012. They're finding so much gas as they drill for oil that, for the moment, at least, they have to burn off a substantial portion of it because the infrastructure hasn't caught up to the point that they can get it to market.

How did this happen? New drilling techniques, such as horizontal drilling and hydraulic fracturing (or "fracking"), combined with oil prices high enough to make these methods economically feasible, are turning the United States into the world's energy juggernaut. For the last three years, it's been saving America from economic ruin.

High-paying jobs in the oil and gas industry are forming the core of a new economy in North Dakota. Employers—including even the local chain restaurants—can't even find enough workers. The number of jobs in the state is up 14.5 percent since the recession ended. Wages are way up too, and the state's seasonally adjusted unemployment rate in October 2012 stood at an astonishingly low 3.1 percent[36]—well below the levels that economists usually refer to as "full employment."

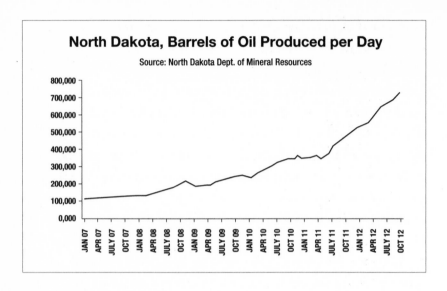

This boom is real, it is historic, and it's not limited to just one state. In Colorado and Texas, Ohio and Michigan, Pennsylvania and Wyoming (among others) the oil is flowing and the gas is bubbling up to the surface. Despite the drop in production on federal land, overall U.S. oil production rose nearly 17 percent between the recession's end in June 2009 and August 2012, according to the Department of Energy. And it will keep rising. Just after the election, the International Energy Agency released projections showing the United States eclipsing Saudi Arabia in oil production before the end of this decade.

As I noted above, President Obama did try to claim some credit for the fossil fuel boom in his campaign speeches. During the 2012 campaign, he touted an IHS Global Insight report on "unconventional" (mostly shale) natural gas production. It showed that directly, indirectly, and through surrounding economic activity, shale gas alone (not including oil) was supporting 649,000 jobs in 2010.[37] A subsequent report in the same series was released in October 2012, showing that between 2010 and 2012, "unconventional" gas exploration had created 250,000 new jobs, for a total of 900,000.[38] It also said that the emerging "unconventional" oil market was supporting 845,000 jobs in 2012, for a total of more than 1.7 million jobs.

The media reacted to all of this with appropriate excitement, but nobody thought to ask: "Doesn't this mean that oil and gas are almost single-handedly saving the economy—and your presidency?"

Whatever his most enthusiastic fans may tell you, Obama definitely did not put that shale under the ground. Nor did he create fracking, nor even (despite his claim to the contrary in his 2012 State of the Union Address) was it the result of government investment.[39]

At best, Obama deserves credit for not doing too much in his first term to hurt the industry. So far, his Transportation Department is the only bureaucracy to do anything of substance to harass it. In July 2012, the Federal Motor Carrier Safety Administration reinterpreted a safety rule in a way that makes it more expensive for the unconventional oil and gas industries to handle their delivery and transportation systems, inspiring an angry response from several dozen members of Congress.[40] Obama's EPA is also expected to produce new "fracking" regulations in his second term, which could pose a much bigger threat.[41]

The oil and gas boom has been great for America, but it has also put a black smudge on many environmental activists' visions of a green future. They don't have as big a problem with gas, which is at least less carbon-intensive than coal, but a cottage industry of fracking scaremongers has already cropped up to decry the methods by which it is being extracted. And if America becomes the new Saudi Arabia of oil, then Obama's goal of making "clean" energy more popular and economically feasible through large subsidies will be set back decades—to the extent that its spectacular bankruptcies haven't already set it back.

For all that, the oil and gas boom worked in Obama's favor in the 2012 election, and in the media coverage he got. His anti-carbon, ocean-lowering aspirations did not prevent a fossil fuel explosion from statistically masking the economic pain produced by large job losses elsewhere.

Unconventional oil and gas is the best thing America's economy has going for it right now. It came out of nowhere in recent years and now supports 1.7 million good-paying jobs in all. IHS Global Insight projects they will create another 1.3 million jobs by 2015. In a period when businesses were loath to make capital investments, unconventional oil and gas accounted for $87 billion in capital expenditures in 2012.

Where would we be without dirty oil and gas and fracking? Probably, we'd have just inaugurated a different man as president.

Story Idea: Amid New Union Push, Right-to-Work States Gain an Edge

In my book *Gangster Government*, I wrote at length about the Obama administration's efforts to stave off the demise of labor unions as a political force. Organized labor now represents less than 7 percent of the private-sector workforce, and Obama is on the job to rescue it from irrelevance. Whatever you think of unions, there's no question where Obama stands.

His intervention in the automakers' hasty bankruptcy processes—which was against precedent and of questionable legality—was primarily designed as a large bailout for the United Auto Workers, which had lost about half of its members in the preceding decade. The administration's defenders repeatedly point out that there were no buyers for the auto companies. But that may not have been so were it not for the requirement, imposed by the Treasury Department, that the UAW sign off on any deal. We will never know for sure, but thanks to Obama's work, the union's benefits fund is several billion dollars richer and the union itself has more remaining members than it would have otherwise.

During his first two years in office, Obama tried but failed to secure congressional support for the Employee Free Choice Act, also known as the card-check law. Had it passed, that bill would have made it much easier for unions to seize monopoly bargaining power in more workplaces with fewer workers' support, and to force companies into federal contract arbitration more quickly.

In a break with seventy-six years of legal precedent, Obama's appointees on the National Mediation Board altered unionization election rules for airlines and railroads in favor of the unions, so that they could take over representation without even getting 50 percent of a company's workers to vote in favor. (This was an attempt to influence one particular unionization election, among Delta's 20,000 flight attendants. It failed when the flight attendants rejected the union anyway in fall 2010, but the precedent might still matter.)

In January 2012, even though the Senate was not in recess, Obama made three recess appointments to the National Labor Relations Board, which has been on a pro-union rule-writing tear. Its new regulations include a requirement—found in no statute— that employers advertise union membership to their employees. The same board persecuted the Boeing Corporation for adding production lines in South Carolina—a right-to-work state, where no one can be forced to pay for union representation—because of repeated strikes by its workers in Washington State.

Obama has moved on from these initiatives to new ground. By the time this book is in stores, his Labor Department is expected to produce new rules forcing employers to give union organizers any and all contact information they have for employees, including cell phone numbers and email addresses.

It's very clear where Obama stands on labor policy—he helps his friends. Unions spent hundreds of millions of dollars and sent entire armies of volunteers to get him elected and reelected.

That makes it more interesting to look at where jobs are being created in his recovery. Because Michigan's just-signed right-to-work law does not take effect until April 2013, there are now twenty-three right-to-work states (Indiana just became one in February 2012), and twenty-seven where unions can compel workers to pay dues as a condition of their employment. According to the Bureau of Labor Statistics, the rate of job creation in right-to-work states during the Obama recovery—that is, since June 2009—has been 26 percent higher than in the other states.[42]

Everyone agrees—and President Obama has said it himself—that employers and entrepreneurs have been keeping capital on the sidelines. Conservatives argue that part of the reason is Obama's policies, including his many efforts to make it easier for unions to gum up the works of businesses. Is it just possible that the statistic above is a meaningful sign of something happening in the labor force? Could it be that job-creators, when given the choice, are doing an end-run around Obama's labor policies by setting up in right-to-work states? After all, that's exactly what Boeing tried to do.

That's a story.

The press did at least confront some elements of this trend, because Mitt Romney offered a similar statistic while wooing primary voters in 2011. But it came only in the form of a fact-check, and the results were somewhat at odds with the facts.

At a public appearance in South Carolina Romney said this:

> [R]ight-to-work states, those 22, have created 3 million jobs over the last 10 years. The union states have lost about half a million jobs. So right to work is the way to go if you want good jobs.

Josh Hicks, writing for Glenn Kessler's *Washington Post* fact-checker, pointed out first that Romney kind of flubbed the numbers to the detriment of his own argument. In fact, right-to-work states had created 3.6 million jobs over the ten preceding years (going by the Labor Department's household survey), whereas the other states had lost 900,000 jobs on aggregate. (The disparity was similar in the Labor Department's other measure, the payroll survey.)

That didn't stop Hicks from giving Romney's statement "two Pinocchios." Hicks pointed out, correctly, that correlation does not necessarily imply causation. He quoted Gordon Lafer, a professor at the University of Oregon, who pointed out that "states with names that start with the letters 'n' through 'z' grew faster over the past decade... That's actually true, but it's not meaningful in policy terms."

But it's a bit careless to dismiss Romney's argument this way for three reasons. First, the statement that right-to-work states create jobs faster appears to be true both over short and long periods of time. It's true over Romney's ten-year period, and it's also true through the Obama recovery period that I cited above.

Second, it's very hard to find any evidence that contradicts the hypothesis of a right-to-work advantage. For example, Thomas Holmes of the Federal Reserve Bank of Minneapolis wrote a 1998 academic paper in which he looked at the forty-five years between 1947 (the year the Taft-Hartley Act allowed states to choose right-to-work) and 1992.[43] Holmes tried to isolate state economic policy differences from non-policy considerations (cost of living, weather, geography, *et cetera*) by comparing counties along the borders of right-to-work states. Holmes found that over the forty-five-year period, in which national non-farm employment grew by about 150 percent in the United States, the counties on the right-to-work sides of state borders enjoyed a 41 percent higher growth rate for manufacturing jobs.

Holmes carefully noted that other pro-business state-level policies could have contributed to this effect—lower taxes, for example,
or a better civil tort climate, or better subsidies for companies that
came in. But given the consistency of the results in multiple states
over nearly any period of time, it's hard to dismiss the relationship
with Pinocchios. All in all, the statistical case is strong enough that
journalists should take it seriously. It would be an awfully big coincidence for right-to-work states to outperform their counterparts so
consistently just by chance.

Third, the numbers are accompanied by plenty of anecdotal
evidence. If you ever hear a CEO talk about how he'd rather operate
in a state whose name starts with the letters "n" through "z," expect
him to be fired. But when the circumstances give them the choice,
you can bet that decision-makers in the business world think about
right-to-work when they're considering expansion. It's no accident
that unionized manufacturing jobs fell by 75 percent between 1977
and 2008.[44] Nor that, on aggregate, non-union manufacturing
employment actually increased by 6 percent during the same period.
The premium that businesses have to pay for a unionized workforce
may seem good for workers, but businesses that pay it instead of
reinvesting profits tend to fall behind their competitors, especially
in a global marketplace.

The Boeing story offers one such example. That company didn't
mind so much paying a modest wage premium for a union workforce
in Washington State—and in fact, it never tried to fire any of its
workers there. But as its executives noted (in comments that ultimately brought the Obama administration down on them), it was
unlikely it would ever be able to meet orders for its new 787 Dream-
liner jets if it had to rely on the members of the constantly striking
Machinists' union.[45]

The pain that even small unions can thus inflict was amply dem-
onstrated in the port strike on the West Coast in late November
2012. An eight-day strike by just six hundred of America's best-paid

clerical workers—members of the International Longshore and Warehouse Union—cost the U.S. economy $8 billion and left more than a million workers in the shipping chain without paychecks.[46] Imagine if a much larger share of American workers were in unions—as Obama's Labor Department is pushing for—and such strikes became more commonplace.

The auto industry, which has brought so much foreign investment to the United States, provides another example. Obama may have saved the UAW in Michigan and Ohio—for now. But as *Reason* columnist Shikha Dalmia notes: "Not a single foreign automaker has built a factory in Michigan, the auto capital of the world, whose highly trained auto work force—you'd think—would give it an unbeatable advantage."[47] Although foreign companies did go to Ohio and Indiana (before it became a right-to-work state), the trend has been to build factories in right-to-work states not previously known for automobile manufacturing: Tennessee (Toyota, Nissan, and Volkswagen), South Carolina (BMW), Alabama (Honda, Mercedes-Benz, Toyota, and Hyundai), Georgia (Kia), Texas (Toyota), and Mississippi (Toyota and Nissan).[48]

When the Chamber of Commerce—best described as the lobbying arm of big business—weighs in on the issue, they invariably weigh in on the right-to-work side. That's what the national and state chambers' members pay them to do. Right-to-work isn't everything for a business—just as low taxes aren't everything—but it's a meaningful something.

There are legitimate policy arguments against right-to-work, and many union supporters make them. But it's pretty clear which one job creators prefer, and it's a rational preference, unlike a state's location on an alphabetical chart.

During the Obama recovery, businesses have been voting with their feet against Obama's pro-union policies. Luckily for Obama, there are plenty of places within the United States where they can go to escape without hurting the jobs numbers or the unemployment rate. And there are plenty of political reporters who will be too busy writing about the War on Women to notice the trend.

The Untold Stories

During the 2012 election, an emaciated version of America's labor market was making a feeble comeback. Amid the horserace coverage, the trends beneath the surface were missed or ignored.

This wasn't entirely a story about Obama. Some of the unhealthy trends, such as the shift from middle-income to low-wage jobs, were underway long before he took office—albeit more slowly than during his recovery. But Obama had specifically pledged to preside over a recovery that would put America's economy on a firmer foundation—not one that would hollow it out.

The Obama recovery—the period after the recession ended—is replacing full-time jobs with part-time jobs. It's replacing high-wage jobs with low-wage jobs. It has seniors holding more and more jobs while young and middle-aged workers can't resume their careers in the jobs they lost in the recession. It has workers going on public assistance and disability insurance because there are few jobs to be had, and the ones out there pay too little to feed a family. It has employers looking for an escape from Obama's labor policies, which they find in right-to-work states.

The Obama recovery is also about hundreds of thousands of excellent, high-paying jobs, inconveniently being created in an industry at whose mention Obama practically spits. It is about the paradox that, even as his green jobs boom went bust, an energy jobs boom occurred in the industry which he routinely demonized, whose taxes he promised to raise, and whose profitability the EPA might soon threaten through regulations on fracking.

These all sound like good stories. Maybe when there's a Republican president, someone will write such stories again.

CHAPTER FOUR

THE WAR ON WOMEN

"Who woke up in the Republican Party one day recently and said, 'I know what we'll go after, let's go after reproductive rights?' What was that about?"

—Brian Williams, anchor, NBC *Nightly News*, March 6, 2012

O f all the ways journalists helped Barack Obama win reelection in 2012, there were few more overt than the media's promotion of the Democrats' accusation that they were waging a "war on women."

The Obama campaign and congressional Democrats decided early on to make "women's issues"—especially abortion and contraception—major campaign themes. At the risk of alienating the many Americans who are not quite so zealous about the need for abortion on demand, they even gave this theme a leading role at the Democratic National Convention in September.

The media did their part, providing Democrats with a platform from which to make their allegations unchallenged. The media sidelined legitimate concerns about religious freedom, just as they blithely assumed that all women are naturally pro-abortion, dismissing the millions of American women who view the intentional taking of unborn human life as wrong and consider pregnancy and motherhood as a blessing, not a threat.

Republicans and conservatives didn't help themselves. A few of them made cringe-inducing gaffes at inopportune moments that reinforced the Democrats' allegations. But most of the media didn't seem nearly as interested in investigating the Democrats' accusations as in amplifying them.

For a political campaign to accuse one of America's two main political parties of being "at war" with half the country is really beyond the pale; for the media to collaborate with such a campaign is a scandal.

"Contraception, It's Working Just Fine, Just Leave It Alone"

Given the media's portrayal of Mitt Romney and other Republicans, Americans would have been justified in believing that Republicans really did want to ban birth control. But it wasn't a Republican who got the ball rolling on this specious narrative of the 2012 campaign. It was the media.

After Rick Santorum won the Iowa caucuses in early January there was some interest in his publicly stated but strictly personal opposition to contraception, based on his Catholic faith. He had been asked to clarify in an interview with Fox News' Bill O'Reilly. This is what he said:

O'REILLY: You say that the states should have the right to ban some contraception. That's right off the bat going to be a big one.

SANTORUM: Well, the states have a right to do a lot of things. That doesn't mean they should do it. Someone asked me if the states have the right to do it? Yes. They have the right to do it, they shouldn't do it. I wouldn't vote for it if they did. It doesn't mean they don't have the right to do it. As you know, Bill, you're a Catholic, Catholic Church teaches contraceptive is something you shouldn't do. So when I was asked the question on contraception I said I didn't support it.[1]

Santorum's explanation was pretty straightforward. He distinguished between his own choice not to use contraception on the one hand and public policy on the other, noting that he did not support and would vote against any ban on contraception.

But those subtleties were lost on Chris Matthews, who followed up by interviewing a former Santorum aide about the clip transcribed above. After playing the clip, he went on:

MATTHEWS: Let me tell you what he said. He's said "My religion should dominate, should trump issues of the Constitution."... He was saying, "Bill O'Reilly, you and I are of the same religion, therefore we should deny a woman's constitutional right to buy birth control or a male to buy birth control." Isn't that what he said? We just showed the tape.

ROBERT TRAYNHAM: I don't think he said that.

MATTHEWS: He just did. Ok, he just did. And that's what scares me. He thinks we should have a theocracy.[2]

The media's distortion of the contraception debate continued much like this, straight through Election Day.

Two days later, at the New Hampshire Republican primary debate of January 7, 2012, this issue finally had its breakthrough when former Clinton communications director and *Good Morning America* co-host George Stephanopoulos badgered Mitt Romney with a bizarre series of questions about birth control.

> STEPHANOPOULOS: Governor Romney, do you believe that states have the right to ban contraception? Or is that trumped by a constitutional right to privacy?

> ROMNEY: George, this is an unusual topic that you're raising. States have a right to ban contraception? I can't imagine a state banning contraception. I can't imagine the circumstances where a state would want to do so, and if I were a governor of a state or... STEPHANOPOULOS: Well, the Supreme Court has ruled—

> ROMNEY:... or a—or a legislature of a state—I would totally and completely oppose any effort to ban contraception. So you're asking—given the fact that there's no state that wants to do so, and I don't know of any candidate that wants to do so, you're asking could it constitutionally be done? We can ask our constitutionalist here. (Points to Ron Paul, to laughter.)

> George, I—I don't know whether a state has a right to ban contraception. No state wants to. I mean, the idea of you putting forward things that states might want to do that no—no state wants to do and asking me whether they could do it or not is kind of a silly thing, I think.

In fact, it was very silly. It certainly wasn't journalism. No one on that stage wanted to ban contraception, nor was any kind of state ban even remotely in the works, nor were these candidates for a state office. No voter was learning anything from this.

The question's sole purpose was to leave people with the same misleading impression Matthews had tried to create. It was an attempt to get candidates to say they did not embrace the "right to privacy" doctrine that eventually led to the *Roe v. Wade* abortion decision, and then—gotcha!—make it look like Republicans wanted to ban contraception.

Stephanopoulos was not ashamed to push on with his interrogation:

> STEPHANOPOULOS: Hold on a second. Governor, you went to Harvard Law School. You know very well this is based on...

> ROMNEY: Has the Supreme Court—has the Supreme Court decided that states do not have the right to provide contraception? I...

> STEPHANOPOULOS: Yes, they have. In 1965, *Griswold v. Connecticut.*

> ROMNEY: The—I believe in the—that the law of the land is as spoken by the Supreme Court, and that if we disagree with the Supreme Court—and occasionally I do—then we have a process under the Constitution to change that decision. And it's—it's known as the amendment process.... But I know of—of no reason to talk about contraception in this regard.

STEPHANOPOULOS: But you've got the Supreme Court decision finding a right to privacy in the Constitution.

ROMNEY: I don't believe they decided that correctly. In my view, *Roe v. Wade* was improperly decided. It was based upon that same principle. And in my view, if we had justices like Roberts, Alito, Thomas, and Scalia, and more justices like that, they might well decide to return this issue to states as opposed to saying it's in the federal Constitution.

And by the way, if the people say it should be in the federal Constitution, then instead of having unelected judges stuff it in there when it's not there, we should allow the people to express their own views through amendment and add it to the Constitution. But this idea that justice...

STEPHANOPOULOS: But should that be done in this case?

ROMNEY: Pardon?

STEPHANOPOULOS: Should that be done in this case?

ROMNEY: Should this be done in the case—this case to allow states to ban contraception? No. States don't want to ban contraception. So why would we try and put it in the Constitution? With regards to gay marriage, I've told you, that's when I would amend the Constitution. Contraception, it's working just fine, just leave it alone.

(APPLAUSE)

STEPHANOPOULOS: I understand that. But you've given two answers to the question.

Do you believe that the Supreme Court should over-turn it or not?

ROMNEY: Do I believe the Supreme Court should over-turn *Roe v. Wade*? Yes, I do.[3]

This was, to put it bluntly, a clown question. The degree to which Stephanopoulos belabored it is demonstrative of the liberal media's obsession with making Republicans appear to support the criminalization of birth control. Romney gave it more of an answer than it deserved in his first sentence, yet Stephanopoulos set a record for candidate-hounding in presidential debates.

By merely asking this question, though, Stephanopoulos dam-aged Republicans and created a Democratic propaganda coup. He did it, conveniently, a few weeks before the Obama administration released its widely expected Obamacare regulations forcing Catho-lic institutions and employers to pay the full cost of all employees' birth control or else pay fines.

Stephanopoulos wasn't just helping Obama advance a meme—he was actually doing advance work for Obama's campaign.

From there, the rest of the media picked up the ball. First came the Associated Press wire service story in the early morning of January 8:

> ROMNEY SAYS DISCUSSION ABOUT
> CONTRACEPTION "SILLY"
> Republican presidential contender Mitt Romney tried
> to avoid answering a question about whether states
> should be able to ban contraceptives…

Then came the opinion columnists.

"Caution: This presidential campaign endangers reproductive health," wrote liberal columnist Clarence Page. "Women's rights to contraception and other reproductive health services seem to face even more than the usual threats from the 2012 Republican presidential candidates. All of which raises new questions about whose freedoms today's conservatives really want to defend."[4]

Anna Holmes penned a piece for the *Washington Post* Style section titled, "GOP candidates revive issue of birth control,"[5] which is kind of an interesting way of putting it, given how the subject was thrust into the national spotlight.

> The fact that the issue of birth control is even up for debate and that its detractors and naysayers aren't being laughed off the public stage is profoundly depressing...[T]he newly explicit GOP attack on reproductive health services underscores what many abortion-rights activists and advocates have known all along: that opposition to abortion is not always about opposition to pregnancy termination or the fantasy of saving cute, chubby babies but to the very idea that women can, and should, make decisions about their own bodies, and that sex is for more than just procreation.

Both Page and Holmes, whose columns were published two days apart, seemed to be singing from the same party hymnal.

Wrote Holmes:

> To be clear: No one in the race for the GOP nomination has called for an explicit ban on contraception...[O]ne only need to deny funding for and otherwise chip away at existing reproductive rights laws in order to make an impact. The strategy: Defund family-planning initiatives and organizations, legislate away health insurance coverage

of birth control or block FDA approval for new preventatives....

Wrote Page:

> But none of the candidates is calling for an outright ban on contraceptives. Instead they would chip away at women's access, especially if it receives federal funding. They would deny funding to family-planning initiatives and organizations. They would legislate away health insurance coverage of birth control. They would block FDA approval for almost any new contraceptive....

However you want to phrase it, at least these two both got the very first part right. Nobody wanted to ban contraception. Yet everyone seemed to know the Republicans' strategy for making it impossible to get contraception, except for the Republicans themselves.

Given the ubiquity and low price of contraceptives, it might have seemed like a strange issue to dwell on. No one lacks access to something that costs $9 per month at Target or Walmart.

But Stephanopoulos, the former Democratic operative, had done more than help introduce an irrelevancy to campaign 2012. He had helped dig out a new trench for the left to fight from in the culture war. Losing ground on abortion, they preferred to shift the subject to birth control. The media created this story, and the Obama campaign reaped the benefits throughout the rest of the year. In an early March broadcast, NBC *Nightly News* anchor Brian Williams said, "One issue that's been percolating through this presidential primary season, a push by some in the GOP to limit women's access to contraceptives and abortion."[6] The media were covering a self-generated story that wasn't actually happening.

Then the broadcast went to correspondent Andrea Mitchell, who explained that presidential candidate Rick Santorum said he opposed contraception. But in doing so, Mitchell failed to make the crucial distinction that while Santorum is personally opposed to contraceptives he has repeatedly stated he would not support banning them.[7]

What few journalists mentioned was that cheap, and often free, birth control is ubiquitous in America, and nobody has ever threatened to take it away.

The only issue that actually arose, with the Obamacare HHS mandate of late January, was whether employers with conscientious objections would be forced to pay 100 percent of the cost. As we will see in a subsequent chapter, those employers' rights of conscience were sidelined in favor of "war on women" propaganda.

And a major part of the issue was not about conscience or birth control, but corporate welfare. With 100 percent coverage, contraceptive manufacturers could get more women to use their most expensive forms of contraception, thus reaping larger profits. But the war on women got a lot more attention than that minor detail.

With the media's help, Democrats did everything they could to make the 2012 election a referendum on the right to contracept—a right that no one was trying to take away. The media made a story out of a non-story, and it helped keep Barack Obama's political foes off-balance.

Origin of a Specious Argument

Democrats have charged Republicans with waging wars against women for decades. The push this time was especially urgent. In the 2010 midterm elections, congressional Republicans had won female voters for the first time since 1982.[8] This set off alarm bells at DNC headquarters.

For the next year, President Obama and the Democrats continued to hemorrhage support, especially among women, who had been particularly hurt by the struggling economy. According to Gallup, by August 2011, Obama's approval rating among women stood at 41 percent, an all-time low.[9]

This is part of the reason why, by early 2011, the "Republican war on women" had already become a regular Democratic talking point. House Democratic Minority Leader Nancy Pelosi of California began using the phrase "war on women" to describe Republican efforts to restrict taxpayer funding for Planned Parenthood, the country's largest abortion business. "There is actually a war on women," Pelosi told hundreds of activists attending the Women Money Power Summit sponsored by the Feminist Majority Foundation in April of that year.[10]

Democratic National Committee Chairwoman Debbie Wasserman Schultz accused Republicans of being "anti-woman" and of waging a "war on women" in pursuit of an "extremely radical social agenda."[11]

And the news media began picking up and repeating not just the theme of a battle over women's rights, but the Democrats' actual propaganda phrase—"war on women." In February 2011, the *New York Times* published an editorial titled, "The War on Women," which accused Republicans of "mounting an assault on women's health and freedom."[12]

The "assault" was actually an attempt by House Republicans to pass a budget that would have, among other things, ended subsidies to Planned Parenthood. Planned Parenthood receives $350 million from taxpayers annually in government grants and contracts even though it has its own robust donor base and makes tens of millions of dollars in yearly profits, mostly from the hundreds of thousands of abortions it performs annually.

At least *Washington Post* columnist Ruth Marcus was a bit more nuanced in her characterization of the GOP attempt to defund Planned Parenthood, labeling it part of the "GOP's war on family planning."[13]

A good example of how the media amplified the "war on women" theme came in the debate over a bill presented in the House of Representatives in 2011, called the "Protect Life Act." It would have amended Obamacare to prevent federal subsidies for abortion coverage. It contained exceptions for rape, incest, and to save the life of the mother. It would have also protected health care workers from losing their jobs because they didn't want to assist in abortions.

Pelosi argued that if it passed, "women can die on the floor and health care providers do not have to intervene."[14] This obviously ridiculous statement was not challenged, but instead repeated by the media.

MSNBC's Martin Bashir called Republican supporters of the Protect Life Act "misogynists" and labeled the bill the "let women die act."[15] In her *Washington Post* blog "On Faith," Sally Quinn wrote, "Some call it the 'Protect Life Act' while others deem it the 'Let Women Die Act.'"[16] Quinn's piece spun so hard as to state that it would allow "hospitals to refuse abortion to a woman, regardless of whether her life was in danger."

The media elites seemed to be playing a game of telephone with one another. Repeat the silly phrase, and keep repeating it, and keep making wilder claims that make it sillier. It's a lot less work than explaining the nuances of an issue to readers.

"Where Are the Women?"

On February 16, 2012, the House Oversight and Government Reform Committee convened a hearing to discuss the effects of the contraceptive mandate on religious freedom. One of the panels was comprised of five clergymen. That no women appeared prompted three Democrats to walk out of the hearing, and a media frenzy to ensue.

"What I want to know is, where are the women?" Democratic Representative Carolyn Maloney of New York asked before walking out.[17] "I look at this panel, and I don't see one single individual representing the tens of millions of women across the country who want and need insurance coverage for basic preventative health care services, including family planning. Where are the women?"[18]

Democratic Delegate Eleanor Holmes Norton of the District of Columbia told journalists outside the hearing that she left because it was being conducted like an "autocratic regime."[19]

Democrats had invited a Georgetown University Law Center student and abortion activist named Sandra Fluke to testify. But Republicans had rejected her appearance because she was not a member of a clergy or an expert on religious liberty.

Two women did in fact testify that day on the hearing's second panel. But it didn't matter: "Where are the women?" was already fast becoming a rallying cry for liberals. News outlets across the country pitched in by displaying photos of the panel full of men and uncritically repeating the Democrats' outrage.

Minority Leader Nancy Pelosi held a press conference later in the day. "Imagine having a panel on women's health and they don't have any women on the panel…Duh." she said.[20]

The incident made headlines for days—and was portrayed in the media as yet more proof of a Republican war on women.

"Birth control hearing on Capitol Hill had mostly male panel of witnesses," blared a *Washington Post* headline.[21] National Public Radio reported, "A photo of the lineup quickly circulated the Internet—appearing on Twitter and Facebook feeds and landing on women's rights advocacy blogs."[22]

Later, a group of Democratic women senators took to the Senate floor to protest the lack of women, which they called an "assault on women." All the major news networks gave the story attention. An ABC News headline quoted Democratic Senator Patty Murray of Washington, who said, "Reading the news this morning was like stepping into a time machine and going back 50 years."[23] The story quoted four female Democratic senators' responses to the panel and only one Republican.

Democrats weren't done, and neither were the media. Congressional Democrats held an unofficial hearing a few days later, and invited Ms. Fluke to testify. They were determined to milk the story for all it was worth, and then some.

Fluke complained that her friends could not receive birth control from Georgetown University, a Catholic institution, and argued that Georgetown should be forced to dispense free contraceptives.

Fluke's appearance would have been quickly forgotten, but for Rush Limbaugh. He's been called the de facto boss of the Republican Party, but apparently he's the de facto boss of the mainstream media as well,[24] at least when the media can capitalize on his remarks. He called Fluke a "slut" and a "prostitute" on air, and that made her the biggest story in the country for weeks.

It catapulted Fluke into the frontlines of the battle over the Obamacare mandate, and helped Democrats keep the "war on women" theme alive. President Obama called Fluke to offer his support and solidarity, comparing her to one of his young daughters.

This silly story outweighed real and serious ones discussed throughout this book. Blame Rush if you want to for using a crude sexual slur, but more blame belongs to a media that would rather deal in easy, frivolous issues than do the hard work of researching and dissecting complicated ones. What was the bigger story, after all: that the Obama administration with its HHS mandate was subverting the First Amendment and the rights of the largest Christian denomination in the country, or that a radio show host had used shock jock language on air?

During the Limbaugh-Fluke dust-up, the media focused on little else. Fluke became a media-created celebrity. CNN's Soledad O'Brien introduced her on air: "We move on to talk about the controversy over birth control. The woman who became, really, the center of that controversy is speaking out today."[25]

CNN's Carol Costello introduced Fluke as the "woman who became the face of the fight over whether insurance plans should cover contraceptives."[26] Later, at the Democratic National Convention in September, CNN's Brianna Keilar noted Rush's slut comments and then asked Fluke if she thought Rush's "views represent Mitt Romney and the Republican Party?"[27] After the election, *Time* magazine nominated Fluke as one of forty finalists for "Person of the Year."[28] If she wins, she'll be in the same company with such greats as Mohandas Gandhi, Ronald Reagan, Lech Walesa, and Pope John Paul II.

Was the public's interest at all commensurate with this media frenzy? Here's an indication for you: In the late stages of the 2012 election campaign, Fluke served as a surrogate for President Obama. She staged an event in Reno, Nevada, to promote his reelection.

Ten people showed up to listen.

And yes, the media were there to cover it.[29]

Is This a Story, or Someone's Talking Point?

Numerous polls throughout the campaign showed contraceptives and abortion coming in last among voters' priorities. An April 2012 Gallup poll found them at the very bottom of a long list of issues voters cared about. "Most voters in the United States say issues such as healthcare, unemployment, the federal deficit, international issues, and gas prices are important to their presidential vote, but less than half say the same about federal birth control policies," Gallup's Frank Newport wrote.[30]

A May 2012 Kaiser Family Foundation poll found that less than one-third (31 percent) of women believed there is an ongoing and "wide-scale effort to limit women's reproductive health choices and services."[31]

Later that month, the Pew Research Center released a poll that suggested a similar conclusion. "With Voters Focused on Economy, Obama Lead Narrows; Social Issues Rank as Lowest Priorities,"[32] ran the headline. According to the poll, "About four-in-ten (39 percent) say that abortion will be very important to their vote, 34 percent rate birth control as very important, and just 28 percent say the same about gay marriage—the lowest percentage for any issue."[33]

Abortion and birth control ranked sixteenth and seventeenth out of eighteen issues in regards to the share of respondents who said the issue was "very important" to their vote.[34] And in a Rasmussen Reports poll on September 21, 2012, abortion didn't make voters' top ten.[35]

Now, compare that to what the news media wrote about and discussed. For fun, I ran searches for certain terms through the Nexis database of U.S. publications and television and radio transcripts, to see how many times certain terms appeared along with one of the two presidential candidates' names during the last two weeks before the election. Here are the results:

Abortion	2,910
Unemployment rate	2,115
Benghazi	1,980
Contraception/Birth Control	1,159
Christopher/Chris Stevens	482
"War on Women"	233
Sandra Fluke (eight months after her big moment)	40

Were the media out of touch with America during the 2012 campaign cycle? Yes and hell yes. If you didn't know better, you'd almost say they were trying to set voters' priorities.

What War on Women?

No two words sum up Republicans' woes in 2012 better than "legitimate rape." Asked by a reporter in August about his opposition to abortion in cases of rape, Missouri Senate Candidate Todd Akin challenged the notion that pregnancy from rape even happens. He said:

> It seems to me, from what I understand from doctors, that's really rare. If it's a legitimate rape, the female body has ways to try to shut that whole thing down. But let's assume that maybe that didn't work or something: I think there should be some punishment, but the punishment ought to be of the rapist, and not attacking the child.[36]

Akin's remark was incorrect, inept, and totally insensitive. Nearly every Republican in the country immediately disavowed him, and many urged him to forfeit the nomination he had just won. Some even urged him to step down as a congressman. Republican donors and super PACs stopped funding his campaign. And the National Republican Senate Committee quickly announced it would not play in Missouri if Akin was on the ballot. Akin's words were also a gift to Democrats, but they were a much more valuable gift because of the media's contribution. This wasn't just a congressman saying something stupid—this was an opportunity for the media to paint the entire Republican Party as anti-woman. And they did.

Washington Post columnist Eugene Robinson said that Akin's comments suggested the Republican view is that unless a woman violently resists a ski-masked assailant who comes through the bedroom window to rape her, "she must have been asking for it."[37] Robinson's headline said Akin's comment brings the "'war on women' back to prominence."[38]

The media made the Akin theme prominent enough that it spilled into the coverage of other races as well. In an October debate, Richard Mourdock, the Indiana State Treasurer and Republican Senate candidate, was asked about the rape exception (almost certainly because the Akin story was so well known by then), and gave this answer:

> I believe that life begins at conception. The only exception I have to have an abortion is in that case of the life of the mother…. I just struggled with it myself for a long time but I came to realize: Life is that gift from God that I think even if life begins in that horrible situation of rape, that it is something that God intended to happen.[39]

Mourdock clearly meant that the creation of all human life is willed by God, but many of the news accounts that followed portrayed him as suggesting that God intended rape. And the media strained to tie Mourdock to Mitt Romney as well. As one ABC News headline put it about a Mourdock ad featuring the Republican presidential nominee, "Romney Hasn't Asked Mourdock to Pull Ad After Rape Comments."[40] Or as a *New York Times* headline put it, "Rape Remark Jolts a Senate Race, and the Presidential One, Too."[41]

So there was a chance to say it again: "What is it with Republicans and rape?"

Akin's comments in particular generated a lot of media attention. An NBC headline stated, "Akin's comments reignite war on women."[42] Piers Morgan, host of CNN's *Piers Morgan Tonight*, said the Akin remark lent credibility to "the argument that the Republican Party is anti-women."[43]

ABC's George Stephanopoulos opened his Sunday show with: "Good morning and welcome to *This Week*. Storms brewing. The

GOP convention threatened by Tropical Storm Isaac and that political hurricane from Todd Akin…"[44]

Broadcasting from the Republican National Convention in late August, CBS's Bob Schieffer asked guest Haley Barbour how Republicans could get the focus back on the economy. Barbour said, "If your first four questions are about it [Akin's comment], it's kind of hard getting the subject back on the economy when you want to talk about Todd Akin." Schieffer shot back, "I want to talk about the news."[45]

But the media were deciding what was newsworthy. And for weeks, it was all Akin, all the time.

Scott Whitlock of the Media Research Center estimated that the ABC, NBC, and CBS evening newscasts and morning shows covered the Akin gaffe for ninety-six minutes in forty-five segments over just the first three and a half days.[46]

By way of comparison: when Notre Dame and forty-two other religious-affiliated institutions sued the Obama administration for violating their religious freedom, that got nineteen seconds of coverage in one segment over the same period of time.

Priorities.

Redefining Rape?

Democrats didn't let any opportunity pass to portray Republicans as misogynists with some kind of sickening fondness for rape. In May 2011, the House of Representatives passed the No Taxpayer Funding of Abortion Act, which included a provision to clarify that Medicaid did not fund abortions in cases of statutory rape.

Under the provision, only cases of "forcible rape" or child sexual abuse would have qualified for taxpayer-funded abortion. Abortion-rights groups immediately charged that Republicans were attempting to "redefine rape."

The accusation was made against Congressman Paul Ryan, once he was the Republican vice presidential nominee, by numerous Democrats, including speakers at the Democratic National Convention in September. But, as *Washington Examiner* Senior Political Columnist Timothy P. Carney pointed out, the term "forcible rape" had been used for decades, by Democrats and Republicans alike. Carney writes:

> For instance, the Democratic House and Democratic Senate in 1994 passed, and Democratic President Bill Clinton signed, a crime bill that included a line "The term 'part 1 violent crimes' means murder and non-negligent manslaughter, forcible rape…"
>
> Also, in 1990, the Democratic Congress passed the "Hate Crimes Statistics Act"—with Ted Kennedy and Barbara Mikulski among the 60 co-sponsors—which required statistics be kept on bias-motivated "crimes of murder, non-negligent manslaughter; forcible rape…"
>
> Was Barbara Mikulski redefining rape? Did Bill Clinton "redefine rape"?
>
> The word shows up in many parts of criminal codes in the U.S. When the District of Columbia passed a hate-crimes law, it distinguished "forcible rape" from other rapes.
>
> Look at California's official crime statistics—they have a category for forcible rape.

You may think distinctions between "forcible rape" and statutory rape are bad policy, but you can't claim that Paul Ryan, Todd Akin, or any other current Republican lawmaker invented the term in an effort to "redefine rape." "Forcible Rape" is already part of our federal criminal code, for better or worse.[47] As a journalist,

Carney wasn't about to take the Democratic assertion at face value. Unfortunately, much of the news media did.

Mother Jones's Nick Baumann authored a piece titled, "Todd Akin, Paul Ryan, and Redefining Rape."[48]

But it wasn't just left-wing outlets that advanced the "redefining rape" narrative. The *Atlantic*'s Caitlin Dickson wrote a piece titled, "Republicans Redefine Rape, Outraging Liberals."[49]

Democrats spent the next two months doing all they could to tie Akin to the Republican presidential ticket. They raised vice presidential candidate Paul Ryan's and Akin's shared sponsorship of the No Taxpayer Funding for Abortions Act to argue that Ryan, too, was an anti-abortion extremist who didn't care about rape victims.

The media ate it up. ABC News' Chris Good reported in August:

> Now with Akin making headlines, Democrats will seek to tie Ryan to the Missouri congressman by highlighting social-issues legislation on which they've partnered. Akin and Ryan cosponsored a 2011 bill, the No Taxpayer Funding for Abortions Act, that would redefine rape as "forcible rape," narrowing the scope of what's considered rape in cases of abortion.[50]

Note how this works: "Democrats will seek to tie Ryan to Akin," says journalist who is doing just that.

As the *Weekly Standard*'s John McCormack noted, Good provided no evidence to support the claim that the bill would "narrow 'the scope of what's considered rape in cases of abortion.'"

"The intent of the word 'forcible' was to prevent taxpayer-funding of abortions in the case of statutory rape—i.e. when a 16-year-old and a 19-year-old have consensual sex, which no one thinks is the moral or legal equivalent of forced sex," McCormack wrote.

> By all indications, the longstanding interpretation of the
> Hyde amendment's exception that allows Medicaid to pay
> for abortion in the case of rape has always excluded "stat-
> utory rape." The word "forcible" wouldn't have "rede-
> fined" rape—it was simply an attempt to codify this
> longstanding interpretation of the Hyde amendment.[51]

Not only that, but Good neglected to mention that the word "forcible" was removed from the final text of the bill—a bill, by the way, that easily passed the House with the support of eleven Democrats. Not that any of that mattered. Much of the media seemed committed to following the Democrats' lead in making Republicans appear to be trivializing rape.

Violence against Facts

In March 2012, congressional Democrats began a push to renew the Violence Against Women Act (VAWA). Originally enacted in 1994, VAWA had always enjoyed bipartisan support and easily passed in each of its re-authorization votes. But Democrats, sensing an opportunity to reinforce the war on women narrative, added provisions to the bill that invited Republican opposition.

The bill included many noncontroversial items, such as continuing grants to local law enforcement and battered women's shelters. But Republicans objected to three provisions. One would allow Indian tribal courts to try certain non-Indians accused of committing crimes of domestic violence on Indian reservations. Republicans said this could deny due process in some cases. Another would give new protections to gay, lesbian, bisexual, and transgender victims of domestic violence, which Republicans said was redundant (and basically pandering). And the third granted more temporary visas to immigrants without, in the Republicans' view, adequate safeguards against fraud.[52]

In short, the reasons for opposition to this bill had nothing to do with violence against women. They had to do with immigration law, due process, and gay politics.

Democrats, as political parties are wont to do, presented a version of the story that was much more favorable to their own political prospects. And for the most part, the media played along, deeming it yet another case of Republicans trivializing or dismissing violence against women.

The media's biased reporting on the legislation was subtle but unmistakable. Compare the *New York Times*' disparate coverage of the passage of the House and Senate versions of the reauthorization.

From April 16, 2012, on the Democratic Senate's bill:

> The Senate voted overwhelmingly on Thursday to reauthorize the Violence Against Women Act and expand its reach to American Indians and homosexuals, after Republicans opted to sidestep an expected partisan brawl.[53]

Here's the first sentence of the *Times*' coverage of the Republican-controlled House vote, on May 16, 2012:

> After a fierce fight, full of gender politics, the House passed a Republican bill on Wednesday to combat violence against women, over objections from President Obama and other Democrats, who said it would reduce protections for many battered women, including lesbians, American Indians and illegal immigrants.[54]

The Senate version of the bill included the three provisions mentioned above. The House version did not. In the very first sentence of the *Times*' piece about the House legislation, the reporter, Robert Pear, mentions the Democrats' complaint that the Republican bill supposedly left women unprotected.

In Pear's nearly 900-word piece on the House Republicans' bill, he mentioned that Republicans opposed the Senate's "more expansive version," but failed to give even the faintest hint at their rationale. Instead, he offered a string of quotes by outraged Democrats making outlandish accusations. He quoted Democratic Representative Gwen Moore of Wisconsin, who said that under the bill, "abusers' rights prevail over the rights of the victim," and labeled it "a direct assault on women's lives."[55]

Pear quoted Democratic Representative Zoe Lofgren of California, who said: "The House bill rolls back protections for battered spouses and victims of serious crimes such as rape and sexual assault. It does so by weakening or repealing provisions that have had near-unanimous support of Democrats and Republicans in years past."[56] He also quoted Democratic Representative Rubén Hinojosa of Texas, who alleged that the bill "shifts power into the hands of abusers."[57]

The closest Pear's piece comes to explaining the Republican position was a couple of quotes by Republican lawmakers who claimed the Democrats were exploiting the law's reauthorization for partisan advantage. Otherwise, the reader is left in the dark: Why would anyone oppose more protections for the most vulnerable? (Because they're Republicans, that's why.)

In the *Times*' coverage of the Senate VAWA vote, reporter Jonathan Weisman gave credence to the Democratic talking point that Republican opposition was part of the "war on women." He even used the words.

Amid partisan brawls over abortion and contraception, some Democrats saw the Violence Against Women Act as the next battle in what they framed as a Republican "war on women."[58]

But Weisman wrote that "Senate Republicans did not rise to the bait," suggesting that if they had stuck to principle and opposed the bill, as House Republicans had, then the "war on women" frame might have fit.

To his credit, Weisman at least explained why Republicans opposed those provisions. But then he quickly pivoted to quotes by Democratic lawmakers suggesting Republicans don't care about women. He quoted Democratic Senator Patrick Leahy of Vermont saying, "Stripping out those provisions would result in abandoning some of the most vulnerable victims... battered immigrants, Native women and victims in same-sex relationships."

This is how media bias frames issues.

The *Times'* War on Women Obsession

Perhaps more than any other print publications, the *New York Times* and *Washington Post* devoted themselves to advancing the "Republican War on Women" meme in 2012. According to *Slate*'s David Weigel, "Between January 1 and April 12, the *New York Times* published 24 references to the 'war on women' and the *Washington Post* published 26 such references."[59]

The *Times* seemed particularly interested in pushing the war. In its February 2011 editorial titled, "The War on Women," the *Times* called House Republican efforts to end taxpayer funding of Planned Parenthood "an assault on women's health and freedom...."[60]

"These are treacherous times for women's reproductive rights and access to essential health care," the *Times* continued. "House Republicans mistakenly believe they have a mandate to drastically scale back both even as abortion warfare is accelerating in the states.

To stop them, President Obama's firm leadership will be crucial. So will the rising voices of alarmed Americans."[61]

In a March 6, 2012, editorial, the *Times* accused the Republican Party of being more "relentlessly nasty, divisive and vapid" than it's ever been. "Republican candidates are so deep in the trenches of cultural and religious warfare that they aren't offering any solutions."

The *Times* predicted that Republicans would soon start paying a price for the "casual cruelty with which they attack whole segments of society." It quoted favorably a Republican senator who said the GOP's policies leave some thinking that they are engaging in "war with women."[62]

The following week, *New York Times* editorial page editor Andrew Rosenthal labeled the Republican Party the "Grand, Old and Anti-Woman" Party. "There's really no other conclusion to reach from the positions Republican lawmakers, and the contenders for the party's presidential nomination, have taken on contraception, abortion and reproductive health services, including their obsession with putting Planned Parenthood out of business," Rosenthal claimed.[63]

On May 19, the *Times* published an editorial titled, "The Campaign Against Women." I'll let you guess whose campaign the *Times* was referring to.[64]

In a July 29, editorial, the *Times* cited a Republican budget proposal that included cuts to Planned Parenthood and Title X birth control funds. "There is a striking overlap between the subcommittee's regressive politics and the policies espoused by the presumptive Republican presidential nominee, Mitt Romney," it stated. "That makes it a window on what a Romney presidency could mean for women's rights and lives."[65]

Another August 22 *Times* piece on abortion and Senate candidates mentioned the "war on women" in its first sentence.[66]

After Romney's strong debate performances, and as polls showed Obama's 20-point lead among women evaporating, the *New York*

Times editorial page reliably stepped up its sex-based attacks on Romney and the Republicans.

In an October 17 editorial entitled, "Mr. Romney's version of equal rights," the *Times* states, "It has dawned on Mitt Romney that he has a problem with female voters. He just has no idea what to do about it, since it is the result of his positions on abortion, contraception, health services and many other issues." The editorial accused Romney of having a "1952 sensibility" when it comes to women's issues.[67]

Why such harsh accusations against Romney? In part because as governor of Massachusetts, Romney vetoed legislation that would have forced Catholic hospitals to dispense abortion drugs to rape victims. The piece also alluded to Romney's support of the right of religious institutions not to be forced to pay for their employees' contraceptives and abortion-inducing drugs.

Two days earlier, the *Times* had published an editorial titled, "If *Roe v. Wade* Goes," arguing that the Romney/Ryan ticket "would turn back the clock" on women's rights.[68] The *Times* concluded that under a Romney presidency "some women would die" from back alley abortions.

Shortly before Election Day, the *Times* published a piece by columnist Nicholas Kristof titled, "How Romney Would Treat Women."[69] In it, Kristof advanced the "war on women" meme, adding that men "have a pretty intimate stake in contraception as well."

Then he went even further, comparing the fight over birth control (remember: a month's supply of the pill costs $9 at Walmart) to civil rights. "Just as civil rights wasn't just a 'black issue,' women's rights and reproductive health shouldn't be reduced to a 'women's issue,'" he wrote.[70]

Kristof conceded that, as a foreign correspondent who regularly reports on real wars on women in Congo, Darfur, and Afghanistan, the current debate seemed "hyperbolic." But then he went back to calling it a "major setback for American women—and the men who love them."[71]

Hyperbolic indeed.

Santorum Stockholm Syndrome?

Rick Santorum did quite well during the Republican presidential primaries. He won ten primaries and the Iowa caucuses. But what the mainstream political press could not fathom was the fact that Santorum won among female voters in many primary states.

A March *Washington Post*-ABC News poll found that two-thirds of Republican and Republican-leaning women voters had a favorable opinion of Santorum, while just 18 percent saw him unfavorably. Santorum's "favorability surplus" in that poll nearly doubled that of Mitt Romney.[72]

Many in the media just couldn't believe that his popularity might be due to, and not despite, the fact the he's a man of deep faith and conservative views on abortion.

On March 14, 2012, the *New Yorker*'s John Cassidy wrote that "one of the most fascinating aspects of the primaries in Alabama and Mississippi was that in both states Rick Santorum got more votes from women than Mitt Romney did—this despite his views on abortion and contraception."[73]

Cassidy went on to favorably quote an emailer who attributed Santorum's popularity among female Republican primary voters to "some form of Stockholm Syndrome," the psychological phenomenon whereby hostages develop positive feelings for their captors, sometimes to the point of defending them.

At the heart of Cassidy's argument is the unstated assumption that women all favor liberal abortion laws, and that they're all naturally repulsed by a faithful Catholic who passionately lives and defends his pro-life beliefs. It reflects how out of touch media elites can be. They have no concept of the tens of millions of pro-life women in America, who view the idea that abortion and artificial birth control are "preventive care" as insulting.

Polls show there are as many pro-life women as there are women in favor of abortion rights—though you would never know it the way the media treat these issues. What's more, women are more likely than men to take a hard-line position against abortion.

A May 2012 Gallup poll found that more women describe themselves as "pro-life" (46 percent) than "pro-choice" (44 percent).[74] A 2002 Public Agenda poll found that men (44 percent) were two percentage points more likely than women (42 percent) to believe that "abortion should be generally available to those who want it."[75] The poll also found that women were more likely than men to think "abortion should not be permitted" (22 percent to 21 percent).[76]

A 2009 CBS News/*New York Times* poll had found that 40 percent of men and 37 percent of women felt "abortion should be generally available." Meanwhile 20 percent of men and 24 percent of women believed "abortion should not be permitted."[77]

How can anyone miss all of these data? It's what comes from living in the bubble.

The Media's Unfair Play on Unfair Pay

Another way the media tried to help Democrats gain an advantage with women was through their constant misrepresentation of the Lilly Ledbetter case. Ledbetter was the plaintiff in the American employment discrimination case *Ledbetter v. Goodyear Tire & Rubber Co.* She became famous for losing her case, after which Congress changed the law on which it was decided.

Ledbetter worked at Goodyear for nearly twenty years. After retiring she sued the company claiming that she had been paid significantly less than her male colleagues. Ledbetter's suit reached the U.S. Supreme Court, which ruled against her because she had not filed her complaint within 180 days of knowing about the unfair pay, as the law specified.

Congress later passed the Lilly Ledbetter Fair Pay Act, which abolished time restrictions on filing claims, and Obama signed the bill into law as one of his first acts as president.

Romney's ambivalence about the law was portrayed as yet more evidence that Republicans were anti-woman. During a question about the law during the second presidential debate, Obama was quick to raise the fact that he signed the bill into law.

Romney then responded that he had placed more women in senior leadership positions than any other governor. But Obama interrupted, "I just want to point out that when Governor Romney's campaign was asked about the Lilly Ledbetter bill, whether he supported it, he said, 'I'll get back to you.' And that's not the kind of advocacy that women need in any economy."[78]

But there was a key fact in the case that the media consistently misrepresented. Politifact, a fact-checking website associated with the *Tampa Bay Times*, wrote:

> In 2007, the Supreme Court had ruled in *Ledbetter vs. Goodyear Tire & Rubber Co.* that the 180-day statute of limitations started from the day an employer made the decision to discriminate—making it impossible for employees who learned of such discrimination later to get relief, such as back pay.

This should be rated "pants-on-fire." The real reason Ledbetter lost her case is that she knew of the pay disparity for more than five years before filing a legal complaint. She admitted as much in her lawsuit deposition, and her legal team never disputed that fact in court.

Ledbetter herself routinely misrepresents this fact when speaking about her case. So do the media. It would get in the way of a good "war on women" story. And we can't have that.

Ledbetter's campaign appearances were part of a broader effort by Obama's campaign to embarrass Republicans and advance the War on Women theme in the area of women's pay.

In March 2011, the White House published a report titled, "Women in America: Indicators of Social and Economic Well-Being." It stated that at all levels of education, women earned 75 percent of what their male counterparts earned in 2009.

"Seventy-five cents on the dollar" became something of a rallying cry in the media.

"Women still lag behind men in pay, report says," ran the headline of an article at CBS.com. "According to the report, young women are now more likely than young men to have a college degree," the article stated. "But whatever their level of education, women earn about 75 cents for every dollar a man earns."[79] The report was also featured in a segment on CBS's *The Early Show*.

The *Chicago Sun-Times*' Lynn Sweet started an online post about the White House report his way: "While U.S. women have made gains, when it comes to salary, a big gender gap still exists, a new Obama White House study found, with females earning about 75 percent of what male counterparts make."[80] The report was followed up with a bill—the Paycheck Fairness Act—that Democrats brought to the floor because they knew Republicans would defeat it. It would have given the federal government unprecedented control over nearly all employers' pay decisions. It would have forced employers to give equal pay for different job classifications, and it would have subjected employers to punitive damages in civil suits for the first time.

Senate Republicans voted against it, as predicted. And with the media uncritically trumpeting the 75 cent figure, the Democrats' had another issue to run with. The problem is that women don't actually make 75 cents on a man's dollar, if you compare apples to apples. Diana Furchtgott-Roth, a columnist for the *Washington Examiner*, is a former chief economist at the U.S. Department of

Labor and a leading expert on pay discrimination. She points out that the White House's 75 percent calculations "do not account for industry, educational field, occupation, or weekly time worked in excess of 35 hours."[81] According to Labor Department data, for example, the average working woman worked 12.3 fewer hours than her average male counterpart in 2011. That alone accounts for half the gap.

In late 2012, Furchtgott-Roth also dissected the findings of an American Association of University Women report titled, "Graduating to a Pay Gap." The report asserted that, "just one year out of college, millennial women are paid 82 cents for every dollar paid to their male peers."[82] The AAUW report, which also got scads of favorable media coverage, recommended more pay equity legislation, of course. But as Furchtgott-Roth noted, if one reads the report's fine print, it actually found that once college majors and occupations are accounted for, women earn 93 cents on a man's dollar. Although the AAUW authors contended that the remaining 7 cents are likely due to discrimination, Furchtgott-Roth suggests that it's simply a result of the report's occupational categories being too broad, placing vastly different professions such as lawyer and librarian into the same miscellaneous category.[83]

> "Other Occupations" includes jobs in construction and mining, a high-paying, male-dominated occupation, and also jobs in food preparation and serving occupations, a low-paying, female-dominated occupation. If a waitress is paid less than a miner, does it follow that it's because she's been discriminated against?[84]

Furchtgott-Roth suggests that one of the reasons the categories were so broad was that the AAUW had an extensive get-out-the vote campaign and wanted to energize young women to go vote for

Democrats. And if there's one thing that can energize young women to vote for Democrats, it's telling them that they're not getting paid what they should be because Republicans are waging a war on women.

The War Continues

How successful was the "Republican war on women" attack line? Again, polls showed most voters were focused on other issues, but Democrats probably feel vindicated by the election's results. Perhaps their attack, in concert with the media keeping the theme alive, finally chipped away at the public's consciousness—as propaganda often does.

According to CNN exit polls, women, who made up 53 percent of the electorate, went for Obama by 10 points.[85] That represented the second-largest gender gap in American history, according to the Center for American Women and Politics at Rutgers University.[86]

Alas, the end of the election didn't mean the end of "war on women" narrative. In November, pundits began advancing the idea that Republican opposition to the nomination of United States Ambassador to the United Nations Susan Rice for secretary of state was part of that war as well.

"Democratic women defend Susan Rice, call out her critics' sexism, racism and mediocrity," wrote Kathleen Geier in the *Washington Monthly*.[87] "McCain uses Susan Rice to re-launch war on women," wrote *USA Today*'s Dewayne Wickham.[88]

Anyone who thinks the end of the 2012 election signaled the end of the so-called "war on women" is sadly mistaken. President Obama has flourished and won reelection by dint of this wedge issue. This meme is sure to be around in his second term, distracting people from ongoing failures to whatever extent possible.

CHAPTER FIVE

IT'S ALL
ABOUT RACE

"The economy is so bad MSNBC had to lay off 300 Obama spokesmen. That's how bad it's gotten."[1]

—Jay Leno

I n 2008, America elected its first black president. And in that election, race was a dog that just never barked.

Yes, more blacks voted for Obama than usually vote Democratic, but that was to be expected. This was historic—he was the first. And you need not like the outcome—I did not—to see and be happy that America is *able* to elect a black president without his race playing any serious role.

Obama's race didn't cause him to do worse among whites. In 2004, Democrat John Kerry won only 41 percent of white voters;[2] in 2008, Obama won 43 percent of them.[3]

Even the so-called "Bradley Effect"—the phenomenon whereby poll respondents lie and say they will vote for a black candidate out of fear that they'll be seen as racists otherwise—did not materialize.

Obama performed pretty much the way the polls predicted he would.

But in 2012, America seemed to go backward. Obama won easily, but with a much more racially polarized electorate. Obama slipped to just 39 percent of the white vote, losing it by 20 points, the widest losing margin for a Democratic presidential candidate since the Reagan landslide of 1984.[4] His share of the Hispanic vote, meanwhile, increased from 67 percent to 71 percent in 2012. His share of Asian voters jumped from 62 percent to 71 percent. And Obama again captured more than 90 percent of the black vote (93 percent). Overall, Obama won the support of more than three in four racial minorities.

The racial polarization was even more astonishing among some demographic subgroups. For instance, 98 percent of 18-to-29 year-old black women, voted for Obama.[5] And relatively few non-white voters supported Romney—88 percent of Romney's votes were cast by whites.

Even more significant was the disappearance of millions of white voters. One estimate put the decrease in the number of white voters between 2008 and 2012 at nearly 7 million.[6] Although the final totals are still being tallied as this book goes to print, it is clear that many white voters stayed home on Election Day.

Many commentators have written about the Republican Party's problems if it remains the "white" party. There is, however, another side to that coin. There are plenty of possible reasons for the increased racial polarization of the 2012 election, but here's one you probably didn't hear the pundits ruminating about: perhaps it had something to do with an abundance of race-obsessed media smears against one of the political parties and its millions of regular voters.

This is not a pretty fact, but it is a fact: the 2012 race featured a relentless propaganda campaign of racial fear-mongering, waged by a handful of prominent media actors. They labored and stretched to turn every innocuous statement by a Republican into some kind of racial innuendo, in an attempt to stoke fear, divide people, and, ultimately, shut down as many arguments as possible against Barack Obama's reelection.

Though surely grounded in the media bias that this book explores, this campaign was not mere journalistic bubble-blindness and self-deception. It was a conscious and malicious effort by a small segment of the media to vilify, intimidate, and belittle those with whom they disagreed politically.

Most media bias is at least amusing. This was not. It was an attack on racial harmony and civility in America's political life. The journalists who took part in it should be ashamed of themselves. They should resign their jobs.

Although its pundits were by no means the only offenders, MSNBC did more for this disgusting campaign than any other news outlet, hands down. An entire cable network dedicated itself to constant race-baiting for a period of months. Nothing like this has happened in my lifetime, and I presume that nothing like it had happened since open racists controlled television and radio microphones in some parts of America more than fifty years ago.

MSNBC's coverage at the Republican National Convention— which predictably failed to air a single speech by any of the numerous black or Hispanic Republicans who took the stage—seemed designed to cast the GOP as a parade of racist horribles.

Four years ago, there were hopes that with the election of America's first black president, a clear benchmark had been reached in the nation's quest to move beyond race in politics. But it hadn't. In fact, Obama's election gave new life to the media's race-based attacks on conservatives—and it was something that a few bad apples in the media seemed intent on promoting even if Obama was not.

Chris Matthews Creates a Monster

Chris Matthews is the host of MSNBC's *Hardball*. But Matthews isn't exactly Mr. Hardball when it comes to Obama. His enthusiasm is well known, undisguised, and over-the-top.

It produced the famous "thrill going up my leg" remark during the 2008 campaign. And it produced, upon Obama's election, Matthews' candid admission that, "I want to do everything I can to make this thing work, this new presidency work"[7] Matthews once compared one of the president's speeches to the troops in Afghanistan to Shakespeare's "Band of Brothers" speech from *Henry V*.[8]

But Matthews takes a very different tone when he talks about people who speak or vote against Barack Obama. His tone in the 2012 campaign set a new standard for bile and acrimony.

In March 2011, Matthews told MSNBC colleague Martin Bashir that "Everything [Obama's] done has been good for this country." Then he accused Republicans of avoiding important issues in order to "go back to the old nativist root, this old dark night of the soul thing that people worry about, a black man in a White House. And they start working on that. 'Oh he's a mau mau. He goes back to a Muslim background.'"[9]

"It's using race," Matthews continued. "It's using paranoid fear of whites of black males against this president whose life has been spotless, has been the American dream."[10] Those remarks captured the full scope of Matthews' commentary: Obama's perfect; those who disagree are racists.

On a different occasion Matthews said this about the plurality of Americans who identify as political conservatives:

> I think they hate Obama. They want him out of the White House more than they want to destroy al Qaeda. Their number one enemy in the world right now, on the right, is their hatred, hatred for Obama. And we can go into

that about the white working class in the south about looking at these numbers we've been getting the last couple days, about racial hatred, in many cases. This isn't about being a better president, they want to get rid of this president.[11]

For context, this was Matthews' "insight" into how Romney was able to move successfully to the center during the general election season. It's something nearly every Republican candidate in the modern era has done, but Matthews needed an excuse to make it a racial issue. Matthews stated on national television that conservatives hate having a black man in office so much that they could tolerate any amount of ideological heterodoxy from Romney. In fact, he said, conservatives hate Obama more than they hate the terrorists who caused 9/11.

Yes, really, that's what he said. And yes, he still has a job.

It's tempting to laugh off such stupidity, but you can't when it's being broadcast all over America and shaping voters' opinions about the candidates.

It isn't the sort of message that persuades, but hate speech is not designed to persuade. And this was definitely hate speech. It was designed to intimidate people into silence on political matters. It is a brutally negative message that strikes dire, groundless fear in the hearts of half the population, and turns the other half off to the political process. This is what voter suppression really looks like.

Matthews is paid a great deal for his political commentary because it's hard work studying data, talking to political insiders, putting current politics into historical context, and developing real insights into what is going on at the White House and on Capitol Hill.

It takes a lot less work for Matthews to issue baseless, off-the-cuff condemnations of the motives of millions of Americans who happen to disagree with him politically. But he still gets paid the same amount if that's all he does, and apparently there's enough of an audience for it to keep him on the air.

Broadcasting outside the Republican National Convention in August 2012, Matthews walled off the word "Chicago"—Obama's adopted hometown and the site of his campaign headquarters—as somehow racist.

"They keep saying 'Chicago' by the way, have you noticed? They keep saying 'Chicago,'" Matthews told his guest, *New York* magazine's John Heilemann. "That's another thing that sends that message—this guy's helping the poor people in the bad neighborhoods, screwing us in the 'burbs."[12]

Heilemann jumped in and finished Matthews' thought. "There's a lot of black people in Chicago."[13]

Never mind that Obama's hometown is known to most people not for its demographic composition, but for its infamous legacy of political corruption—a legacy mostly created by white people, by the way—and that Obama publicly associated and aligned himself with the city's brand of politics. But hey, if it helps protect Obama from his past, then Matthews is happy to carelessly throw accusations of racism at anyone who even mentions the town.

In an interview after the election, Congressman Paul Ryan told a Wisconsin television reporter, "I think the surprise was some of the turnout, some of the turnout in urban areas which definitely gave President Obama the big margin to win this race." Ryan said, "When we saw the turnout that was occurring in urban areas that [was] unprecedented, it did come as a bit of a shock.... So those are the toughest losses to have—the ones that catch you by surprise."[14]

Ryan might have said this because he noticed that turnout in cities was up when returns came in to the campaign on election night. He might have also said it because the share of voters from "big cities" in his home state of Wisconsin had increased by about

40 percent from 2008, according to the exit polling, and those voters had given Obama an incredible 83 percent of their votes.[15]

Nope, announced Chris Matthews. It's "more of this dog whis-
tle stuff."[16] There's no need to analyze the logic. Republicans are
just so racist that they can't even discuss election results without
dog-whistling.

There was a moment after the election when Matthews seemed
to waver in his convictions. When Susan Rice, Obama's UN ambassador, was floated as a possible nominee to replace retiring Secretary
of State Hillary Clinton, many Republicans objected. They cited in
particular her wide dissemination of false information about the
attack that killed America's ambassador to Libya. Richard Wolffe,
however, an MSNBC regular and author of two fawning books
about Obama, pinpointed Republican Senator John McCain's
opposition to Rice as rooted in racism:

> RICHARD WOLFFE: I think it's Susan Rice . . . [N]ow
> that John McCain has sunk his teeth in, he's made it
> about presidential authority, and, frankly, it's outrageous
> that there is this witch hunt going on the right about these
> people of color—let's face it—around this president. Eric
> Holder, Valerie Jarrett, now Susan Rice. Before it was
> Van Jones. This is not about who is hawkish in the same
> way John McCain is about foreign policy because if you
> look at Iran and Libya, Susan Rice checks those boxes.[17]

This was too much even for Matthews.

> MATTHEWS: So, you think McCain is being—McCain
> and people like Lindsey Graham—McCain, who had his
> own daughter attacked, was accused of having an ille-
> gitimate child when, in fact, he adopted a young girl from

South Asia. You're saying that McCain's being driven by racial prejudice here?[18]

Was this the moment when Chris Matthews finally noticed the monster he had spent the last several months creating? Did it suddenly dawn on him that he was guilty of turning the sort of drivel then coming out of Wolffe's mouth into respectable political commentary?

Who knows? At least Wolffe provided some entertainment value with his reply:

> WOLFFE: ...Look at what John McCain said about Condi Rice's nomination.... Back then—four years— eight years ago, John McCain said the people—the Democrats who were questioning Condi Rice's credentials they were engaged with bitter innocence, they needed to move on. Why has he changed his tune? What is it about Susan Rice?[19]

Indeed, what is it about Susan Rice that had made McCain change his tune? It must be that Susan Rice is black. Condi Rice, on the other hand, is...also black.

To put it in Pulitzer's terms, how did Chris Matthews form and shape the future of the Republic during this election season? If one's goal were to sow racial distrust on purpose—to exacerbate it, to keep the flames of discord burning as brightly as possible for as long as possible—one couldn't do much better than to put Chris Matthews on television more often.

"Food Stamp President"

In late 2011, presidential candidate and former House Speaker Newt Gingrich began referring to Obama as "the food stamp president," because the number of food stamp recipients had shot up so rapidly during Obama's first term. In fact, it had grown 65 percent—to 46 million—between 2008 and late 2011.[20]

Democrats suggested that the term was racist, and so was Gingrich. "Unfortunately, there's still people in this country who think that the president can't be their president because of his race," said Democratic Representative Steve Cohen of Tennessee. "Some even refer to him as a food stamp president."[21] Democratic Congresswoman Sheila Jackson Lee of Texas made a similar criticism of Gingrich on the floor of the House of Representatives.[22]

First of all, most food-stamp recipients are white.[23] It is certainly possible to imagine someone trying to use a term like "food stamps" to cast racial aspersions, but it would be hard to imagine them having much success.

More important, food stamp policy was a legitimate issue that Obama had raised. He was the one who had made the food stamp program (properly known as SNAP) a centerpiece of his stimulus plan. That wasn't Gingrich's idea, or any Republican's, and in fact Obama and his surrogates had spent significant time defining and defending food stamps as a means to economic recovery. That was one major reason food stamp enrollment was soaring. The other reason was that the economy continued to be consistently lousy throughout Obama's recovery.

As part of his 2009 stimulus package, Obama had spent $20 billion to expand the SNAP program, on the Keynesian theory that food stamps have a high "multiplier" effect and stimulate economic activity.[24] As NPR reported in July 2009, "The federal food stamp program is being beefed up in hopes that it will help jolt a sagging economy back to life."[25]

U.S. Secretary of Agriculture Tom Vilsack called the food stamps program "economic stimulus" that was "putting people to work" and "exciting in terms of job growth" because "if people are able to buy a little more in the grocery store, someone has to stock it, package it, shelve it, process it, ship it. All of those are jobs. It's the most direct stimulus you can get in the economy during these tough times."[26] A number of liberal economists like Mark Zandi contended that yes, food stamps were in fact the most efficient way government could stimulate the economy.

So, for the record, long before Newt Gingrich announced that he was running for president, Obama made food stamps a central part of his economic stimulus plan. That meant putting millions of additional people on SNAP. And as we saw in an earlier chapter, the failure of his stimulus to create jobs has kept SNAP growing rapidly throughout the "recovery" period, and it was setting new records every month in 2012.

For the Republican primary voters to whom Gingrich was appealing, the idea of food stamps as an economic cure is precisely the kind of backward thinking that permeates Washington. These were conservatives, far less inclined to believe in Keynesian "magic multipliers" and more likely to view an increase in government dependency as a sign that government is doing something wrong. From a conservative perspective, food stamps, cash welfare, and housing assistance are safety-net programs that temporarily alleviate suffering. They do not create wealth or jobs, nor do they put anyone on a permanent path to self-sufficiency.

For the conservative voters to whom Gingrich was appealing, the fact that a sitting president thinks that food stamps are a serious economic solution to a labor market depression is in fact grounds to question Obama's competence in economic matters. None of that has anything to do with race.

When Chris Matthews (who else?) confronted Gingrich about the "food stamp" line during a broadcast of his show outside the Republican National Convention, suggesting that it was a racial issue, Gingrich responded by flipping the race script on him.

A food stamp president is a guy whose policies are so destructive that he creates the longest unemployment since the Great Depression and he puts more people on food stamps—most of them white—than anybody else. Why do you assume food stamp refers to black? What kind of racist thinking do you have? Wait a second! Why, aren't you being a racist because you assume it refers to black?[27]

Matthews wasn't the only MSNBC host to go after Gingrich about "food stamp president." MSNBC's Martin Bashir, in predicting that Gingrich wouldn't win the Republican nomination, said that "he could badly damage race relations in the process. So here is a simple plea: Let's cut out the food stamps rhetoric right now before things get any worse."[28]

In other words, a serious and hard-to-defend economic position that Obama explicitly staked out as part of his stimulus package must be taken off the table—otherwise, you're a racist. Got that? No discussions of Obama and Chicago politics, and no discussions of the fact that far, far more people are going on food stamps than are finding jobs in Obama's recovery.

This is how you intimidate people, so that you don't need to address their arguments.

Creating the Race Issue

With the primary campaign in full swing, former CNN correspondent Bob Franken weighed in on the Republican field on Al Sharpton's MSNBC show, *Politics Nation*. He said that the GOP candidates were making "appeals to the extreme white wing of the Republican Party." He continued:

That is to say that there continues to be among many conservatives a real resentment against blacks.... I think this is very intentional, it is pandering, there's sort of a wink-wink that this base should be reminded that Barack Obama, President of the United States, is one of them, an African-American. Yes, I think this is very intentional. I think it is part of a hateful campaign that is being very methodically run in the hope it's going to appeal to voters who would love to see us return to the good old days of Jim Crow.[29]

Really. "Many conservatives" resent blacks? "Many conservatives" want to go back to Jim Crow? To segregated movie theaters and violence and intimidation against blacks—all of the things that were outlawed nearly fifty years ago, by the grace of God, and which voters under age fifty never experienced?

Did Franken think before he said this? Is this really the sort of thing Franken thinks conservatives talk about when they go out for a beer—that they sit around and obsess about what sort of harm they can do to African-Americans? Or is this just a typically irresponsible, hyperbolic, blanket condemnation of millions of his fellow Americans, for which he knows he will never be held accountable?

The fact is, it's a lot easier to call people who disagree with you "racists" than it is to defend a president with Obama's record. For some of the journalists who loved Obama most, accusations of racism were a convenient shortcut. If that meant trivializing racism—the real form of which does indeed exist—then it was a price worth letting someone else pay.

Already in 2008, some journalists preemptively—and unnecessarily—mounted the "if-he-loses-it's-racism" defense of Obama. In August 2008, Jacob Weisberg wrote a piece for *Slate* titled, "If Obama Loses: Racism is the only reason McCain might beat him."[30] Jonathan Freedland of Britain's *Guardian* newspaper had written that if Obama lost in 2008, the world would conclude that America is racist.[31] (So, vote however you want. No pressure.) Peter Beinart wrote in the *Washington Post* that race would be central because "McCain needs it to be. He simply doesn't have many other cards to play."[32]

In fact, McCain didn't play the "race" card in 2008. The only people who kept invoking it were the media.

Of course, the fact that racism isn't there won't stop everyone from finding it. When McCain ran a light-hearted attack ad portraying Obama as a frivolous celebrity candidate, using pictures of Paris Hilton and Britney Spears to drive home the point, *New York Times* columnist Bob Herbert saw racism. McCain's ad was an attempt, Herbert wrote, "to exploit the hostility, anxiety and resentment of the many white Americans who are still freakishly hung up on the idea of black men rising above their station and becoming sexually involved with white women."[33]

Oh, well.

During the 2012 presidential campaign, the media were much more determined to find racism at the bottom of any and all opposition to their favored candidate.

In May 2012, Michelle Obama appeared on ABC's *The View*. Co-host Barbara Walters, the longtime broadcast journalist, asked her, "Do you think, in this campaign, which is getting fairly ugly, that racism is still going to be a part of it?"[34]

The First Lady showed class by deflecting the question. Walters showed none by pressing her: "But do you think that racism is going to play a part in this campaign?"

Mrs. Obama answered diplomatically: "You know, racism is still an issue in this country. But I'll tell you right now, Barack Obama is President of the United States. And he's done a phenomenal job. And this country—this country put him in office."

Walters wasn't really asking a question—she was making a statement. Racism was going to play a part in the campaign. She and others in the media would make sure of that.

Early in 2012, *New York Times* editorial page editor, Andrew Rosenthal, wrote that Republican attacks on Obama had "racist undertones."[35] "Nobody likes to talk about it but it's there," Rosenthal wrote. "Talking about race in American politics is uncomfortable and awkward. But it has to be said: There has been a racist undertone to many of the Republican attacks leveled against President Obama for the last three years, and in this dawning presidential campaign."

The examples he cited were hardly persuasive. He mentioned how Republican Congressman Joe Wilson of South Carolina had shouted, "You lie!" during Obama's speech before a joint session of Congress in 2009. He mentioned House Speaker John Boehner's rejection of Obama's request to speak before a joint session of Congress—the same night as a Republican presidential debate. This "level of disrespect," Rosenthal wrote, "would be unthinkable were he not an African-American."[36]

Such a short memory. Recall that Democratic Senate Majority Leader Harry Reid of Nevada called President Bush a "liar" and a "loser." Twelve thousand San Franciscans signed a petition to name a sewage plant after him.[37] Thousands of Americans, including one of Obama's former White House advisors, signed a petition asserting that high-level officials in Bush's government "had foreknowledge of impending 9/11 attacks and 'consciously failed' to act."[38]

So no, Obama is not the first president to be criticized, rebuked, disrespected, or given the cold shoulder by his opponents. In fact, he's probably had it pretty good compared to his predecessor. But when you search for racism in every remark, and in every slight, it's not that hard to find it.

Some in the media are determined to put even standard political jabs out of bounds when it comes to Obama. When Mitt Romney and other Republicans made television ads replaying Obama's "You didn't build that" remark about business owners, you probably didn't think of racism. But Jonathan Chait of *New York* magazine saw right through the Republicans' crafty code. Chait noted that Obama had spoken those words in a "black dialect." And so by replaying them, Republicans were playing into whites' fears of an angry black man. "From the moment he stepped onto the national stage, Obama's deepest political fear was being seen as a 'traditional' black politician, one who was demanding redistribution from white America on behalf of his fellow African-Americans," Chait wrote.[39]

MSNBC's Touré Neblett went even further when Mitt Romney called the president "angry and desperate" and said Obama should take the "campaign of division and anger and hate back to Chicago."[40]

"You notice he [Romney] says 'anger' twice," Neblett said. "He's really trying to use racial coding and access some really deep stereotypes about the angry black man. This is part of the playbook against Obama. The other-ization, he's not like us. I know it's a heavy thing to say. I don't say it lightly. But this is *n-gg-rization*, 'You are not one of us,' and that 'you are like the scary black man who we've been trained to fear.'"[41] Neblett's despicable neologism recalled an incident in 2011 when MSNBC blogger John Aravosis wrote that Romney was using as a campaign slogan "Keep America American," which, he said, had been used by the Ku Klux Klan in the 1920s. Later, MSNBC anchor Thomas Roberts commented on the story, calling the slogan "a central theme" and "rallying cry" for the KKK.[42] Aravosis had gotten it wrong. The phrase Romney had actually used was "keep America *America*." MSNBC later apologized for running the story, but it gives you some idea of how prepared they were to pounce.

Kevin Baker of *Harper's* magazine might win the prize for making the silliest accusation of racism during the campaign. In one of the presidential debates, Romney mentioned that he's got five sons, so he's "used to people saying something that's not always true but just keep repeating it and ultimately hoping I'll believe it."

According to Baker, Romney had slyly found "a way to call [Obama] a boy, comparing Obama's statements to the sorts of childish lies his 'five boys' used to tell. How the right's hard-core racists must have howled at that! Mitt, at long last, has secured his base."[43]

Baker obviously didn't remember, but Obama once used exactly the same device to compare members of Congress to procrastinating schoolchildren who couldn't get their homework done on time. During the debt ceiling debate in 2011, Obama told a group of reporters:

> You know, Malia and Sasha generally finish their homework a day ahead of time. Malia is 13, Sasha's 10. It is impressive. They don't wait until the night before. They're not pulling all-nighters. They're 13 and 10. You know, Congress can do the same thing. If you know you've got to do something, just do it.[44]

The MSNBC cries of racism extended even to Republicans' comments about Obama's enthusiasm for golf. Obama plays a lot of golf—he played more than one hundred rounds in his first four years in office.[45] His affinity for the links prompted Republican Senate Minority Leader Mitch McConnell of Kentucky to quip, "For four years, Barack Obama has been running from the nation's problems. He hasn't been working to earn re-election. He has been working to earn a spot on the PGA Tour."

It was the typical sort of barb that politicians from both parties use to poke the other side. But oh no, when MSNBC pundits are on their seek-and-destroy mission to find racism, sinister motives can always be invented. Lawrence O'Donnell plunged right in.

O'DONNELL: Well, we know exactly what he's trying to do there. He is trying to align to Tiger Woods and surely, the—lifestyle of Tiger Woods with Barack Obama. Obviously, nothing could be further from the truth…

Even Martin Bashir—not the sort to defend Republicans—was a bit incredulous about this one.

BASHIR: Lawrence—don't you think—don't you think that what he's really trying to do is to suggest that the president is not paying attention to the central issues that come with the responsibility he has? Is he really—Mitch McConnell really making a connection with Tiger Woods who, of course, has become infamous for chasing various cocktail waitresses around Las Vegas and so on?

O'DONNELL: Martin, there are many, many, many rhetorical choices you can make at any point in any speech to make whatever point you want to make. If he wanted to make the point that you just suggested and I think he does want to make that point, they had a menu of a minimum of ten different kinds of images that they could have raised. And I promise you, the speech writers went through, rejecting three or four before they landed on that one. That's the one they want for a very deliberate reason. That—there's—these people reach for every single possible racial double entendre they can find in every one of these speeches.[46]

If O'Donnell hadn't said this for real, it could have been in *The Onion.*

Voter I.D. Laws

Days before the election, *Washington Post* columnist Colbert King wrote, "A Romney takeover of the White House might well rival Andrew Johnson's ascendancy to the presidency after Abraham Lincoln's assassination in 1865." King continued:

> A Romney win would be worrisome...because of his strong embrace of states' rights and his deep mistrust of the federal government—sentiments Andrew Johnson shared. And we know what that Johnson did once in office.... Johnson stood by as Southern states enacted "black codes," which restricted rights of freed blacks and prevented blacks from voting. Romney stood by last year as Republican-controlled state legislatures passed voter-identification laws, making it harder for people of color, senior citizens and people with disabilities to exercise their fundamental right to vote.[47]

It is a bit difficult to believe that a sane person can compare a requirement to show an I.D. when voting—a perfectly reasonable request that Americans must comply with to do a whole host of other things every day—is in any way like the sort of terrorism and state-sanctioned racism that was once routinely inflicted on blacks in the South when they tried to exercise their right to vote. But King wasn't alone in linking voter I.D. laws to racism. In fact, there were some days when it seemed that MSNBC covered little else besides "Voter I.D. racism."

In 2011 and 2012, at least thirty-seven states passed or considered some form of voter identification law in order to prevent people from voting illegally under others' names.[48]

Most Americans support voter I.D. laws. Most other countries, including Mexico, have them. Some state voter I.D. laws are more stringent, and others more lenient. The law in Hawaii—President Obama's home state and a Democratic bastion—requires poll workers to request a photo I.D. from voters, although voters who lack one can also prove their identity by giving their birth date and address.[49]

But because these laws are supported mainly by Republicans, and a liberal think tank study says that racial minorities are more likely not to have photo I.D.s, the media engaged in a campaign to portray them as racially discriminatory.[50]

That accusation was made by America's highest-ranking law enforcement official. Attorney General Eric Holder called voter I.D. laws a "poll tax" during a speech to the NAACP in July 2012.[51]

Poll taxes were once used to disenfranchise poor black voters, and they are explicitly forbidden by the Twenty-fourth Amendment to the Constitution. But I'm sure you don't expect me to explain how journalists then challenged or pilloried Holder for this ludicrous comment—because they didn't, of course.

An August 2012 *Washington Post* poll found that 74 percent of respondents supported requiring voters to show photo identification at the polls. Forty-eight percent said they felt voter fraud was a "major problem," and 33 percent said it was a "minor problem." Only 14 percent said it was "not a problem." The *Post* poll also showed that voter I.D. laws were supported by large majorities of both Republicans and Democrats, *and of all ethnic groups.*[52] Justin Danhof of the National Center for Public Policy Research pointed out that in the four days after this *Washington Post* poll result was released—August 13 through August 16, 2012—MSNBC ran nineteen stories on voter I.D. laws. Not one mentioned this *Washington Post* poll.[53]

They did interview Democratic Representative John Lewis of Georgia, a civil rights activist who was beaten badly in the Selma march. After noting that several states had passed voter I.D. laws,

Lewis was asked, "That march almost killed you, and Republicans deny there is any connection here between these moments and that time in history. What's your reaction?"[54]

Now there's a thoughtful, fair question for you.

Some Democrats and pundits suggested that voter I.D. laws could even cost Obama the election by keeping minorities from the polls. On the anniversary of the Voting Rights Act, August 6, CNN's Zoraida Sambolin began a segment about voter I.D. this way:

> With America's first black president up for re-election this November, the conversation about voting rights has been reignited. Thirty states are currently enforcing some form of voter I.D. law, which many civil rights advocates say is an effort to suppress the minority vote.

Later Sambolin asked a panel of commentators, "Do you think that having an African American president is actually reigniting some of these old prejudices?"[55]

On another MSNBC show, Thomas Roberts pushed the "poll tax" canard with Democratic Congresswoman Sheila Jackson Lee of Texas. He said:

> One issue impacting minority voters is voter I.D. —early voting restrictions. In your home state, a federal appeals court tossed out a voter I.D. law last week saying that it was an "unforgiving burden on the poor." Governor Rick Perry responded saying, "chalk up another victory for fraud." With 19 states now involved in this fight, why does the Republican Party—the party of smaller government and less taxes—want to institute more red tape and basically a poll tax on Americans to vote?[56]

For all the scaremongering over voter I.D. laws, not one story has been written since the election about a voter who was disenfranchised by any of the states that had such laws in effect on election day.

In fact, in a report published days ahead of the election, Reuters news service found that voter I.D. laws in Georgia and Indiana, two states where such laws had been in place for numerous election cycles, did not, in fact, discourage minority voters, nor did they lead to lower turnout. The report concluded that Democratic concerns about voter disenfranchisement "are probably overstated."[57] Which is probably understated, considering that MSNBC seemed to spend most days of its election coverage comparing Voter I.D. laws to cross-burnings.

MSNBC didn't report the Reuters study either, naturally. And the media's obsession with voter I.D. laws vanished immediately after Election Day, as post-election exit polls showed record turnout among racial minorities.

Welfare Reform

In July 2012, President Obama moved to grant states permission to dilute the work requirements in the 1996 welfare reform law, Temporary Assistance for Needy Families, or TANF. Under new rules devised by the Department of Health and Human Services, the work requirements that were the heart of the successful and popular law were no longer legally binding on states.

Ever since the welfare reforms of 1996, states have had to report to the federal government on what percentage of their TANF recipients are fulfilling the program's work requirements. States that fall far short can be penalized, and so officials in some states figured out ways to game the system. They would count exercise and weight loss and smoking cessation programs as "work," for example, in order to increase their participation rates, according to a 2005 study by the Government Accountability Office.[58]

Congress cracked down that year when it reauthorized the program. Obama was effectively undoing that change, allowing states, if they wanted, to expand the work requirements once again to include things that aren't work.[59]

The Romney campaign aired a television ad criticizing this unilateral executive move. Many conservatives, including some of the legislative experts who had helped reform welfare in 1996, argued that the administration didn't have the legal authority to change the law in this way. But because the criticisms dealt with welfare programs, they were attacked—you guessed it—as racist code.

National Journal's Ron Fournier wrote, "Romney's team knows, or should know, they are playing the race card."[60] The *New York Times* suggested that Romney's message on the welfare changes reflected "a campaign infused with a sharper edge and overtones of class and race."[61]

MSNBC's Rachel Maddow said that the ad's use of the word "welfare" six times "is...a blunt allusion to the populist, racist politics of white economic racial resentment."[62]

Touré Neblett wrote a piece for *Time* magazine where be deemed racial "code words," as "linguistic mustard gas, sliding in covertly, aiming to kill black political viability by allowing white politicians to say 'Don't vote for the black guy' in socially-acceptable language."[63]

Sometimes a code word, Neblett wrote, "comes directly out of a candidate's mouth. Sometimes it comes from supporters, or can be found in advertisements."[64] According to Neblett, the word "welfare" is racist because "when a candidate says 'welfare' many whites think of their tax dollars being given to blacks."[65]

Obama, who as a state senator in the 1990s gave a speech about how he opposed welfare reform, unilaterally weakens that same welfare reform. And the media is there, ready and able to intimidate anyone who tries to discuss it as a political issue. This doesn't seem like a very productive method of political discourse, does it? And the real shame is that journalists, whose work usually facilitates discourse, were the ones trying to crush it with spurious charges of racism in an effort to protect a sitting president.

Trivializing Racism[66]

By trying to warn of racism behind every bush, the liberal pundits were trying to invent a nobler cause in their own minds than the one they were actually serving.

In crying "racist" over nearly every word or argument a Republican utters, these journalists engage in a political fantasy of sorts. They can pretend they live in a bygone era—that they're standing alongside freedom riders and marchers in the segregated South. Their fantasy lets them confer upon themselves all the glory and righteousness of the civil rights struggle, without their ever having to face the insults, the discrimination, the fire hoses, the lynchings, the beatings, and the state-sanctioned terrorism that far braver Americans fought against decades ago.

This fantasy helps these pundits cope with the everyday reality of their jobs defending an incumbent president whose White House has produced no lasting economic successes, but plenty of divisive, bitter, and hyper-partisan political maneuvering.

The problem with the pundits' civil rights fantasy is that there is a cost to their trivialization of racism. As we editorialized at the *Washington Examiner*:

> The racialization of every innocent comment is not just tedious. It is also damaging to democracy and to society in two important ways. First... America imposes a lasting societal stain upon those found guilty of racism. The abusive politicization of this healthy stigma, all just to protect a single politician from defeat, is a short-sighted

attempt to squelch legitimate political conversation, and with it democracy.

Second, this dishonest behavior...actually weakens the legitimate societal shaming of real racism—which still exists, by the way, and which does sometimes include the use of "coded language." Those who lightly and carelessly attribute racism in this way are only undermining legitimate societal hatred of real racism. If they ever succeed in racializing every innocent statement and act, they will only cause Americans to stop taking real racism seriously. The boy who cried wolf, as everyone knows, was eventually devoured.[67]

If you think the campaign has ended to turn the mere mention of "racism" into a valid, conversation-ending argument, you have another thing coming. Liberal pundits carried the "racist" theme right through the election into Congress's lame duck session.

After the election, when the possibility of Susan Rice's nomination as Secretary of State arose, the full-court press continued. Yes, she had gone on television and disseminated the White House's false account of the Benghazi attacks, but...well, racism, so stop it.

The Grio, which is part of the NBC News website, published a story that stated, "The Republicans really need to lay off U.N. Ambassador Susan Rice. The image of a party of angry old white dudes going after an accomplished black woman will not give them the image makeover they need."[68]

MSNBC's Neblett called Republican senators John McCain and Lindsey Graham, the two leading voices against Rice, "old, white establishment folks" and criticized them for "wrongly and repeatedly attacking a much younger black woman moments after an election in which blacks and women went strongly blue."[69]

The editors of the *Washington Post* editorial page wrote that a letter by ninety-seven House Republicans opposing Rice's potential nomination as secretary of state was "bizarre" because Rice is "a Rhodes scholar and seasoned policymaker who, whatever her failings, is no one's fool."[70] Then they raised the specter of racism.

> Could it be, as members of the Congressional Black Caucus are charging, that the signatories of the letter are targeting Ms. Rice because she is an African American woman? The signatories deny that, and we can't know their hearts. What we do know is that more than 80 of the signatories are white males, and nearly half are from states of the former Confederacy. You'd think that before launching their broadside, members of Congress would have taken care not to propagate any falsehoods of their own.[71]

We can't know what was in the hearts of the *Post* editorialists that day, but it doesn't seem to have been a well-reasoned argument.

On CNN, Soledad O'Brien asked Democratic congressman Jim Clyburn of South Carolina if critical comments about Rice had a sexist or racist component to them. Clyburn said he felt they were "code words."[72]

He said, "During this recent campaign we heard Senator Sununu calling our President 'lazy,' 'incompetent,' these kinds of terms that those of us, especially those of us who had grown [up] and [were] raised in the South, we would hear these little words and phrases all of our lives and we'd get insulted by them."[73]

This kind of commentary is a sign that America's politics will only get uglier in the future—and also a major reason why.

It was Obama who offered perhaps the best response to claims that those who oppose him must be motivated by race. Appearing on CBS's *The Late Show* early in his presidency, he was asked by host David Letterman whether criticism of his health care reform efforts were grounded in racism.

Obama quipped, "I think it's important to realize that I was actually black before the election." [74]

It's something that a few of Obama's biggest supporters in the media are capable of selectively forgetting.

CHAPTER SIX

THE IMPERIAL OBAMA PRESIDENCY

O ne of the most memorable observations Bernard Goldberg made in *Bias* was about Bill Clinton's greatest unsung achievement: he eradicated homelessness the moment he was sworn in.

Well, not really. But he did nearly eliminate its coverage in the news. After twelve solid years of news stories on homelessness, many of them blaming the problem on the policies of Republican presidents Ronald Reagan and George Bush, the media suddenly lost interest in the topic.

So here's another story that only matters when Republicans are in the White House: the abuse of executive power.

The media went on endlessly when George W. Bush tried to fire some of his own U.S. attorneys. And perhaps they were right to.

But with Obama as president, it isn't even that big a deal that he ignores actual constitutional imperatives, such as congressional approval for going to war and the Senate's advice and consent for appointments.

With a stroke of the pen, Obama can institute regulations that abridge a large religious minority's First Amendment right to live according to its beliefs, and the media will dutifully bury the story.

What about all those war on terror abuses the media reported during the Bush era? The CIA renditions? The terror suspects being held permanently without trial? The unmanned drone strikes on terrorists, which kill civilians as collateral damage?

Not only can Obama evidently engage in these same practices, but he can even expand them and it won't even come up in the next interview. He is praised for trying to bring Gitmo detainees to the continental United States, so that he can hold them here without trial, arguably setting an even worse precedent than holding them at Gitmo. He can kill a sixteen-year-old American citizen in a drone strike, and most of the population never even hears about it.

Story Idea: Unprecedented Attack on Religious Freedom

On January 20, 2012, Health and Human Services Secretary Kathleen Sebelius announced what has since become known as the "HHS mandate" of Obamacare. The health care law, which passed Congress in 2010, states that all insurance plans must cover "preventive health services" without co-pays. But the rule Sebelius was issuing specified that "preventive health services" includes all contraceptives, sterilizations, and abortion-inducing drugs approved by the Federal Drug Administration.

Employers were given a year to comply by adding this to their employees' health insurance plans. And that was that.

The Catholic Church and other religious organizations regard these drugs and devices as gravely immoral. The Obama administration's decision not to provide a meaningful conscience exemption—even if only for religious employers such as Catholic hospitals and universities, let alone for any Catholic employer—was unprecedented. If they insisted on following their religion's teachings, Catholics who engage in business would now be fined, and so would obviously religious institutions like Catholic schools, Catholic charities, and Catholic hospitals. In the case of the religious institutions, Obama was requiring them under penalty of law to act as hypocrites—to do something they were duty-bound to denounce in public as morally wrong.

For ordinary Catholics, the provision evoked the fines levied against Catholics in Elizabethan England who failed to attend Church of England services. It was an affirmative command from government to do something that violated their consciences, or else pay a price.

Perhaps a better analogy is to say that it was like a rule requiring all delis—including Kosher delis owned by observant Jews—to serve pork. Even if most Jews do eat pork, it would still be un-American to impose such a requirement.[1] That would seem obvious by the standards of the First Amendment and America's founding belief in religious tolerance.

Yet the Obama administration proceeded to treat the Catholic Church and observant Catholics as if they had no conscience rights at all. The administration's supporters actually made the case that what the Church professed to believe didn't matter, because most Catholics didn't follow Catholic teaching on contraception anyway. The Obama administration had decided that the Church's beliefs were outdated, so the Church and observant Catholics would no longer be allowed to adhere to them unmolested.

The HHS mandate would never have passed Congress as part of the Obamacare statute. And it was completely unnecessary for achieving the bill's goals. Unlike the individual mandate, which requires all Americans to purchase government-approved health insurance, the HHS mandate wasn't necessary to make Obamacare function. It was a throwaway provision, the purpose of which seemed chiefly political—a way to score points with important parts of Obama's left-wing base, and throw some extra cash to drug companies.

But for many religious believers, especially Catholics who observe their Church's teachings faithfully, it was about to become a big headache. Catholic organizations and employers were suddenly faced with a dilemma. They could disregard the doctrines of their faith; they could drop health insurance for their employees and pay fines; or they could go out of business.

The new rule provided a "religious exemption" so narrow that only an actual religious order could qualify. Even the Catholic University of America—the nation's only university whose charter comes from the pope himself—did not fit the exemption, to say nothing of nearly 250 independent Catholic colleges and universities, and countless Catholic hospitals and charitable organizations. Yet the Obama administration lauded itself in its press release anyway for striking "the appropriate balance between respecting religious freedom and increasing access to important preventive services."[2]

The U.S. Conference of Catholic Bishops had a different view. They labeled the mandate "literally unconscionable" for violating the Constitution's First Amendment guarantee of religious freedom.[3]

This should have been a big, big story for the media in an election year. Catholics make up about a quarter of the electorate. In the last several elections, their vote has been a reliable bellwether. And even fallen-away and marginally observant Catholics are bound to have an opinion—one way or the other—about a president's attack on an institution they grew up with. For Catholics who attend mass every week—11 percent of the American electorate in 2012, larger than the entire Hispanic electorate—it certainly mattered.

But when Catholic leaders and others first began to raise their voices in January 2012, the media did not seem very interested. It took the bishops ten days to get even a brief mention on CBS *This Morning*. News shows for the other two major networks, NBC and ABC, were silent on the controversy for two weeks.

Even after the media were finally dragged into covering the story, the religious freedom angle—the real story—was essentially ignored. It became instead a story about birth control.

The controversy got a bit more play in print and online, but nearly every organ of the mainstream media failed to represent the stakes properly. To take just one example, *New York Times* reporter Laurie Goodstein wrote that the mandate battle "threatens to embroil the Catholic Church in a bitter election-year political battle while deepening internal rifts within the church. On the one side are traditionalists who believe in upholding Catholic doctrine to the letter, and on the other, modernists who believe the church must respond to changing times and a pluralistic society."[4]

Of course, the issue here was not whether Catholics obey their church's teaching. The issue is whether it is the government's place to decide which teachings they would be allowed to follow. Until Obamacare, American believers had always been free to follow their church's teachings or not to follow them, and nobody was singled out for civil punishments or (if you prefer) special taxes based on their choice.

When the story finally broke the surface, the Obama administration responded by crafting what it and the media called an "accommodation." On February 10, 2012, the administration announced that religious institutions could avoid paying directly for coverage of contraceptives and abortion-inducing drugs, if they wanted, and instead have employees make segregated payments to their insurers to cover them.[5] It didn't seem to matter to anyone that most of these institutions, like most large businesses, self-insure, so there is no separate insurer to pay for anything. Not only was the idea of religious freedom as an "accommodation" ridiculous to begin with, but this didn't actually accommodate most of the organizations affected.

When this problem was pointed out, the administration simply threw up its hands. Lucky for them, so did the journalists. After the "accommodation" was announced, the story was again almost entirely ignored.

The Media Research Center (MRC) conducted a study of the major news networks' coverage of the administration's alleged alteration. According to the MRC, the networks CBS, NBC, and ABC all "characterized the President's February 10 statement as an 'accommodation,' a 'change of course' and a 'compromise with Catholic leaders,' even though church officials never agreed to it and the administration hadn't actually compromised its position."[6]

Many of the broadcasts included sound bites from leading abortion rights advocates and liberal Catholic Democrats. And ABC News assured viewers that "both the Catholic Health Association and abortion rights groups approved" of the new rules.[7] Note that the Catholic Health Association is a liberal group and an early backer of Obamacare.

The U.S. Conference of Catholic Bishops, the church's authoritative voice in America, rejected the supposed compromise.[8] Their opposition was buried—reported only on weekend editions of "the CBS *Evening News* and ABC's *World News*, and not at all on the NBC *Nightly News*."[9]

At least it made the news. A few months later, this failure to reach a compromise prompted dozens of Catholic dioceses and other religious institutions—forty-three in all, including the University of Notre Dame, which had invited Obama to speak at its commencement in 2009—to file twelve federal lawsuits against the Obama administration for violating their religious freedom. CBS News gave the lawsuits a nineteen-second mention. The other major news networks didn't even bother to inform their viewers about the lawsuits at all.[10]

"You'd think the largest legal action in American history in defense of religious liberty would be a major news story," Media Research Center President Brent Bozell rightly noted. "For the *Washington Post*, there was a little one-column story buried on Page A6...*USA Today* had a tiny headline and 128-word item at the very bottom of A2. The *New York Times* had a perfunctory 419-word piece on Page A17."[11]

Another abortion-related controversy that occurred around the same time offers an instructive comparison in how the press sets its priorities. On February 1, 2012, the Susan G. Komen Foundation, America's largest breast cancer charity, announced that it would no longer donate to Planned Parenthood, the nation's largest abortion business. The Media Research Center's Matthew Balan found that "over the course of about 60 hours, ABC, CBS, and NBC emphasized the [Komen] controversy with a whopping 13 morning and evening news stories."

The media leapt to defend Planned Parenthood's right to breast cancer donors' money. The coverage was heavily slanted, with 76 percent of the quotes coming from Planned Parenthood's backers.[12] It might be too much of an understatement to point out that the media were far less zealous about Catholics' First Amendment right to practice their religion than they were about protecting Planned Parenthood's presumed right to tap Komen's cash.

Put yourself in an editor's chair—which is really the bigger story? Especially as it appears that the Supreme Court will now likely hear a case on the religious freedom question? But the sad fact is that even as suits against the HHS mandate wind their way through the courts—one reaching the appellate level in the 8th Circuit, where the Department of Health and Human Services was temporarily enjoined from enforcing the mandate—there remains a virtual media blackout. If you want to follow these stories, you have to dip into pro-life niche news sites such as LifeNews.com (a great site, by the way, but not really a substitute for a mainstream media that covers what's important).

No one is asking the media to give the bishops or religious groups special treatment. But they are supposed to serve the public. And the public isn't better off for having been misled on this serious story, and then having it ignored completely once Obama has washed his hands of the problem.

A March public opinion survey by the Henry J. Kaiser Family Foundation, a nonpartisan health care research organization, found that half of respondents said they thought the mandate controversy was "mostly driven by election-year politics."[13] It's easy for people to form such an opinion when no one bothers to tell them the story.

Spun Story: Obama's Un-Recess Appointments

In early 2012, President Obama did something that presidents are forbidden to do under the Constitution. With the Senate still in session, he unilaterally appointed four officials to executive posts at the National Labor Relations Board and the Consumer Financial Protection Bureau.

These posts required Senate confirmation. But in an unprecedented act, Obama bypassed the Senate in appointing them.

The Advice and Consent clause of the U.S. Constitution has always been understood to confer upon the U.S. Senate the right to approve or disapprove the president's nominees to various positions established by law—senior cabinet posts, judgeships, and ambassadorships, for example.

The Constitution does provide an exception for when the Senate is in recess:

> The President shall have Power to fill up all Vacancies that may happen during the Recess of the Senate, by granting Commissions which shall expire at the End of their next Session.

Today, the recess appointment power is almost never used for genuine emergencies where positions would otherwise go unfilled. It is nearly always used, instead, for controversial nominees. And it is something presidents of both parties use routinely—usually to thwart the will of the other party when it controls the Senate. It is an accepted practice—but only when the Senate is in recess.

And the Senate was not in recess when Obama made these "recess" appointments, which were designed to score points in an election year, particularly with organized labor, a constituency vital to his reelection.

These "recess" appointments were a clear abuse of power. And sure, a few appointments to obscure panels might not seem like that big a deal. But if a president can get away with this, what's to stop him or future presidents from say, changing immigration or education laws without congressional approval? What's to stop him from going to war without congressional approval? In fact, Obama did all of these things in his first term. The steady increase of presidential power is a troubling trend that Obama did not initiate. Yet his bold participation in this abuse was downplayed by the media, even as Obama proudly billed himself as the president who "can't wait" for Congress to act.

When I say that Obama's use of the recess appointment was unprecedented, I am being a bit technical. The only near equivalent came in December 1903, when President Theodore Roosevelt waited for a momentary gap between the first and second sessions of the 58th Congress to "recess-appoint" more than 160 officials, mostly to military posts. His action was condemned, and a subsequent Senate Judiciary Committee report, in 1905, explained the founders' use of the word "recess" as follows:

> It was evidently intended by the framers of the Constitution that it [Article II, sec. 2] should mean something real, not something imaginary; something actual, not something fictitious. They used the word as the mass of mankind then understood it and now understand it. It means...the period of time when the Senate is not sitting in regular or extraordinary session as a branch of the Congress or in extraordinary session for the discharge of executive functions; when its members owe no duty of attendance; when its chamber is empty; when, because of its absence, it can not receive communications from the President or participate as a body in making appointments....[14]

Moreover, the report states, the recess appointment power

> ...was carefully devised so as to accomplish the purpose in view, without in the slightest degree changing the policy of the Constitution, that such appointments are only to be made with the participation of the Senate. Its sole purpose was to render it certain that at all times there should be, whether the Senate was in session or not, an officer for every office, entitled to discharge the duties thereof.

Roosevelt's abuse of this power was never repeated. In the years following, courts and attorneys general offered opinions that have loosely governed recess appointments ever since. In the ninety years before Obama became president, the most lenient interpretation was that, within sessions of Congress (intra-session), presidents can make recess appointments only when Congress is adjourned for at least three days. Obama's own Solicitor General, Neal Katyal, had in fact articulated this standard during a Supreme Court case in 2010.[15]

At least Roosevelt could make an argument that there had to be a recess, if only for a moment, between two sessions of Congress. Obama went further. Before 2012, no president had ever made a "recess appointment" when the Senate was, by every reasonable definition, in session.

The White House's defense of these appointments was weak, and sharp journalists should have seen through it. It rested on the notion that the Senate is only in session when it's actually conducting real business—its brief "*pro forma*" sessions supposedly didn't count. A legal memo from Obama's Justice Department argued:

> The convening of periodic pro forma sessions in which no business is to be conducted does not have the legal effect of interrupting an intrasession recess otherwise long enough to qualify as a "Recess of the Senate" under the Recess Appointments Clause.[16]

This opinion is completely without precedent. Not even Theodore Roosevelt made this argument.

Not only was the Senate's session for real, it was in fact constitutionally required. The Constitution explicitly states that neither house of Congress can adjourn for more than three days without the other's consent (Art. I, Sec. 5). The House (controlled by Republicans) had not let the Senate go into recess, so the fact that the Senate was doing "no business" was irrelevant. (Also, it's worth mentioning that the Senate doesn't do any business most days even when most senators are there.)

Unfortunately, in early 2012, the Senate was in no position to protect its constitutional prerogatives. The president's party controlled the chamber and had no interest in fighting Obama during an election year—not even if the constitutional balance of powers was at issue. The Republicans, a minority in the chamber, were powerless. Short of trying to impeach Obama—a politically disastrous idea—they had no leverage.

The best lawmakers could do was hope for the courts to strike down all of the appointees' official acts—and in fact, those cases were just getting underway at the federal appeals court level as this book was being finished.[17]

Congress was neutered, and the courts are slow, but there was another power out there—another force capable of counteracting this presidential power grab in an election year. That was America's free press. It was the only institution capable of cutting through the highly technical features of this debate and shaming a president who was clearly abusing his power in an unprecedented way.

The Fourth Estate, if it cared about the perennial problem of "the imperial presidency," could take its stand. It could discourage such abuses now and into the future by making Obama pay for this politically. Neither party's presidents should do this sort of thing. It certainly doesn't serve the public good.

This is what newspaper editorial boards are made for. And unfortunately, the most important ones were way too busy rooting for Obama's reelection to waste their time speaking truth to power.

The *Washington Post*'s editorial had this headline: "Obama's justifiable 'power grab' on recess appointments."[18] It made this incredible argument:

But so what? Both the consumer bureau and the labor relations board are agencies of the U.S. government, created by Congress, and it is inexcusable that congressional obstructionism would leave them unable to function.

A small detail that the *Post* missed is that Republicans did not obstruct the three appointments to the labor relations board. They never had the chance to, because Obama *hadn't even announced them* as nominees until he "recess-appointed" them.

The *Los Angeles Times* bravely confronted this unprecedented expansion of executive power by calling it "a rational response to an increasingly gridlocked Congress."[19]

And then there's the *New York Times*. Sure, they're always very liberal, but you could at least expect their editorial board to recognize an abuse of power when they see it, right?

Oh, who am I kidding?

"The validity of recess appointments, like Senate filibusters, depend on the eye of the beholder," wrote editorial page editor Andrew Rosenthal. His blog post on the topic failed to address or acknowledge any of the constitutional issues involved, although it did take a cheap shot by comparing Republicans to "Southern segregationists" and their filibusters from more than five decades ago.

Rosenthal went on:

> We supported the Democrats under Mr. Bush when they held pro-forma sessions to block his recess appointments, because we believed his choices were egregiously bad. I know this looks hypocritical, but I can't bring myself to support the Republicans for doing the same, or get outraged about the president's refusal to accept the pro-forma loophole.[20]

Rosenthal is right about exactly one thing: This does indeed look hypocritical. The *Times*, as it does routinely, put partisanship ahead of facts. As noted above, the Senate was definitely in session because the Constitution required it. And the Constitution, which is not a "loophole," also says that the Senate makes its own rules. President Obama is not the arbiter of when it is or is not in session.

These are editorialists I'm quoting—people who write opinions. They do the same job I do at the *Washington Examiner*. I don't have a problem with the fact that some or even most editorial boards are liberal—nor even that nearly all of the editorial boards at the most influential national newspapers are well to the left of center.

But whether you're liberal or conservative, there are still standards in opinion journalism. Opinions have to be informed by facts. Editorialists are supposed to do more than just cheer on one side and boo the other as if they were at a sporting event. They are supposed to provide a critical voice, and they have a duty to inform the public rather than act as partisan hacks.

The fact that Andrew Rosenthal loves Obama doesn't justify his embrace of abusive and precedent-setting expansions of presidential power. If the courts allow this travesty to pass, do you doubt that Rosenthal will man the barricades the moment a Republican president does exactly what Obama did?

This is also a shame because in their partisanship, these journalists missed a great trend story. Obama's decision to abuse the recess-appointment in 2012 was in fact a continuation of his earlier, highly inventive (though legal) use of the recess appointment power.

As my *Washington Examiner* colleague Byron York observed, Obama was already using recess appointments in 2010 in a possibly unprecedented way. Most recess appointments that are made in defiance of Congress—for example, Bush's appointment of John Bolton as UN Ambassador in 2005—have taken place when nominees have been or will be rejected by the Senate. The president resorts to the recess appointment either because the nominee is expected to lose a vote or (as in Bolton's case) the other party prevents him from getting one.

But during his first term, Obama used the recess appointment for nominees who were yet to be blocked by anyone. Despite promises that his would be the most transparent administration in American history, Obama used recess appointments simply to spare his nominees the Senate's vetting process.

In July 2010, for example, Obama recess-appointed Donald Berwick as head of the Medicare and Medicaid programs. When he did this, there had not been so much as a single confirmation hearing scheduled by Democratic Senate Finance Chairman Max Baucus of Montana. Democrats controlled the Senate with 59 of its 100 seats. Yes, some Republican opposition was expected to Berwick's nomination, but Republicans had done nothing to prevent him from getting a hearing.

The real issue was that Obama didn't want there to be any hearings at all. The recess appointment came almost immediately after Republican senators submitted written questions about Berwick's finances. He had been paid millions of dollars by a non-profit group with murky funding sources.[21] Once he had been recess-appointed, Berwick simply refused to answer those questions when asked in subsequent committee hearings. He quit one month before his temporary term expired.

Obama repeated this pattern with three of the four illegal recess appointments of January 2012. The nominees to the National Labor Relations Board had not even been named before they were "recess-appointed."

The mythology is that journalists relish exposing abuses of power. The reality is, when the president is someone they like, they're far more likely to look the other way, or even to congratulate him for his "rational response to an increasingly gridlocked Congress."

Story Spun: A First-Person War

America goes to war too often. That's my opinion—take it for what you will—but I believe the Founding Fathers would agree.

In The Federalist No. 69, Alexander Hamilton described the Constitution's division of war powers by citing the British system as a counter-example. The powers that England vested in just one man—the king—were to be divided under the U.S. Constitution between the president and the Congress:

> The President is to be commander-in-chief of the army and navy of the United States. In this respect his authority would be nominally the same with that of the king of Great Britain, but in substance much inferior to it. It would amount to nothing more than the supreme command and direction of the military and naval forces, as first General and admiral of the Confederacy; while that of the British king extends to the declaring of war and to the raising and regulating of fleets and armies—all which, by the Constitution under consideration, would appertain to the legislature.[22]

James Madison, the father of the U.S. Constitution, described the reasoning behind giving Congress, not the president, the power to declare war, even though the president is named in the Constitution as commander in chief of the armed forces.

> The constitution supposes, what the History of all Governments demonstrates, that the Executive is the branch of power most interested in war, and most prone to it. It

has accordingly with studied care, vested the question of
war in the Legislature.[23]

This quote, from a 1798 letter to Thomas Jefferson, has been
cited frequently by anti-war thinkers, but its context is cited far
less often. Madison was particularly worried about presidents
negotiating agreements with foreign powers and then using them
as a pretext to force the nation into wars against the better judgment of Congress:

> [I]f again a Treaty when made obliges the Legislature to
> declare war contrary to its judgment, and in pursuance
> of the same doctrine, a law declaring war, imposes a like
> moral obligation, to grant the requisite supplies until it
> be formally repealed with the consent of the President and
> Senate, it is evident that the people are cheated out of the
> best ingredients in their Government, the safeguards of
> peace which is the greatest of their blessings.

America has learned in recent years that even Congress, which
should be more reluctant to make war, is probably too quick to pull
the trigger when it is given a chance. The fact that Democratic
Senator John Kerry of Massachusetts became the "anti-war" presidential candidate two years after writing, speaking, and voting in
favor of the same war he was campaigning against provides a stark
illustration of this fact.

But it's even worse with presidents. Madison's warning applies
today as much as it ever did. Certainly every president thinks long
and hard about the consequences of taking lethal action. Whenever
you send tens of thousands of twenty-year-olds into the field with
guns, bad things are bound to happen—even beyond the intended
combat deaths and the inevitable accidental civilian deaths that

every war brings. But whether they have their eyes on thwarting America's enemies or on restoring order where chaos has broken out, presidents usually don't think so hard about war that they actually avoid it.

That is why the Constitution provides a safeguard. As another of our nation's presidents once said,

> The President does not have power under the Constitution to unilaterally authorize a military attack in a situation that does not involve stopping an actual or imminent threat to the nation.

That quote is from Barack Obama, then a senator, speaking to the *Boston Globe* editorial board in December 2007.

By March 19, 2011, Obama had adopted a very different stance on this question. He made his own declaration of war, repeatedly employing the first-person singular as he did so. He was announcing the United States' entrance into a conflict that most certainly had no "actual or imminent threat to the nation" involved. And his decision came to the consternation of leaders in Congress, and at least some members of both parties.

Terry Jeffrey, the editor in chief of CNSNews.com, described the scene well:

> [W]hen Barack Obama announced he had ordered the U.S. military to intervene in Libya's civil war, he did not do so from the Oval Office or the well of the U.S. House of Representatives, but from the capital city of Brazil.
>
> In that speech, delivered March 19, 2011, Obama repeatedly used the first-person pronoun, I, in explaining who had decided America would intervene in Libya.

"Today I authorized the Armed Forces of the United States to begin a limited military action in Libya in support of an international effort to protect Libyan civilians," Obama said.

"I want the American people to know that the use of force is not our first choice, and it's not a choice that I make lightly," said Obama.[24]

Obama's rationale for going to war was a United Nations resolution, "which calls for the protection of the Libyan people" from their now-deceased and unlamented longtime dictator Muammar Gadhafi. Obama went to war without congressional approval, based on a foreign diplomatic body's deliberations—just the sort of circumstance that James Madison had so presciently feared.

You wouldn't know it from watching the major news networks. On March 29, 2011—ten days after Obama announced he was deciding all on his own to take the United States to war—all three major networks were given ten minutes with him.[25] The Media Research Center's Brent Baker compiled all of the questions they asked.[26] Not one of their questions had to do with the fact that Obama had gotten the United States of America into a war without the involvement of Congress.

I won't reproduce all of the questions they asked, but here's a sample just from ABC's Diane Sawyer:

- "If Gadhafi ends up in a villa someplace in Zimbabwe with no war crimes trial, is that okay with you?"
- "Have you made, or would you make any calls to say 'take him'?"
- "What about the famous quote from another beleaguered President, Abraham Lincoln, who said he had

been driven many times to his knees because his own
wisdom and that around him 'was insufficient for the
day'?" (Obama responded: "I do a lot of praying.")

- "Just a final question: *How much do you think Kentucky will win by?*"

The emphasis on that last question is mine.

At least Erica Hill of the CBS *Evening News* asked one difficult
question—though not on the legality of presidents declaring war:

- "The supreme allied commander for NATO said
today that there are flickers of al Qaeda and Hezbol-
lah amongst these [Libyan] rebels. How do we know
what their end goal is? And how do we know they
won't, in fact, turn on the U.S. and on our allies?"

Not one question about the president getting America into a
war all by his lonesome. *Not one.*

Sixty days later, the Libyan war drew on and Obama was
approaching a deadline. The War Powers Resolution, passed in
1973, was an attempt by Congress to remedy presidential abuses in
war-making and reclaim legislative prerogatives. It was meant to
force presidents, when they found themselves involved in conflicts
that hadn't already been approved by Congress, to get congressional
approval within sixty days.

As it approached this deadline on Libya, the Obama White
House began referring to the war as a "kinetic military action," and
pretended congressional approval wasn't necessary. The *New York
Times* cited "some lawyers"—likely within the White House—floating the idea that they could simply pause hostilities briefly, start
them again, and thus buy themselves another sixty days of war.[27]

This suggestion was, to put it mildly, offensive to the spirit of the law, if not the letter as well.

Not all media outlets suppressed this story, and a few reliably liberal editorial boards even earned some credit—though not too much—for not completely flip-flopping on the issue. The *New York Times* editorial board, for example, was at least intellectually honest enough to recognize Obama's attempt to circumvent the War Powers Act as bordering on "sophistry."

> [M]r. Obama cannot evade his responsibility, under the War Powers Act, to seek Congressional approval to continue the operation.
>
> The White House's argument for not doing so borders on sophistry—that "U.S. operations do not involve sustained fighting or active exchanges of fire with hostile forces, nor do they involve the presence of U.S. ground troops," and thus are not the sort of "hostilities" covered by the act....
>
> ...But the 1973 act does not apply solely to boots-on-the-ground, full-out shooting wars. It says that 60 or 90 days after notifying Congress of the introduction of armed forces "into hostilities or into situations where imminent involvement in hostilities is clearly indicated," the president must receive Congressional authorization or terminate the mission.
>
> No word games can get him off the hook.[28]

Great stuff. But what's amusing about this editorial is that even as the *Times* editors leveled substantive criticism at Obama's policy, they managed to reserve their harshest condemnation for congressional Republican leaders who were, at that point, leveling the same substantive criticisms. The *Times* sniffed out hypocrisy in Republican House Speaker John Boehner of Ohio. A spokesman for Boehner had said that it was the Speaker's position that he "has an institutional obligation to enforce the laws of the land," which seems reasonable enough. But because Boehner had criticized the War Powers Act in the 1990s, the *Times* concluded that Boehner's effort to uphold the law "looks a lot like every other maneuver by Republicans determined to block Mr. Obama at every turn—no matter the cost." The cost in this case would be what, exactly? Not allowing a president to ignore the law?

The lesson from the *New York Times* editorial board is that if you don't love Obama enough, you're not allowed to criticize him.

Throughout America's involvement in the Libya conflict, the press utterly failed to hold Obama accountable for engaging in a war without congressional approval. During the 2012 presidential campaign the media barely mentioned our role, and certainly Obama was never grilled on the dubious constitutionality of his actions. If the press is supposed to be one of the people's guardians against political abuses of power, they singularly failed; and worse, as per the *New York Times*, they actually criticized Republicans who kicked up a fuss about imperial presidential sophistry.

A Story Spun: "Gitmo North"

Conservatives, you're not alone. You're not the only ones frustrated by the media's love for Barack Obama and its willingness to bury stories that might embarrass him or hurt his political standing.

Many on the Left feel the same way. In some cases, they share their frustrated opposition to Obama's policies with certain strains of conservatism. Because in the end, the media are even more partisan than they are ideological.

Obama was elected on a platform of closing the Guantánamo Bay prison—the U.S.-controlled enclave in Cuba where more than 160 captured terror suspects and "enemy combatants" are held. The issue is a big deal for people both on the anti-war Left and the libertarian Right.

Obama did a lot of moral posturing on Guantánamo throughout the 2008 election and after his inauguration.

"As president," he had promised in August 2007, "I will close Guantánamo, reject the Military Commissions Act, and adhere to the Geneva Conventions."[29] His promise led to the Democratic Party's adoption of a 2008 platform that explicitly promised to close the prison.

But as with his wildly over-ambitious promises on the economy, Obama never delivered. In fact, his administration never even proposed to end the actual constitutional abuses that Guantánamo represents. As a result, in 2012, the Democratic Party platform was quietly scaled back to supporting something Donald Rumsfeld had actually tried to do during the Bush era: "substantially reducing the population at Guantánamo Bay without adding to it."[30]

Based on his actions and not his words, Obama's position on Guantánamo goes something like this: It's embarrassing that we run it, so we should shut it down. But we'll still hold people without charging them or giving them trials of any kind—military or civilian. It's just that now, instead of holding them in the isolated, tropical environment of Guantánamo Bay, we'll start holding them indefinitely in prisons within the continental United States. Is it better that we will be holding people without trial *in Illinois*? Who knew that Obama could out-Bush President Bush?

Don't take my word for it. Take that of the American Civil Liberties Union, which denounced Obama's Guantánamo closure plan as an attempt to establish "Gitmo North."

The creation of a "Gitmo North" in Illinois is hardly a meaningful step forward. Shutting down Guantánamo will be nothing more than a symbolic gesture if we continue its lawless policies onshore.

Alarmingly, all indications are that the administration plans to continue its predecessor's policy of indefinite detention without charge or trial for some detainees, with only a change of location... [W]hile the Obama administration inherited the Guantánamo debacle, this current move is its own affirmative adoption of those policies.[31]

Glenn Greenwald, a left-wing journalist and attorney who writes chiefly about human rights issues for the British *Guardian* newspaper, cared enough about the abuses themselves—not just about their value as a political issue—that he proved somewhat annoying to Obama fans during the election. He penned a piece for Salon.com in which he exposed the myth, a conceit shared by many Obama supporters, that Obama had valiantly tried to shut Guantánamo down but was blocked by right-wingers. Greenwald's devastating piece pointed out that in fact:

When the President finally unveiled his plan for "closing Guantánamo," it became clear that it wasn't a plan to "close" the camp as much as it was a plan simply to relocate it—import it—onto American soil, at a newly purchased federal prison in Thompson, Illinois. William Lynn, Obama's Deputy Defense Secretary, sent a letter to inquiring Senators that expressly stated that the Obama administration intended to continue indefinitely to imprison some of the detainees with no charges of any kind. The plan was classic Obama: a pretty, feel-good, empty symbolic gesture (get rid of the symbolic face of Bush War on

Terror excesses) while preserving the core abuses (the powers of indefinite detention), even strengthening and expanding those abuses by bringing them into the U.S.[32]

This is why it was a thoroughly bipartisan majority in Congress—not a partisan one—that defeated Obama's attempt to close Gitmo.

The *New York Times*, in a May 2012 article, provides a typical example of the revisionist history the media give this event. It chalks up the thwarting of Obama's plan entirely to Republicans:

> Though President George W. Bush and Senator John McCain, the 2008 Republican candidate, had supported closing the Guantánamo prison, Republicans in Congress had reversed course and discovered they could use the issue to portray Mr. Obama as soft on terrorism.

And yes, this is *part* of the truth, but it fails to explain the full political reality, let alone provide an accurate context to Obama's feel-good, do-nothing policy on the issue. Republicans did indeed decry the detention of terrorists on American soil in spring 2009. With the wind of public opinion very much at their backs, they warned of creating new terrorist targets in the American heartland.[33]

But to accept this as the real issue is to forget that the GOP was nearly irrelevant in May 2009. Democrats controlled the House by a wide margin, and at that point held 59 of 100 Senate seats. Yet Obama lost his bid to close Gitmo in a Senate vote of 90 to 6. Many Democrats simply did not want to help establish "Gitmo North."

The ever-liberal Democratic Senator Russ Feingold of Wisconsin, as Greenwald notes, wrote a letter to President Obama in which he stated:

My primary concern…relates to your reference to the possibility of indefinite detention without trial for certain detainees. While I appreciate your good faith desire to at least enact a statutory basis for such a regime, any system that permits the government to indefinitely detain individuals without charge or without a meaningful opportunity to have accusations against them adjudicated by an impartial arbiter violates basic American values and is likely unconstitutional…. [T]hose policies and legal precedents would be effectively enshrined as acceptable in our system of justice, having been established not by one, largely discredited administration, but by successive administrations of both parties with greatly contrasting positions on legal and constitutional issues.[34]

The story of Gitmo was spun in a way that helped Obama with his base instead of hurting him. It never became an issue in the mainstream 2012 election coverage. Perhaps that's because Mitt Romney once promised to "double Guantánamo"(whatever that means), and so there was little daylight between the candidates.

But since when has the press needed the opposition party's seal of approval to decide that something is a story?

To look at it in raw political terms, Obama made big promises on Guantánamo that got his base excited. Not only did he fail to deliver, but in a 2011 executive order he also embraced indefinite detention wherever it "is necessary to protect against a significant threat to the security of the United States."[35] This story mattered especially to Obama's base, which he had to turn out in large numbers to win the 2012 election. Yet the liberal-leaning press did not pursue this liberal story because the press, again, are more a partisan force than an ideological one. They accepted Obama's posturing as real, his real policy as irrelevant. Actually, they went one better than that. The press began to rewrite history to make Obama look like a do-gooder who was stymied by evil Republicans. The sad fact is, the media were not interested in the truth about Guantánamo. They propagated a myth that served Obama's purposes quite well.

Story Idea: Obama Supports the Death Penalty for Minors

Abdulrahman al-Awlaki, a sixteen-year-old Colorado native, was living in Yemen with his grandparents in September 2011. One day, he slipped away, leaving a message that he had gone to look for his father, Anwar.

Abdulrahman hadn't seen Anwar in two years, because his father, also a U.S. native, was an al Qaeda terrorist whom Barack Obama had added to his "kill list." Abdulrahman gave up his search when he learned that his dad had been killed in a drone strike on September 30, 2011.

The elder Al-Awlaki was a preacher of hate, who had called on Muslims not only to kill Americans, but also to kill other Muslims who opposed such violence. He had influence in the United States, even after he had fled to Yemen. The now-famous underwear bomber, once he was cooperating with police, identified Anwar al-Awlaki as the mastermind behind the plot to bring down his airliner. Al-Awlaki had also helped incite Army Major Nidal Hassan, the Fort Hood shooter, who murdered thirteen of his military colleagues while shouting the Islamic mantra, "God is the greatest" ("*Allahu akbar!*").

On October 14, 2011, two weeks after his father's death, sixteen-year-old Abulrahman al-Awlaki was killed by a drone as well. As subsequent reports had it, he was not targeted for death, but he and a few other Yemeni boys were collateral damage in a strike supposedly aimed at al Qaeda's Ibrahim al-Banna. (Al Qaeda—not exactly a reliable source of information—later claimed that al-Banna is still alive. But exacerbating people's doubts is the fact that administration officials tried at first to justify the strike by claiming that Abdulrahman was a twenty-one-year-old terrorist. At least his age was corrected when his grandfather released his Colorado birth certificate in response.)

At the site of the Hofstra University debate in October 2012, former White House spokesman and then-Obama campaign surrogate Robert Gibbs was confronted by an aggressive, left-leaning interviewer about Abdulrahman's death. This is what he said:

> GIBBS: I would suggest that you should have a far more responsible father if they are truly concerned about the well-being of their children. I don't think becoming an al Qaeda jihadist terrorist is the best way to go about doing your business.

Now, does this comment strike you as more or as less of a national story than Todd Akin's stupid comment about female reproductive biology, which dominated the news for weeks? This one was released just two weeks before the 2012 general election. And you've probably never even heard about it until now.

President Obama was never asked about his longtime aide blaming sixteen-year-old Abdulrahman's death-by-drone on his family life. Not only did he never have to defend or disown Gibbs' comments— can you imagine a Republican president being treated that way?—but he never had to defend his policy, either, even though he personally makes the final decisions about the kill list. The same press that was frothing at the mouth over Mitt Romney's tax returns and how he once traveled with his dog on the roof of his car have never once asked Obama about the killing of this sixteen-year-old American boy.

Obama is not the first president to agonize over the life and death decisions that come with the office. Obama is not the first president to fight and kill terrorists. He is not the first to use weaponized drones over the skies of nations with whom we are not at war—although he's done it quite a bit more than Bush did. He is not the first to authorize military operations that were expected to result in civilian casualties. But he might be the first to do all of these things and receive such deferential treatment from the media as he does so.

Steve Coll, in reviewing Daniel Klaidman's book *Capture or Kill*, pointed out in the *New Yorker* that Obama is also, apparently, the first president to claim an explicit right to assassinate a particular American citizen abroad—to single him out for death, even if found unarmed; to kill him in a country where we are not at war; to kill him without a jury trial. This is kind of a big deal if you care about the Constitution.

Coll notes that this is part of a larger approach to engaging terrorists that makes the title of Klaidman's book something of a misnomer. In fact, the Obama administration seems to prefer killing over capture almost every single time:

> In fact, the book makes clear that the Obama Administration has judged again and again—almost routinely—that capturing terrorist suspects outside of Afghanistan (where there is a friendly host government and an extensive prison system) is not feasible.[36]

Another reason the Obama administration prefers killing over capture—a problem more unique to Obama—is the political problem of what to do with terrorists once you've caught them. After all, he can't exactly send them to Guantánamo after all that bluster about closing it, can he?

Coll makes one other point that very few Obama-loving journalists seem to consider:

President Obama and his advisers have opened the door to violent action against American citizens by future Presidents when the facts may be much less compelling.[37]

Coll's tacit assumption that the Obama administration isn't already killing American citizens without due cause is a gift that most presidents would not automatically receive from the press—especially after the administration was caught claiming that the sixteen-year-old American they killed was a twenty-one-year-old terrorist.

In May 2012, top U.S. security officials sat with the *New York Times*' Jo Becker and Scott Shane for what became a major front-page story on drone assassinations of terrorists.[38] Obama was quoted second-hand saying that the choice to put Anwar al-Awlaki on his kill list was "an easy one." The subsequent killing of Awlaki's sixteen-year-old son was not even mentioned.

The *Times* story did contain a few good nuggets, though. One was the extent of Obama's personal involvement in assassinations. He had asked to be notified of strikes beforehand whenever there was a decent chance that civilians would be killed, so that he could "decide personally whether to go ahead."

Buried in the forty-second paragraph of the piece was, arguably, the most important news item. It addressed the reason administration officials kept claiming that the number of civilian deaths from the drone strike program was in the "single digits."

> ...Mr. Obama embraced a disputed method for counting civilian casualties that did little to box him in. It in effect counts all military-age males in a strike zone as combatants, according to several administration officials, unless there is explicit intelligence posthumously proving them innocent.[39]

Mitt Romney couldn't even honor Polish war dead without reporters shouting such crucially important questions at him as, "What about your gaffes?" Why was President Obama never asked directly about Abdulrahman? Were Brian Williams, Diane Sawyer, and the all-star talking heads who interviewed Obama in calendar year 2012 incapable of asking whether he regretted it? Or did it just not matter?

The fact that Mitt Romney and many Republicans don't disagree with the drone assassination policy is not a very satisfactory answer. Again, a public-spirited, disinterested press does not need permission from either political party to take on an issue that might make a party or a president look bad.

Story Idea: The Curious Case of Executive Privilege

People have already written books on Operation Fast and Furious.[40] I don't intend to go into all of its details here. Suffice it to say that it was a federal law enforcement action conceived without much regard for human life. It pushed gun shop owners to sell weapons to dubious buyers so that the guns could be tracked to border drug gangs. It ended with a lot of deaths, just as one might expect.

As of December 14, 2010, it still seemed like a good idea to many people. Dennis Burke, the U.S. Attorney for the district of Arizona, dashed off an ungrammatical email to a few members of his staff:

> AG' office is now expressing interest in the AG coming out for it Will you send me 4 or 5 lines abt it that I can brief Monty on it—esp time window. Thx.

The "Monty" referred to here is Monty Wilkinson, chief of staff to Obama's Attorney General, Eric Holder. The event the "AG" had wanted to attend was a planned takedown of bad guys to be captured in Operation Fast and Furious.

A week later, on December 21, 2010, Burke sent another email to Monty. "I would not recommend the AG announce this case," he wrote. "I can explain in detail at your convenience."

The sudden change came about because on December 15, a Border Patrol agent named Brian Terry had been killed in a shootout with bandits along the Mexican border. Found at the scene were weapons that had entered the Mexican drug underworld courtesy of the United States government, through the same Operation Fast and Furious.

Fast and Furious put thousands of weapons into criminals' hands and promptly lost track of them. Hundreds of the guns involved in this operation subsequently turned up at crime scenes on both sides of the border, and Attorney General Holder has since acknowledged that those weapons still missing will probably be used in crimes for years to come.[41] Mexican officials, who were never even told about the operation, have claimed that 150 of their citizens were killed or wounded with guns from Fast and Furious.[42]

Border Patrol agent Brian Terry's death forced everything into the open—that and the fact that, just a few weeks after it happened, Republicans took control of the House of Representatives. Its dormant oversight committee, which under Democratic control had spent the first two years of the Obama presidency holding important hearings on such topics as "gender restroom equality," finally started doing some oversight.

Republican House Oversight Chairman Darrell Issa of California and Republican Senate Judiciary ranking member Chuck Grassley of Iowa demanded answers about Fast and Furious, as details began to emerge thanks to whistleblowers' accounts.

On February 4, 2011, Assistant U.S. Attorney Ronald Weich sent a letter to Grassley denying that there had been anything untoward in ATF's weapons trafficking operations along the southern border:

At the outset, the allegation...that ATF "sanctioned" or otherwise knowingly allowed the sale of assault weapons to a straw purchaser who then transported them to Mexico—is false. ATF makes every effort to interdict weapons that have been purchased illegally and prevent their transportation to Mexico.

But nine months later, as documents and whistleblowers suggested the contrary, the Department of Justice had to retract the letter. This statement above, in particular, was false, as were some other statements in the letter—for example, that the whistleblowers who exposed Fast and Furious suffered no retaliation (emails later surfaced showing at least one senior ATF official promising retaliation, with creative use of the F-word).

Congress then demanded answers on how it had been deceived for the better part of a year. Grassley and Issa demanded documents related to what was starting to look like a cover-up. Attorney General Eric Holder spent the next six months stonewalling against the release of the documents.

In June 2012, with Issa's committee about to hold Holder in contempt of Congress, President Obama took the extraordinary step of claiming executive privilege over the documents. Holder was found in contempt of Congress anyway the following week, and the documents in question were not released.

Executive privilege is typically invoked to protect sensitive national security information and policy discussions among a president's senior advisors. But it is a hazy area of law in which courts have been loath to intervene. President George W. Bush's highest profile executive privilege claims related to the energy task force of his first term and the firing of U.S. attorneys in his second. In both instances, the media made Bush pay a political price. In the first case, the media accused Bush of covering up the influence of energy industry lobbyists on his administration (the case went to the Supreme Court where the invocation of executive privilege was upheld). In the second case, the press turned the firing of the U.S. attorneys into a long-running story of a potential abuse of executive power.

In Congress, Democrats rejected the rationale behind Bush's executive privilege claim over the U.S. attorney scandal, and voted to find two of his top aides—Josh Bolten and Harriet Miers—in contempt of Congress anyway. Democratic Senate Judiciary Chairman Patrick Leahy of Vermont made the argument that executive privilege did not apply because Bush had not been personally involved in firing the U.S. attorneys at issue.

"The president's lack of involvement in these firings—by his own account and that of many others—calls into question any claim of executive privilege," Leahy said.[43]

Of course, the exact same can be said about Fast and Furious. No one had asserted that Obama had been personally involved in the law enforcement operation or the subsequent cover-up. Yet here he was, protecting the perpetrators from congressional oversight with an extensive claim of executive privilege. Holder, who had maintained that his department had nothing to hide, was now hiding under President Obama's desk.

"If Fast and Furious was really a 'low level, rogue operation' then executive privilege shouldn't have been asserted in the first place," observed Katie Pavlich, author of *Fast and Furious*.[44]

When Obama inserted himself into the scandal with his executive privilege claim, it was a risky move—at least in theory. The media might have reported, accurately, that he was putting himself between the public and the information about how his administration had, by its own admission, given false information to Congress about a matter in which many people died. Who was involved? Who knew what, and when?

But there was no real risk. The national political media, which had never really given the story much play to begin with, dropped it altogether after Obama made the claim of executive privilege and Holder was voted in contempt. As ever, when Obama declared a story was over, the media, too, decided a story was over.

Had Obama manipulated a friendly news media once again? It certainly seemed that way. The story was kept out of the news until after the election. Then, sure enough, a few weeks after Obama won, the Justice Department began negotiating with House Republicans to release the documents. Law enforcement officials who had been involved in the scandal were suddenly fired, transferred, or demoted.[45]

Because the media let him get away with it, Obama's executive privilege gamble pushed all publicity regarding a major scandal off until after he'd been reelected. It was, in reality, barely a gamble at all, because the mainstream media seem to regard Obama as their editor in chief.

Guardians of the Republic

President Obama is by no means the first chief executive to test the limits of presidential power. The past several decades, in fact, have been characterized by the exaltation of the presidency at the expense of Congress. Presidents have an increasingly free hand to set both domestic and foreign policy—and even to start wars without reference to Congress, the only directly elected branch of the U.S. government.

In *Gangster Government*, I outlined a number of ways that Congress can try to reassert itself. Without so much as a president's signature, Congress could abolish the recess appointment, give oversight and subpoena powers permanently to the opposition party (as some other nations do), and draft legislation with less deference to the bureaucracy.

Unfortunately, for a variety of reasons—partisanship, a preoc-cupation with fundraising, and the cozy get-along atmosphere in Washington, to name a few—Congress is unlikely to step up any time soon. That's where the media should be filling in the gap.

The imperial presidency is as much a problem today as it was in the Nixon era. Even if today's executive transgressions are less flashy than they once were, they are especially meaningful because the size and scope of government have increased so dramatically.

The press is supposed to be the guardian of our republic. When presidents usurp power, conscientious journalists are often the only ones in a position to push back. Yet with a president as wonderful as Obama in office, the will to push often just isn't there.

CHAPTER SEVEN

THE
ROMNEY-MONSTER

L et it never be said that Mitt Romney didn't benefit from liberal media bias during the 2012 campaign. Without it, he never could have won the first presidential debate so decisively.

It was his best moment, and he had the media to thank for it.

Here's why: up until that debate, the Obama campaign had spent months running millions of dollars in ads trying to define Romney and his positions. Most of the claims they made were false, but the media had largely parroted them anyway in its coverage.

The media even used Team Obama's buzzwords and talking points—Romney was leading a Republican "war on women"; he was "out of touch" with ordinary Americans; he was the "outsourcer-in-chief," he was a heartless plutocrat who cared only about people like himself—rich people.

But in that first debate on October 3, 2012, the media filter was removed for the first time. And in that environment, Obama—who had relied so heavily on media bias to lend credibility to his propaganda, and to distort even basic facts about Romney's positions—was blown away.

Each time Romney contradicted him and set him straight—explained that no, that's not my position—Obama seemed unable to accept the rejection. Obama's propaganda had gotten such broad airing, he believed it himself. And that's why he lost that debate.

There in that first presidential debate, and to a lesser extent in the two others, voters got a chance to see the real Romney. And he appeared, well, presidential—even more presidential, some pundits suggested, than the president himself.

Romney was the Republican nominee for a reason. He had had a successful business career. He had helped rescue the 2002 Winter Olympics. He had worked with an overwhelmingly Democratic legislature in Massachusetts to pass important laws. He was a loyal husband, a devoted father, and a man of impressive generosity. Americans hadn't heard those stories.

Nor would they. The debates offered voters only ninety-minute glimpses of the man who hoped to become their new president. And the media did their best to steer viewers' attention away from who he was as a person.

No time for that stuff when there were so many columns and stories to write calling Romney names and dehumanizing him.

Yes, dehumanizing. Literally, even! *New York Times* columnist Charles Blow told an MSNBC audience that Romney "does not have a soul."

> If you opened up, you know, his chest, there's probably a gold ticking watch in there and not even a heart. This is not a person. This is just a robot who will do whatever it

takes, whatever he's told to do, to make it to the White House. And he will take whatever push in the back from whatever nasty person is pushing him and move him further in that direction.[1]

What sort of policies does one get from a soulless president? Policies that kill people, of course.

"What the press should be focused on is what are the consequences of repeal of Obamacare. And the consequences...are death," *Newsweek* senior editor Jonathan Alter told MSNBC's Ed Schultz about Romney's pledge to repeal Obamacare. "Repeal equals death. People will die in the United States if Obamacare is repealed. That is not an exaggeration. That is not crying fire. It's a simple fact....They [the Obama campaign]...can bring death into the conversation and say, 'No, we're not calling Mitt Romney a murderer. What we are saying is that if he's elected President, a lot of people will die.'"[2]

When the media weren't depicting Romney as a soulless robot who will kill people, they were disparaging him as a "vulture capitalist," a school-yard bully and an abuser of small animals.

The name-calling didn't end there, either. *Newsweek* published a cover story entitled, "Romney: The Wimp Factor: Is he just too insecure to be president?"[3] The story was like a bleeding shark—it put the media into a self-generated frenzy for days.

Face the Nation host Bob Schieffer asked Democratic National Committee head Debbie Wasserman Schultz: "Is Mitt Romney a wimp?"[4]

CBS Correspondent Jan Crawford even confronted Romney about the aspersion. "I just got a copy of the *Newsweek* cover that's going to be hitting the newsstands tomorrow that calls you a 'wimp,'" she said in an interview. "Have you seen this?...Has anyone ever called you a 'wimp' before?"[5]

When Romney selected Wisconsin congressman Paul Ryan as his running mate, the media cast Ryan in the role of Romney's evil sidekick, referring to him variously as a "scrooge," a "sociopath," and a "zombie-eyed granny-starver."

All the demagoguery set expectations low for Romney's public unveiling. A pre-election CNN/ORC International poll found that 59 percent of respondents felt Obama would win the debate, while just 34 percent thought Romney would win.[6] A Quinnipiac poll gave Obama a twenty-six-point advantage.[7] It's no wonder Obama's backers went into such a panic when he was crushed.

Fortunately for Obama, though, one of Romney's lighthearted quips got nearly as much attention in the media as his commanding performance.

When asked during the debate what he would cut from the budget, Romney listed several items, including funding for PBS, which airs Sesame Street and employs debate moderator Jim Lehrer. Romney said:

> I'm sorry Jim. I'm gonna' stop the subsidy to PBS. Im gonna' stop other things. I like PBS, I like Big Bird, I actually like you too.

Big Bird became the subject of a roundly criticized Obama campaign ad, as well as numerous opinion columns. *The New York Times'* Charles Blow wrote a column titled, "Don't Mess with Big Bird."[8] Other headlines included "Mitt Romney's Big Bird Attack Threatens Thousands of U.S. Jobs,"[9] "Mitt Romney's Big Bird Blowback," and "The Presidential Debate's Biggest Loser: Big Bird."[10] It was coverage like this that helped ensure that in the heat of the campaign Romney received many more negative stories and far fewer positive ones than Obama did, according to the Pew Research Center.[11]

But the coverage got worse when it mattered most—during the final days of the campaign. Pew Research Center's Project for Excellence in Journalism found that Obama enjoyed a surge in positive coverage during the crucial last days of the race. "During the final week, from October 29 to November 5, positive stories about Obama (29 percent) outnumbered negative ones (19 percent) by 10 points," the study found. "For Mitt Romney in the final week, the tone of coverage remained largely unchanged from the previous two weeks. Negative stories in the press outnumbered positive ones 33 percent to 16 percent."[12]

Benghazi Bungle

On September 11, 2012, the eleventh anniversary of the 9/11 attacks, tensions were rising in Egypt. The U.S. Embassy in Cairo released a statement apologizing for an obscure internet video produced in America that was critical of Islam and had upset some Egyptian Muslims. The statement also criticized "continuing efforts by misguided individuals to hurt the religious feelings of Muslims." The embassy was attacked that day—the walls were scaled and an Islamic flag associated with al Qaeda groups was raised in place of the American flag, which was burnt. Protestors chanted, "Obama, Obama, there are still a billion Osamas."

The U.S. Embassy in Cairo tweeted that it still stood by its initial statement denouncing the anti-Islamic video and apologizing for it—feeble groveling in the face of violent terrorist sympathizers who did not notice and did not care. But the person running the embassy's Twitter account was essentially throwing Americans' free speech rights under the bus, and trying to blame the First Amendment for an attack that looked a lot more like a celebration of 9/11.

Three years earlier, on June 4, 2009, President Obama had given a speech in Cairo in which he had gone out of his way to praise as many aspects of Arab and Islamic culture as possible. It was all part of a major attempt by the Obama administration to ingratiate America (or at least himself) with the Islamic world, with which Obama, having grown up in part in Indonesia, felt he had a special connection.

The violence in Cairo provided evidence that Obama's charm offensive had accomplished little in three years. The only remarkable thing had been his naïve belief that it would, given that America has been unpopular in the Muslim world for decades. Later that day came the attack on the U.S. Consulate in Benghazi.

At first glance, the real story seemed to be that all of Obama's attempts to curry favor with the Arab world—including a policy of putting "daylight" between the United States and Israel in order to appear more even-handed in negotiating a lasting peace in the Middle East—seemed to have come to naught. Another story might have been how the State Department appeared confused about whether Americans' First Amendment rights were worth defending abroad. A third story might have been about whether the consulate was adequately defended, especially given that it had been subject to earlier attacks (as it turned out, this was a very serious question).

None of these issues became the big story. Instead, the media turned this into a story about a Romney gaffe. I don't know that I've ever seen anything quite like it.

After it was clear that at least one American had died in the Benghazi attack, Romney released a statement:

> I'm outraged by the attacks on American diplomatic missions in Libya and Egypt and by the death of an American consulate worker in Benghazi. It's disgraceful that the Obama administration's first response was not to condemn attacks on our diplomatic missions, but to sympathize with those who waged the attacks.[13]

The next day, the Obama campaign reacted with predictable outrage—at Mitt Romney. Obama campaign press secretary Ben LaBolt said he was "shocked" that Romney would launch a political attack in the middle of an international crisis.[14] And that, dear reader, is the story the media chose to run with. The story about how Mitt Romney attacked the embassies—or something like that.

After it became clear four Americans, including the U.S. ambassador to Libya, had died in the attacks, Obama finally used stronger language, saying he "strongly condemn[ed] the outrageous attack."

Romney later made televised remarks in which he called the Cairo embassy statement about the anti-Islamic video as "akin to an apology" and a "severe miscalculation."

The Obama administration implausibly blamed both attacks (which, remember, occurred on the anniversary of 9/11) on the YouTube video. Instead of investigating this claim, the media zeroed in immediately on Romney's criticism.

"Unless the Romney campaign has gamed this crisis out in some manner completely invisible to the Gang of 500 [Mark Halperin's term for political insiders], his doubling down on criticism of the President for the statement coming out of Cairo is likely to be seen as one of the most craven and ill-advised tactical moves in this entire campaign," said *Time*'s Mark Halperin.

The *New York Times* said Romney's "knee-jerk response showed an extraordinary lack of presidential character." The *Los Angeles Times* called it "an outrageous exercise in opportunism."[15]

The narrative instantly shifted from the actual news—the crucial errors of the Obama administration that left four Americans dead, and the administration's hesitant response to the attacks—to the propriety and timing of Romney's response.

As my *Washington Examiner* colleague Philip Klein wrote,

That instant conventional wisdom is a pretty fortunate turn of events for Obama, given that it diverted focus from his administration's bungled handling of the entire situation and the failure of his broader foreign policy posture....

In 2004, John Kerry routinely attacked President Bush's handling of Iraq when things weren't going well.... And the media dutifully reported on Bush's foreign policy blunders in Iraq. But now, instead of scrutinizing Obama's handling of a foreign policy crisis, the media has decided that the real story in Egypt and Libya is a Mitt Romney gaffe.[16]

Of course, it's pretty easy to write a story about someone's gaffe. It's a lot harder to find, through reporting, a more accurate picture of what was really happening in Egypt and Libya, or at least of how the people actually controlling the foreign policy of the United States government—that is, the Obama White House—were bungling the situation. Incredibly, the lack of curiosity and unquestioning acceptance of this unlikely YouTube story would continue straight through the election.

But at least reporters were all over the "Romney bungled it" beat.

Candy's Intervention

The media consistently misrepresented the Obama administration's response to the events in Benghazi. The most prominent example came at a crucial moment, in the second presidential debate on October 16, when moderator Candy Crowley of CNN sided with President Obama on false remarks about Libya.

At one point during the town hall style debate, Obama claimed that he had labeled the attack "an act of terror" in a speech in the

Rose Garden the day after the attack took place. This prompted the following exchange.

ROMNEY: I—I think interesting the president just said something which—which is that on the day after the attack he went into the Rose Garden and said that this was an act of terror.

OBAMA: That's what I said.

ROMNEY: You said in the Rose Garden the day after the attack, it was an act of terror. It was not a spontaneous demonstration, is that what you're saying?

OBAMA: Please proceed governor.

ROMNEY: I want to make sure we get that for the record because it took the president 14 days before he called the attack in Benghazi an act of terror.

OBAMA: Get the transcript.

CROWLEY: It—it—it—he did in fact, sir. So let me—let me call it an act of terror...

OBAMA: Can you say that a little louder, Candy?

CROWLEY: He—he did call it an act of terror. It did as well take—it did as well take two weeks or so for the whole idea there being a riot out there about this tape to come out. You are correct about that.

Crowley had it wrong, and in fact after the debate she acknowl-edged that Romney had been "right in the main," but that he had "picked the wrong word." Obama had said in the Rose Garden that "No acts of terror will ever shake the resolve of this nation." But he had not called the Benghazi attack terrorism explicitly, and was probably making a reference to "the acts of terror" that took place on September 11, 2001.

This was a critical moment in the campaign—the moment Rom-ney seemed to run out of steam.

Crowley may have messed up, but don't be too hard on her. She, like nearly all other Americans, had no way of knowing that just hours after his Rose Garden speech, Obama been asked point-blank by CBS's Steve Kroft, on camera, whether the Benghazi incident had been a terrorist attack, and had refused to say it was.

> KROFT: Mr. President, this morning you went out of your way to avoid the use of the word terrorism in connection with the Libya Attack. Do you believe that this was a ter-rorism attack?

> OBAMA: Well it's too early to know exactly how this came about, what group was involved, but obviously it was an attack on Americans. And we are going to be working with the Libyan government to make sure that we bring these folks to justice, one way or the other.

This portion of Kroft's *60 Minutes* interview with Obama cer-tainly seems to give all the necessary context to his Rose Garden comments, if there was any ambiguity. Obama was not, in fact, saying that the attack on the U.S. Consulate had been a terrorist strike. And Obama's act during the debate, suggesting that he'd maintained it was terrorism all along, was not truthful.

This segment of the interview tape would have clarified what had happened in the debate. But CBS did not release it. This portion of the CBS interview was suppressed until November 4, when it was quietly posted online.[17] Instead, immediately after the debate, CBS released the less revealing portion of its interview that immediately followed it, which was still ambiguous but looked like it might back up Obama's side of the story.

> KROFT: It's been described as a mob action, but there are reports that they were very heavily armed with grenades, that doesn't sound like your normal demonstration.

> OBAMA: As I said, we're still investigating exactly what happened, I don't want to jump the gun on this. But you're right that this is not a situation that was exactly the same as what happened in Egypt. And my suspicion is there are folks involved in this who were looking to target Americans from the start. So we're gonna make sure that our first priority is to get our folks out safe, make sure our embassies are secured around the world and then we are going to go after those folks who carried this out.

After giving this interview on September 12, Obama and his top diplomats spent two weeks advancing the notion in public that the Benghazi attack had been a "spontaneous demonstration" provoked by an Internet video.[18] UN Ambassador Susan Rice spread this idea on five Sunday shows. Obama himself mentioned the video six times in his United Nations address of September 25. Secretary of State Hillary Clinton, standing near the flag-draped coffins of the four dead Americans at the ceremony transferring their remains, also blamed the video:

This has been a difficult week for the State Department and for our country. We've seen the heavy assault on our post in Benghazi that took the lives of those brave men. We've seen rage and violence directed at American embassies over an awful Internet video that we had nothing to do with.

It would be more than two weeks before the president called the Benghazi attack an act of terror or terrorism.

Romney had been right about Obama and Benghazi. Perhaps media bias helped Romney win that first debate, but it probably cost him the second one.

The Bain Blame Game

In 1984, Mitt Romney co-founded Bain Capital, a private equity investment firm. For fifteen years, Romney presided over Bain as its president and managing general partner. During that time, he and his associates helped rescue and improve the value of companies like Staples, Domino's Pizza, and Sports Authority.

Obama signaled early on that his campaign would focus on Romney's tenure at Bain. He announced during a press conference in May 2012 that Bain was "not a distraction" but rather "what this campaign is going to be about."[19]

The Obama campaign devoted much of its advertising against Romney to attacks on Bain, and the media covered them all as if Bain was the most important issue of the election, persistently trying to link Romney to Bain investments that resulted in layoffs and outsourcing. They tried to depict Romney as a hypocrite because on the campaign trail he bemoaned the toll that outsourcing had taken on the American economy and vowed to protect American workers by holding China accountable.

MSNBC host Ed Schultz described the private equity firm as "strip-mining" companies. Former MSNBC anchor David Shuster told a Current TV audience that Bain was practicing "vulture capitalism." Reuters referred to Romney as "a former corporate raider," a term for which it later apologized.[20]

The *Weekly Standard*'s Jay Cost unpacked one example of the media's single-minded focus on Bain. On July 6, 2012, the Labor Department released a terrible jobs report from June. Hiring was weak and unemployment was unchanged. Economists were predicting that the U.S. economy might fall back into recession. But because any bad economic news would hurt a vulnerable president, Cost wrote, "the media—following cues from the Democratic party…pursued an alternative storyline: Mitt Romney is rich! He worked at a firm dealing in high finance! His money is invested overseas!"[21]

"There was a bad narrative out there for the Democratic Party, but it has been replaced with a bad narrative for the Republican Party," Cost wrote. "After all, Mitt Romney has basically been running for president for five years. *Why are these stories about Bain Capital cropping up now?* It is not as though the 'scoops' in these stories were that hard to come upon; everything is in publicly available documents filed with the federal government."[22]

It's not that the Bain story did not deserve any attention, but the media did little to teach people about the high-risk, high-reward business of private equity, the realities of globalization, or anything that put this in context. They covered the story exactly the way Obama's campaign wanted it to be covered.

The Obama storyline was that Bain bought companies, cut workers' pay, and eventually laid everyone off. In some cases, it is true that Bain failed to turn companies around—though how often did you hear that Bain saved a high percentage of the firms it bought?

Even in cases where the failing companies finally went into bankruptcy (some of these companies emerged from bankruptcy stronger) and where Bain was unable to perform its turnaround magic successfully, it still might have deserved credit for staving off job losses that would have otherwise happened sooner.

Nor did the media show much grasp of the idea that capitalism is a risky business. Businesses don't just inevitably grow the way government does, and Bain, as a company, was highly successful, or as a somewhat critical *Wall Street Journal* story had it, "Romney at Bain: Big Gains, Some Busts."[23] But the media are terrible at describing the fine points—especially when they want to be.

One of the big stories of the campaign should have been the dire state of the economy. The media spun that into the allegedly dire state of employees whose companies were bought by Bain.

Consider the story of Joe Soptic. In 1993 Bain Capital became majority shareholder at Kansas City's Worldwide Grinding Systems steel mill. The company, which later became GS Technologies, went bankrupt in 2001. Seven-hundred and fifty people lost their jobs, and many were left without health benefits and with reduced pensions.

The Obama campaign made the company a centerpiece of its attacks on Romney, and the story was treated like a scandal for Romney by much of the media. As one Reuters headline put it, "Special Report: Romney's Steel Skeleton in the Bain Closet."[24] The Democratic National Convention featured three speakers who were former employees at companies controlled by Bain, including GS Technologies Inc. All told stories involving laid off workers, plant closings, benefit reductions, and shattered lives.

An ad produced by pro-Obama PAC Priorities USA Action featured Soptic, who worked at the steel plant for twenty-eight years. Once the plant closed, Soptic was forced to find new work as a janitor at a school, where his health plan did not cover his wife. Soptic's wife later died of lung cancer. The ad made it appear as if she wasn't able to get the medical attention she needed because her husband had been laid off from the steel plant. The ad traded on the idea that Romney was a Gordon Gekko-like corporate raider who cared only about Bain's profits. As William Cohan wrote in a Bloomberg News article, "The real point is how a man who wants to be 'CEO of America' left a trail of destroyed lives when he was only chief executive officer of a single private-equity firm."[25]

Never mind that the plant was on the verge of bankruptcy already when Bain took over, so that Soptic was likely employed much longer there because of Romney. Never mind that dozens of other U.S. steel companies had gone into bankruptcy during that period or that sent all of their production overseas much earlier. Never mind that Romney had left Bain by the time the steel company finally did file for bankruptcy in 2001. And never mind that Soptic's wife had quit a job that provided health insurance. These details were left out or downplayed in stories about the steel company. The media are terrible with details—especially when they want to be.

One anti-Bain story, from the *Boston Globe*, alleged that Securities and Exchange Commission (SEC) documents showed that Romney had presided over Bain Capital longer than he was insisting, and that he headed Bain at a time of increased outsourcing.[26] Here was an opportunity to cast doubt on his integrity.

Romney had always claimed that he left Bain in February 1999, when he departed to run the Winter Olympics in Salt Lake City, Utah. But the Obama campaign breathed life into the idea, based on a misreading of documents, that he left in 2002, which would have meant that he led Bain when a lot of outsourcing occurred.

At one point, Obama's deputy campaign manager Stephanie Cutter accused Romney of possibly committing a felony for misrepresenting his position at Bain to the SEC.

The SEC documents showed that Romney was listed as an owner of shares in Bain, but that didn't mean he had any managerial role there. *Fortune* magazine later obtained a series of post-1999 "offering documents," none of which showed Romney listed among the "key investment professionals" at Bain. *Fortune* noted, "the contemporaneous Bain documents show that Romney was indeed telling the truth about no longer having operational input at Bain—which, one should note, is different from no longer having legal or financial ties to the firm."[27]

FactCheck.org stated that Romney did not actively manage Bain Capital after February 1999. "We see little new in the *Globe* piece," Brooks Jackson, co-author of the FactCheck article, told *Politico*. "So far nobody has shown that Romney was actually managing Bain (even part-time) during his time at the Olympics, or that he was anything but a passive, absentee owner during that time, as both Romney and Bain have long said."[28]

But the Obama campaign and its media allies weren't about to allow the facts to get in the way of a good line of attack. Politico media reporter Dylan Byers described what the SEC report would mean for the coverage of the presidential campaign:

> The report, which was blasted out to reporters late Saturday by the pro-Obama super PAC Priorities USA Action, is further evidence—if any was needed—that both the media and Team Obama intend to keep the issue at the top of the news cycle well into next week, if not longer.[29]

Of course, they could only keep it there because the media let them.

On August 23, more than a month later, CNN's Jim Acosta called the SEC documents a "headache…that keeps coming back time and again for Mitt Romney.... The Bain documents resurfaced as yet another distraction for Romney, who went to New Mexico to detail his new energy plan."[30] It should have been obvious that Romney would get zero coverage that day for his energy plan.

The Gaffe Machine

When the media weren't obsessing over Romney's relationship with Bain Capital, they were detailing his alleged campaign trail gaffes.

In late July, Romney spent a week burnishing his foreign policy credentials by meeting with leaders in England, Israel, and Poland. The media portrayed the trip as one long gaffe, or in the words of *Washington Post* columnist Eugene Robinson, a "gaffepalooza."[31]

Hélène Mulholland of Britain's the *Guardian* newspaper wrote, "Mitt Romney gets cold reception from UK media after Olympic gaffe: 'Romneyshambles', 'party-pooper', 'worse than Palin'—British papers are unimpressed by Republican's charm offensive."[32]

Time magazine asked, "After Gaffe-Filled Foreign Tour, Europe Asks: 'Is Mitt Romney a Loser?'"[33]

After one of Romney's supposed flubs, Bloomberg's Julie Hirschfield Davis asked, "Was this Mitt Romney's 'potatoe' moment?" referencing former Vice President Dan Quayle's infamous[34] misspelling of "potato" during a children's spelling bee.

What did Romney do to invite such scorn?

Not much, as it turned out. While in England, Romney questioned how prepared London was for the Summer Olympic Games, whose opening ceremonies began during his stay. Here Romney's alleged gaffe was really a statement of fact. Romney, as reported in the *Daily Telegraph*, "told NBC News he saw 'a few things that were disconcerting' about London's preparations. 'The stories about the private security firm not having enough people, supposed strike of immigration and customs officials, that obviously is not something which is encouraging,' he said."[35]

In fact, there had been a "cock-up," as the British say, in the security arrangements for the Olympics. The British government had signed an enormous contract with a private security firm to cover the Olympics, but the company failed to meet its obligations and confessed that its performance was a "humiliating shambles."[36] The British government was forced to rely on its armed forces to fill the gap. This was widely covered in the British press, and considered something of a scandal.

The *Washington Post*'s Erik Wemple provided some much-needed perspective on this. In a piece titled, "Media should consider mentioning that Romney was right about Olympic preps," he wrote:

> A nightly newscast on the major networks [in Britain] wasn't complete...without a segment on how the security contractor wasn't doing its job, the government had to send in troops and so on. There was even some celebrated, and overblown, video of some security goon sleeping on the job. That clip got so much attention because of the consensus that things were in disarray.[37]

Romney's comments about London's Olympics preparations might have been undiplomatic—though he was talking to NBC not the BBC—but they were hardly a "gaffe." Romney went on to Jerusalem and committed something that looked a bit more like a diplomatic blunder when he cited cultural differences as a reason for Israel's economic superiority to the Palestinian-controlled territories. Next he went to Poland and visited the Polish Tomb of the Unknown Soldier, where an exasperated Romney aide yelled "shove it" at reporters who were peppering Romney with questions about his alleged mishaps.

So Romney was a foreign policy novice and gaffe machine—that was the story the media ran with. A Media Research Center analysis of all twenty-one ABC, CBS, and NBC evening news stories about Romney's trip found that nearly all of them (eighteen, or 86 percent) emphasized "diplomatic blunders," "gaffes," or "missteps."[38]

This was the same media that in 2008 described in glowing and uncritical terms candidate Barack Obama's trip to Europe. Back then, headlines like "Why Europe Loves Barack Obama"[39] and "Obama Wows Berlin Crowd with Historic Speech"[40] were common.

A fair and honest observer would have to say that Romney's trip really didn't go perfectly, but it certainly wasn't 86 percent blunders. In Israel, he was embraced. In Poland, he met with Cold War hero and former Polish president Lech Walesa. Walesa, who had refused to meet with President Obama in 2011, practically endorsed Romney. "I wish you to be successful because this success is needed to the United States, of course, but to Europe and the rest of the world, too. Governor Romney, get your success—be successful," Walesa told Romney.[41]

Walesa's endorsement, on the few occasions when it was brought up in the news, was downplayed. "What Mr. Walesa says doesn't carry a lot of weight with Poles or Polish-Americans. He thinks differently than most people," John Micgiel, director of the East Central European Center at Columbia University, told ABC News.[42]

The ABC News story went on to state that Solidarity, the trade union that Walesa helped found and led in defiance of Poland's Communist government, had dissociated itself from his comments; then it quoted current Solidarity leaders bashing Romney over his "attacks on trade unions and employees' rights."

"The 47 Percent"

Romney did indeed commit his share of true, honest-to-goodness gaffes. He said some ghastly things that should have and did give voters pause about his candidacy. It's part of the reason he lost.

In mid-September, the liberal political magazine *Mother Jones* released a surreptitious video of Mitt Romney's off-the-cuff remarks at a May fundraiser with rich donors. In the video, Romney predicted that 47 percent of the electorate would vote for Obama "no matter what" because they are dependent on government and pay no income taxes. "My job is not to worry about those people," Romney said. "I'll never convince them they should take personal responsibility and care for their lives."

Romney's remarks were not only insensitive, they were also incorrect. Many of the "47 percent" of Americans who pay no income taxes are retirees, enlisted members of the military, and other low-wage workers who do take "personal responsibility and care for their lives" —and who in fact also pay payroll taxes. Many of them are reliable Republican voters, or at least occasional ones.

After the election, *USA Today* found that Romney won overwhelmingly in the three U.S. counties most dependent on government. "Three Kentucky counties—Owsley, McCreary and Wolfe—are the only places that rely on government programs such as Social Security, food stamps and Medicaid for more than half of income," the paper's study found. Romney won them by 65, 61, and 22 points, respectively.[43]

Romney's "47 percent remarks" fed into the idea—strongly pushed by the Obama campaign—that he was unconcerned about people on the margins of society. And you can bet the media reminded the public of it every chance they got. According to a study by the media watch-dog NewsBusters, during the three days immediately following the video's release, the broadcast network morning and evening shows produced forty-two stories about the tape.[44]

The media's reaction to Romney's 47 percent remarks was summed up best by Bloomberg's Josh Barro, who wrote a piece titled, "Today, Mitt Romney Lost the Election."[45] The story went viral on social media, as well. According to one study, within the first 24 hours of its release, the video of Romney's "47 percent" remarks had been viewed more than 2.4 million times.[46]

But here's something interesting that you may remember. Romney's gaffe was very similar to one that President Obama made in 2008. In April of that year, Obama spoke to a group of wealthy San Francisco donors about working class voters in flyover country. In his words:

> You go into these small towns in Pennsylvania and, like a lot of small towns in the Midwest, the jobs have been gone now for 25 years and nothing's replaced them. And they fell through the Clinton administration, and the Bush administration, and each successive administration has said that somehow these communities are gonna regenerate and they have not.
>
> And it's not surprising then they get bitter, they cling to guns or religion or antipathy toward people who aren't like them or anti-immigrant sentiment or anti-trade sentiment as a way to explain their frustrations.[47]

Romney had written off nearly half the electorate as hopeless, using very insulting terms. Ditto for Obama. Both of them did it behind closed doors and in front of wealthy donors who probably just ate it up.

What sort of coverage do you suppose they each received?

According to LexisNexis, Obama's comments were referenced in fifty unique television segments in the six and a half months between the day they were first reported and Election Day. In the seven weeks between the release of Romney's taped comments and the election, his comments were referenced in eighty-three segments.

A Pew Research Center poll from October found that 49 percent of respondents said Romney's "47 percent" remarks drew too much coverage, while 28 percent said they received the right amount of coverage. Only 13 percent said they didn't get enough attention.[48] It would have been hard to give them much more.

Convention Coverage

The Republicans held their national convention in Tampa, Florida, during the week of August 27, 2012. The media did their best to portray the event as something akin to the cantina scene in the movie Star Wars, a parade of deceitful and detestable characters.

The *Daily Beast*'s Michael Tomasky predicted that the convention would be a "toxic waste dump of hate and lies and race-baiting."[49] (This was true, but only in the MSNBC video booth.)

NBC's Matt Lauer worried that the convention was not appealing to a wide audience. In an interview with Fox News host Bill O'Reilly, the *Today* co-host asked, "When you talk about the conservatives and we talk about the gender gap and how important women are…do you think this convention is reaching out to the people who are going to decide this election, independents, moderates and women?"[50]

On *Morning Joe*, former *Boston Globe* columnist Mike Barnicle asked former RNC chairman Michael Steele, "what percentage of Republican delegates who go to the convention do you figure are total nutcases?"[51]

The *New York Times* opinion columnists were particularly brutal. Maureen Dowd called the convention a "colossal hoax," while Frank Bruni opined that for gay Republicans being at the convention was like "a fleeting moment inside the tent, only to be flogged and sent back out into the cold."[52]

"The Zombie-Eyed Granny-Starver from Wisconsin"

The media came down especially hard on Paul Ryan's acceptance speech on the convention's penultimate evening. The liberal media claimed the speech was full of falsehoods—that is, things they disagreed with. The *New York Times'* Charles Blow accused Ryan of lying and asked, "What does it mean when a party that trafficks in American greatness trades in human horridness?"

The media seemed to hold Ryan in particular contempt throughout the campaign. They made him out to be a cruel, heartless scrooge, all because he had offered the first serious budget proposal produced by either party to address the national debt and deficit.

Consider *New York Times* columnist Maureen Dowd's description of Ryan:

> I'd been wondering how long it would take Republicans to realize that Paul Ryan is their guy.... Who better to rain misery upon the heads of millions of Americans? He's Scrooge disguised as a Pickwick, an ideologue disguised as a wonk. Not since Ronald Reagan tried to cut the budget by categorizing ketchup and relish as vegetables has the G.O.P. managed to find such an attractive vessel to mask harsh policies with a smiling face....Ryan should stop being so lovable. People who intend to hurt other people should wipe the smile off their faces.[53]

Even journalists who aspire to objectivity couldn't hold back their disdain. When Ryan visited NBC's Today show, co-host Ann Curry assailed him with questions and accusations about his budget. Here's how their chat began.

> ANN CURRY: The Center of [sic] Budget and Policy Priorities...says 62 percent of the savings in your budget would come from cutting programs for the poor, that between eight and ten million people would be kicked off of food stamps, that you would cut Medicare by $200 billion, Medicaid and other health programs by something like $770 billion. Where is the empathy in this

budget?... Do you acknowledge that poor people will suffer under this budget—

RYAN: No. No.

CURRY: —that you have shown a lack of empathy to poor people in this budget?[54]

Here's what MSNBC's Martin Bashir said about Ryan's budget proposal:

> If his [the House GOP] budget were ever to come to pass, then Meals on Wheels would be killed, transportation services to the disabled would be destroyed, food stamps would be eviscerated. I think many Americans would end up in soup kitchens like that. So I don't think we should be critical. I think we should be grateful that what Mr. Ryan has shown us is exactly what will happen to people if the kind of vicious and callous budget that he would wish to impose on American people ends up coming to pass.[55]

Esquire's Charles Pierce called Ryan "the zombie-eyed granny-starver from Wisconsin," whose selection as Romney's running mate signaled that Romney had "finally surrendered the tattered remnants of his soul not only to the extreme base of his party, but also to extremist economic policies, and to an extremist view of the country he seeks to lead." Pierce also called Ryan "an authentically dangerous zealot...a smiling, aw-shucks murderer of opportunity, a creator of dystopias in which he never will have to live."[56]

Bill Maher called Ryan a "heartless, smirking bastard." And liberal talk radio host Thom Hartmann diagnosed Ryan as a "socio-path," insisting that "I use that word very, very, very carefully." Hartmann then compared Ryan to a serial killer:

And sociopaths are people who are typically, you know—
Smart sociopaths can be incredibly charming. Ted Bundy,
who was a sociopath and a serial killer, his sociopathy
came out as a murderer.[57]

The Dog on a Roof Campaign

Throughout the campaign, the media relentlessly portrayed
Romney as being heartless toward his fellow man. So why not man's
best friend as well?

In 1983, the Romneys set out on a 12-hour drive from Massachusetts to Mitt's family's vacation home in Ontario, Canada. With
five boys filling the back of the car, the family dog, Seamus, an Irish
Setter, was placed in a dog crate that was fastened to the roof of the
car.

Romney always maintained that Seamus enjoyed being in the
crate on the roof. But during this particular trip, Seamus was suffering from diarrhea, which forced Romney to pull off the road and
hose down the car.

This anecdote was first reported by the *Boston Globe* in 2007.
A lot of people found it amusing, and there were a lot of people who
were put off by it. It was funny—good fodder for late night come-
dians. In the spring of 2012, David Letterman mentioned the incident almost every evening.[58] The "Dogs against Romney" Facebook
page had more than 100,000 likes by Election Day.

It wasn't *that* big a deal. Well, it *wasn't* that big a deal, but a lot
of people in the media decided that it would be, even if it meant they
had to repeat the story *ad nauseam*. Which they did.

According to one estimate, *New York Times* columnist Gail
Collins mentioned Seamus in at least fifty columns.[59] (That's what
columnists do when they're out of ideas.)

"Crate-gate," as it came to be known, generated so much attention in the media that even that nickname now has its own Wikipe-
dia entry—with thirty-five footnotes!

In April 2012, ABC News' Diane Sawyer quoted Ann Romney as saying it was the most wounding thing that had so far happened in the campaign.[60] (She had, on other occasions, pointed out that there was a windshield on the crate, and that it's not really all that different from riding on a motorcycle or in the bed of a pickup.)

The *Washington Post*'s Philip Rucker interviewed Democratic strategist Chris Lehane about why the Seamus story received so much attention. "It's a signifier," Lehane said. "There are certain events that happen over the course of someone's life that play into a larger story line and feed into a caricature. Seamus the dog story just plays into a negative story line about a guy who you may not completely trust."[61]

Or...could it be that the story received so much attention because people like the *Washington Post*'s Philip Rucker did so many interviews on it?

Don't think for a minute that the Dog-on-a-Roof story didn't damage Romney. A March 2012 poll by Public Policy Polling found that 37 percent of respondents said Obama would be a better president for dogs, while just 21 percent felt Romney would be better. Thirty-five percent of respondents said the incident would make them less likely to vote for Romney.[62]

It's also a good thing for Romney that dogs don't vote.

Mitt the Bully

If "Crate-gate" seemed trivial, the media frenzy created by a nearly half-century-old story about Romney's bullying of a prep school classmate was far less so. It was, frankly, malicious and pretty bizarre.

On May 10, 2012, the *Washington Post* published a 5,500-word front page story—a story that's about say, the length of this book's final chapter—titled, "Mitt Romney's prep school class-mates recall pranks, but also troubling incidents."[63]

Reporter Jason Horowitz's piece is an illuminating and mostly evenhanded account of Romney's teenage years at Cranbrook School, a prestigious prep school outside Detroit. Horowitz interviewed many of Romney's old classmates and discovered that as a youth, Romney was something of a prankster. But one anecdote made him look like a bully.

As a senior, Romney led a group of boys in pinning down and cutting another student's hair, which they felt had grown too long.

Later in life, the bullied boy revealed that he was a homosexual. In 2004, he died of cancer—which meant that he wasn't there to say anything about Romney, either to defend him or to say, "Aw shucks, it was so long ago"—or to say he'd been scarred for life by the incident.

Even so, this story proved irresistible to many journalists eager to imply dark motives behind Romney's prank of fifty years ago. ABC World News anchor Diane Sawyer led off her program on May 10 with:

> Tonight on *World News*, campaign curve ball. Mitt Romney's high school classmates accuse him of bullying a vulnerable student. How does the candidate respond tonight?...Good evening. As we begin, there is a surprising turn of events on the campaign trail. Presidential candidate Mitt Romney, accused of bullying a very vulnerable fellow student when he was in high school.[64]

The *New Yorker*'s Amy Davidson compared Romney's youthful bullying to Robert Byrd's affiliation as a young man with the Ku Klux Klan.[65] Ashley Parker and Jodi Kantor began their piece in the *New York Times* this way:

> The day after President Obama endorsed gay marriage, Mitt Romney found himself responding to allegations

that as a teenager he harassed a prep school classmate who later came out as gay.

The account put Mr. Romney, who has struggled on the campaign trail to cast off his rivals' image of him as privileged and insensitive, on the defensive about events nearly 50 years ago.[66]

The incident not only reinforced the image of Romney as coldly indifferent to the vulnerable, but it also gave the media a chance to portray him as violently "homophobic." It was the perfect opportunity to dehuminize him, using a fifty-year-old incident from high school.

The Weird Mormon Guy

Given that Romney was the first Mormon major-party nominee for president, his religion played a surprisingly minor role in the 2012 election. But some journalists just couldn't stop themselves from bashing Romney's faith.

During the primaries, the media often talked about Romney's faith as a possible liability for him among conservative Evangelical voters, some of whom consider the Church of Latter-day Saints to be a cult. But polls showed it was a bigger problem for political liberals.

According to a 2011 Gallup poll, 27 percent of Democrats said they wouldn't vote for a Mormon of their own party for president, while just 18 percent of Republicans said they wouldn't vote for a Mormon.[67] A Quinnipiac poll showed that 46 percent of Democrats and 29 percent of Republicans said they would be uncomfortable with a Mormon president.[68]

The media talked so much about Romney's faith in the lead up to the 2012 election that when the *Washington Post* and Pew Research Center conducted a public opinion poll asking more than 1,000 Americans what one word they associate with Romney, "Mormon" was cited more than three times as often as any other.[69]

But Romney's faith was more often a problem with liberal pundits than with voters. *Slate*'s Jacob Weisberg wrote that Romney's faith should disqualify him for the presidency. The *New York Times*' Maureen Dowd and Charles Blow mocked Romney's Mormonism. In response to Romney's comments about America's high out-of-wedlock birthrate, Blow tweeted, "Let me just tell you this Mitt 'Muddle Mouth': I'm a single parent and my kids are *amazing*! Stick that in your magic underwear."[70]

MSNBC host Lawrence O'Donnell was a frequent and fiery critic of Mormonism. During one tirade he said:

> Mormonism was created by a guy in Upstate New York in 1830 when he got caught having sex with the maid and explained to his wife that God told him to do it. Forty-eight wives later, Joseph Smith's lifestyle was completely sanctified in the religion he invented to go with it, which Mitt Romney says he believes.[71]

Touré Neblett accused Republicans of engaging in the "otherization" of Barack Obama. But that term more aptly describes what the media helped Obama's campaign do to Romney. They made him seem totally foreign to ordinary Americans. They dehumanized him.

Election Day exit polls found more voters believed Romney would be a better steward of the economy. But Obama won the empathy vote hands down. Obama won by 10 points on the crucial question, "Who is more in touch with people like you?"[72] Among voters who most valued candidates who "care about people like me," Obama won by a staggering 63 points.[73]

The media succeeded in their goal of making Romney an unacceptable alternative even to a failing president. It was an impressive feat of invective and spin.

CHAPTER EIGHT

FIGHTING BACK WITH GOOD IDEAS

"Yes, the media are liberal. But what can I do about it?" If you're asking that question, you're on the right track already.

In 1964, Barry Goldwater suffered the most crushing popular vote defeat of any presidential candidate in history. At that time, conservatives were barely relevant in politics, and the media were no less liberal than they are today.

Yet somehow, over the forty-nine years between then and now, conservatism has ascended—often in spite of conservatives themselves—to something much greater than mere relevance. Conservatism produced one of America's greatest presidents in Ronald Reagan and achieved, at least for now, a structural majority in state governments and in Congress. More important, it is creating policy success stories all over America right now—not just in places like Texas, Indiana, and beet-red North Dakota, but even in Wisconsin, Rhode Island (where a conservative governor worked with Democrats to reform Medicaid), and the District of Columbia.

The media environment we live in has changed significantly over the last five decades. It's not just that Fox News and talk radio now exist. With the rise of blogs and then social media, individuals have also gained a voice they never had, breaking the media's old monopoly on public influence. So just think—if conservatives came that far in an era when all most of them could do was throw something at a young Dan Rather's smug face on the television set—just think of what we can achieve now, even with a media so in love with President Obama.

The conservative movement did not come this far over fifty years by whining about obstacles. It overcame them.

Conservatives exhibit a disturbing inferiority complex. I think of Don Corleone, grabbing Johnny Fontane and shouting, "You can act like a man! What's the matter with you?" That's my message to you, dear reader. Act like a man—or a woman—who doesn't crave the approbation of elite media spin masters. They won't give it, and you don't need it.

The liberal media has influence, but to some degree it is only as powerful as you let it be. It draws its power from how you and everyone else regard it. If people see only one political view suffusing political coverage and dominating the commentary on all three network news broadcasts, two of the three cable networks, and in nearly every major newspaper, they may think—how can that view not be right?

But liberals don't dominate the news media because their views are more persuasive or mainstream than yours, nor because the facts line up on their side, nor because all of the smart or well-educated people agree with them.[1] Liberals dominate the media because they are more likely than conservatives to settle for the relatively low pay and—especially today—dim job prospects that exist in journalism. And once they get here, liberals are more likely than conservatives to persevere in newsroom environments where everyone else thinks the way they do. It's that simple.

The Double Standard

Conservatives can console themselves with the fact that they have the right ideas. But they also need to learn that that's not enough. In a world where the most influential voices are utterly contemptuous of conservatism, no matter the facts, conservatives are always held to a higher standard. If your politics are right-of-center, you cannot get away with expounding theories and arguments that lack sound evidence the way liberals can. When liberals make lazy assertions that lack intellectual rigor, the media not only refuse to challenge them but in fact often help trumpet their message.

This is not primarily a reason to complain—it is a reality to which conservatives must adapt.

Yes, the double-standard is real. There is no more dramatic expression of it than the contrast between the coverage received by the Tea Parties of 2009 and 2010 and the Occupy protest movement of late 2011.

The one protest movement was peaceful, and its chief effect on the national commentariat was to inspire deep concern about the uncivil tone of the political conversation. The other movement, which routinely featured serious violence, inspired the national press to worry about the problem of income inequality.

Tea Partiers got together here and there beginning in 2009. They held rallies and confronted lawmakers—sometimes rudely but always peacefully. It was what one would expect to see when Americans become more involved in the political process. The worst anyone could say was that some Tea Partiers—perhaps unwisely—made a big show of exercising their right to carry guns openly, including at a protest outside one presidential town hall.[2]

But despite the guns, no one was ever shot at a Tea Party event, which is more than one can say of Occupy. One resident of the Occupy Oakland encampment actually did shoot and kill another.[3] In Cleveland, a group of five men who met at the Occupy protests later plotted a terrorist bombing of a local bridge, in an extremely harebrained scheme to disrupt the nation's unjust economy.[4]

Occupiers in Oakland set fires in the streets and tried to take over empty buildings. Some of the anarchists among them, to the cheers of the surrounding crowds, shattered the glass of a bank storefront. To mixed cheers and boos, they completely laid waste to a Whole Foods store, with all of the action caught on tape and posted to YouTube.[5]

Occupiers threw bottles and rocks at policemen. At their flagship protest in downtown Manhattan, Occupiers taunted frightened schoolchildren as young as four (perhaps they deserved it, their parents were probably stockbrokers) with chants of, "Follow those kids!"[6] Enough rapes and sexual assaults at Occupy protest sites were reported to police that Occupy leaders had to organize safe zones. But not all of them were so conscientious—Occupy leaders in Baltimore circulated a memo subtly encouraging their comrades to avoid involving the police in such cases.[7]

Those small businesses unfortunate enough to be near Occupy encampments were crushed as their customers were scared away for months—and that's if their bathrooms weren't also destroyed.[8] And needless to say, the public spaces that communities had previously enjoyed were utterly defiled. The $400,000 stimulus-paid renovation of McPherson Square, across the street from the *Washington*

Examiner's offices, was completely undone. (The grass there, newly laid just before the Occupiers arrived, had to be replanted and had only just finished recovering as this book went to print.)

These tales of the lawlessness and mayhem that was Occupy were covered by local reporters, who are far less likely to let ideology get in the way of good stories that directly affect their communities. They seldom made their way into the national news media, which was far more preoccupied with sympathetic coverage of the problem of income inequality.

And here, in the realm of ideas, was another way—probably the most important way—the coverage set back the truth.

The Occupiers' mission was to bring "income inequality" into the public's consciousness. It was a phenomenon allegedly attributable to greed, banks, and big business. It supposedly even caused the economic downturn. The argument goes that people who lacked means took out massive loans because they had studied IRS income tables and learned that others were making much more than they were. As a result, they quickly found themselves unable to make their payments, thus setting off the chain reaction that led eventually to financial collapse.

For the most part, instead of questioning this doubtful hypothesis, the media responded to the protests with an outpouring of stories on what a big problem income inequality is.

PBS *NewsHour*'s Jeffrey Brown solemnly announced that according to a new report from the Congressional Budget Office, "household income grew by 275 percent between 1979 and 2007 for the wealthiest 1 percent of the population.... By contrast, the bottom fifth of the population saw its income grow by just 18 percent."[9]

A boisterous-as-always Ed Schultz mused that "the income inequality in this country is so great, if it doesn't stop, we will never turn this around."[10]

"Since the mid-1980s the top 10 percent of Americans have increased their share at the expense of everybody else," wrote Eduardo Porter in the *New York Times*.[11]

"The West today is somewhat corrupt, uneasy about its own value system," observed Zbigniew Brezinski, former National Security Adviser to President Carter, on MSNBC's *Morning Joe*. "The United States is becoming rapidly one of the most socially unjust societies in the world.... The income disparities between the rich and the poor in the United States are now the most severe in the world." To which journalist Andrea Mitchell replied, "The disparities between rich and poor in this country are the underlying tension."[12]

"Income inequality is getting worse," said *U.S. News and World Report*'s chief economics correspondent Rick Newman "The data clearly shows that the haves have more, and have nots have less. We have a dysfunctional situation in Washington. Nobody is doing a thing about these problems."[13]

Set aside for a moment the question of whether inequality matters—especially if all income groups have been making gains in both income and standard of living. Reporters should have investigated the data rather than parroting the conclusions of the activists. Was income inequality really ballooning? Was it concentrating wealth permanently in a few hands? Was this really a permanent structural problem in our economy...or was it in large part statistical spin?

The numbers the media typically cited in flogging income inequality ignored both taxes and government transfer payments. This makes income inequality look much larger in any given year, but does it really help anyone get at the truth? If you're willing to omit $700 billion in annual Social Security income, for example, you can remove millions of middle-income retirees from the middle class, which you can then claim is shrinking as the population ages and a greater share takes retirement. By omitting taxes and government transfers—the government's current involvement in leveling the economic playing field—one merely creates a circular argument for more government leveling of incomes. Presidents Bush and Obama both signed measures that reduced the share of the tax burden borne by the lowest income earners, and both said they were effectively giving workers a pay raise. Whose agenda is served if the effects of their policies are ignored?

The data behind the media coverage also nearly always looked back to 1979 as the benchmark year. That's where that "275 percent...for the wealthiest 1 percent" number comes from. But the choice of 1979 is a bit of a trick. As Alan Reynolds of the Cato Institute has been pointing out tirelessly over the last decade, the 1980s changes to the tax code—which made the top individual tax rate lower than the corporate rate—suddenly caused wealthy taxpayers to report a much larger amount of business income on individual rather than corporate tax returns.[14] According to the Congressional Budget Office, the average business income on the tax returns of the top "one percent" rose by 150 percent (adjusted for inflation) between 1979 and 1988, a good share of which only occurred on paper.

Finally—and more understandably—many of the media reports centered on income data that the Congressional Budget Office released in October 2011. This data ended in 2007—the last year of the housing bubble and the one with the most dramatic inequality. The Congressional Budget Office released another report in July 2012 with data through 2009. This later report, which includes taxes and transfers, tells a very different story about income inequality. Naturally, it didn't receive nearly as much attention as its predecessor.[15]

With taxes and government transfer payments taken into account, the economic downturn that began in 2008 has erased whatever increase there was in income inequality over the previous 20 years—and then some.

As this chart shows, by 2009—two years before the first Occupy protestor threw a glass bottle at a policeman in the name of economic justice—America's income distribution was already more egalitarian than it had been in 1988.

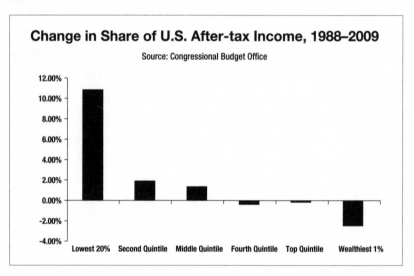

How did this happen? Did all of that income inequality just go away? Or had the problem been somewhat exaggerated in the first place, because of a protest movement that captured the imaginations of a lot of journalists and commentators?

There is plenty of income disparity, to be sure, and it might have even widened again somewhat since 2009. But none of the charts here depict a fundamentally unfair society where income is rapidly concentrating at the top. How much of the dire commentary on the emerging American plutocracy was just so much hype?

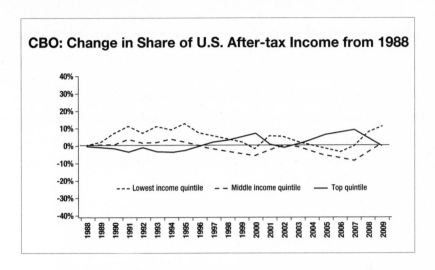

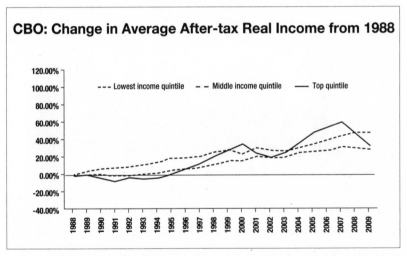

Most of the rhetoric and coverage of income inequality focused on the "one percent." But even here, the story is not quite what the media made it out to be.

According to the CBO data, only about one-third of the top one percent's income is from salaries—in fact, the average salary in that group fell between 2000 and 2007, and has since fallen further. The reason the top one percent surged to its 2007 peak—the alarming point at which the growth of income inequality seemed irreversible—is that its capital gains income tripled between 2002 and 2007. But then it fell back even further—by 73 percent—between 2007 and 2009.

In other words, a large share of "one percent" earners last decade got there not by earning large salaries or even business income, but by selling an historically large amount of assets into a bull market *en masse*. What do you suppose people were selling for big money between 2004 and 2007?

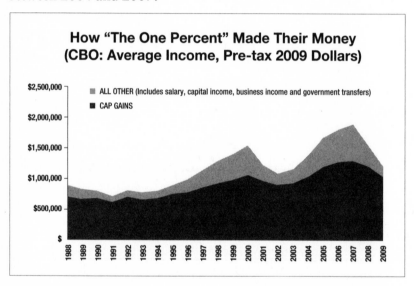

How "The One Percent" Made Their Money (CBO: Average Income, Pre-tax 2009 Dollars)

There's no way to know for sure from these data, but how much of the surge in income inequality last decade simply resulted from sales of homes at bubble prices? People talk about income inequality as a long-term structural problem. But how many Baby Boomers made the one percent and even pulled up its average income for a single year last decade, just by earning a relatively decent salary and selling a nearly-paid-off home in an expensive city at or near the market peak?[16]

In 2007, at the height of "income inequality," the one percent had an average income 115 percent above their 1988 level (which is more precise but less dramatic than the exaggerated 275 percent number cited above). They stopped selling assets when the markets tanked (or sold them for much less) and had a total 2009 income that was only 35 percent above their 1988 level. The bottom three quintiles' average income had made greater gains on aggregate over the same period. A substantial amount of the "income inequality" craze boils down to the timing of those sales.

The media readily fell prey to one other major fallacy about income inequality, upon which the entire problem may in fact rest: namely, the idea that the top one percent of earning households is an actual group of people who just rake it in, year after year. In fact, as our home-selling Baby Boomer demonstrates, earners are moving targets who shift between income groups.

There is a lot of commentary on income mobility, but according to the last government study on the topic, it had not decreased noticeably, not even during the "Unequal 2000s." According to a 2007 report from the U.S. Treasury Department—a report that was available online in late 2011 for anyone who wanted to read it—less than half of the households who were among the top 1 percent of 1996 were there again in 2005.[17] Meanwhile, 58 percent of households from the bottom 20 percent in 1996 had moved to higher income brackets by 2005. More than half of those upward movers had risen into the middle income quintile or higher. Finally, the report noted that with appropriate statistical adjustments, income mobility between 1996 and 2005 was about the same as it had been between 1979 and 1988.[18]

This 2007 Treasury study, released four years before the first Occupy protestor called for revolution, pokes a huge hole in the popular media hypothesis of 2011 that income inequality was rapidly and permanently concentrating wealth in a few hands while the masses labored on with little hope of improving their situation.

Just as people enter the top income percentiles, so do they enter at the bottom.[19] The five U.S. states with the greatest income gaps between rich and poor, according to the liberal Center on Budget and Policy Priorities, are New Mexico, Arizona, California, Georgia, and New York.[20] What these states have in common are large populations of undocumented immigrants, who tend to hold low-income jobs. (Georgia had the fastest-growing "unauthorized" population last decade, according to the Department of Homeland Security.[21]) How much of income inequality is a reflection of undocumented workers who replenished the ranks at the bottom of America's wage scale last decade, anchoring the average pay for the lower quintiles? Is this another contributor to the hype? The rich get richer, while the poor…come to America?

Adapting to the Double Standard

It would be difficult to mock the media's endless coverage of income inequality as much as it deserves. But it illustrates my point: Conservatives make fools of themselves often enough, and they get nailed for it. Liberals make fools of themselves, and the media glorifies their folly.

This is not intended as a lament or complaint so much as a call to action. The conservative press that does exist—and is flourishing in some places—is not enough to counteract the overwhelming liberal dominance of the mainstream media, nor will it be any time soon. So for the time being, conservatives must accept the double standard to which they will be subjected. From the tale of Occupy, learn that you will always need to show more discipline than the other side in how you think about and discuss ideas, as well as in how you conduct yourself in public.

And don't just resign yourself to the media double standard, *take advantage of it.* It is a gift—an opportunity to become better and stronger, to articulate the ideas that will win people over in the increasingly educated and data-driven society that America is becoming.

Familiarize yourself with the other side's strongest arguments. Do not be satisfied with destroying straw men. Make sure you understand and agree with the rationale for the positions you take. Where possible, look at the hard data, or at least read bloggers and writers who do on a regular basis. If you're interested in the political debate—and if you're reading this book, that means you are—take time every now and then to peruse those boring white papers that the major think tanks produce. Go out of your way to avoid living down to the media's stereotype of conservatives as ill-informed, prejudiced yahoos.

This advice may seem obvious, but you'd be surprised how far people have risen in conservative politics without heeding it. Republican Congresswoman Michele Bachmann of Minnesota, for example, has no fewer than two law degrees (a J.D. and an LL.M), so she should know something about argumentation from fact. Yet, in her eagerness to attack an opponent during a presidential primary debate, she pulled out a "somebody-told-me" anecdote to cast doubt on the safety of vaccinations. She barely won reelection to her safe Republican seat in Minnesota last year.

And we saw earlier how Todd Akin, a sitting congressman who won the nomination for Senate in Missouri last year, attempted to pass himself off as an expert in reproductive biology, with devastating results for his candidacy and his party's fortunes.

Conservatives should not only avoid imitating these examples, but more important, be cautious about whom they support in politics. Stop nominating people who habitually speak without bothering to think or to study issues. The media cannot destroy conservatism, but bad conservatives can.

No, Todd Akin was not the choice of the big conservative groups in Missouri in 2012. But he did persuade just enough Republican primary voters to trust him as the true conservative—and the rest is history. Nor was Akin the first unworthy candidate to win this way. Delaware's Christine O'Donnell comes to mind especially as someone whose nomination—won with the vocal support of some prominent conservatives who should have known better—set back the movement significantly. Thanks to her especially, but also others like Nevada's Sharron Angle, the mere mention of a Tea Party candidate brings titters from the mainstream media and gives moderates an opportunity to scold and claim that conservatives cannot win.

Mind you, I don't believe this is true of all or even most of the "Tea Party" candidates who have won nominations and gone on to lose elections. In my opinion, it is worth nominating conservatives, even sometimes where it increases the chances of losing an election, because if they are good candidates, their arguments can still seep into the electorate. But there must be basic standards for candidates. You wouldn't hire a lawyer who knows nothing about the law, just because he tells you he's the most conservative lawyer. Why would you help nominate a mush-head, just because he or she claims to be—or even is—the most conservative mush-head?

Whomever you support in politics, know in advance that the media will chew him up and spit him out the first chance they get. They did it to Mitt Romney, who, for all of his faults, was not the least talented politician ever to run for president. Bear that in mind when you throw your support behind someone. Make sure it's someone who will hold up reasonably well under the coming assault.

The Battle of Ideas

One can never completely disregard media bias or its effect on the American populace. It does make a difference. But conservatives are too likely to view the media as all-powerful. They aren't. The big newspapers lay their pages out one at a time, just like anyone else. There is no shortage of examples where the truth has won out in spite of misguided, ideologically driven media coverage.

President Reagan's defeat of the Soviet Union resulted almost entirely from policies that drew scorn and contempt from the nation's most prominent television news anchors and commentators and newspaper editorial boards. Reagan ignored the prevailing wisdom, which had settled for a permanently tense global conflict with an aggressive enemy who thrived on lies, repression, terrorism, and fear. This conventional wisdom lost, and Reagan won.

Welfare reform became possible—and President Clinton was forced to sign it after vetoing it twice—because social science reality had caught up with liberal good intentions. By 1996, the documented acceleration of permanent dependency and family decline due to perverse welfare incentives had made the case for reform overwhelming. It finally happened over dire media predictions of people dying in the street *en masse*, none of which ever came to pass.

The liberalization of gun laws in many states over the last decade has failed to produce the epidemic of violence that so many sneering pundits predicted. In Washington, D.C., once a hopelessly violent dystopia, the murder rate has plummeted, uninterrupted, right through the 2008 Supreme Court ruling that struck down its total ban on citizen gun ownership. As for the flood of guns that was going to hit the city's streets, D.C. police now recover fewer, not more, firearms per year than they did in any of the five years preceding the decision.[22]

Michigan—the home state of organized labor—has finally adopted a right-to-work law. This welcome development follows the public-sector union reforms in Wisconsin, which have created a model for the nation. Governor Scott Walker, by standing up to the biggest special interest in his state, has suddenly freed up millions of dollars in local governments' budgets and ended the death spiral that underfunded public pensions once threatened. Not only that, but the voters ratified his actions by retaining him in a recall election and by electing a Republican majority in the state legislature in 2012.

Breakthroughs in medical science have mightily strengthened the argument for restricting abortion—an issue where the media are especially far to the left of the American mainstream. Four-dimensional ultrasounds and dramatic incidents during fetal surgeries have proven beyond dispute the humanity of the unborn. Science has debunked the notion that abortion is some kind of harmless medical procedure that merely removes "tissue," so that even those advocating the pro-choice position on abortion must now accept that it takes a human life. This is one reason Gallup's polling shows fewer people embracing that position, regardless of how they vote.[23]

And the number and rate of abortions in America is falling, with the largest one-year decline in a decade occurring in 2009. The federal Centers for Disease Control and Prevention (CDC) attributes this in part to pro-life laws passed in the states, requiring parental involvement in minors' decisions and establishing basic health and safety standards for abortion facilities.[24]

The biggest conservative policy advance at this moment is taking place in education. It is being wholeheartedly embraced by many people who would never call themselves conservatives, and who have probably never voted Republican in their lives. The quality of public schooling in America—especially for the poor and minorities in big cities—had simply become so terrible in the grip of the unionized education bureaucracy that the problem could no longer be ignored.

And again, Washington, D.C.—arguably America's most liberal jurisdiction and for years the nation's worst in terms of public education—has become the focal point of sweeping conservative education reforms.[25] Public charter schools, which set their own curricula and operate outside union control, have grown in the last decade to the point that they now educate 43 percent of all D.C. public school students. That number is only growing as parents vote with their feet and overwhelmingly choose charter schools over the traditional public system. In the neighborhoods where charter schools directly compete with government-run public schools, they easily outperform them in reading and math proficiency, and especially in four-year high school graduation rates.[26] The District's unionized, government-run schools are withering on the vine, closing by the dozen. And as conservative education policy wonks had always predicted, competition is working—the old public school system is making a belated (though also encouraging) effort to reform itself before it disappears altogether.

So no, conservative arguments aren't just as good as liberal ones. They're better, no matter how little weight the mainstream media give them. They have proven themselves in real life, both in the past and all over America today. Yes, even in the Obama era.

In the wake of Mitt Romney's defeat in the 2012 election, there was an abundance of talk about how the Republican Party is dead—doomed by demographic changes. I agree that Republicans must take those changes seriously, but I also believe that it is nonsense to take such a fatalistic view. It assumes that, even as an increasingly educated and information-savvy American populace takes on the challenges of the future, it will continue to be dominated by identity politics rooted far in the past.

In the heat of the campaign moment, it sometimes feels as though ideas have lost their place altogether in our politics. It seems like they have been superseded by truly unimportant things like "gaffes" and "memes" and personal controversies—or by ephemeral notions of which party, as President Obama once put it, is a friend or enemy, and which one the voters in this group or another should reward or punish.

But that feeling is just the effect of media frivolity. In reality, and especially in the long run, ideas matter far more. Good ideas will ultimately trump any apparent structural advantage that either political party enjoys today. That includes demographic changes, gerrymandering, and even the structural advantage that the Left enjoys thanks to liberal dominance of the media.

I don't have a fix for liberal media bias. But even if it can't be fixed—so what? No amount of slanted coverage—whether it comes in the form of subtle bias or the overt propaganda from 2012 that was designed to drive fear and resentment—can forever overcome the soundness of a truly good idea.

The party that wins the future will be the one that makes the strongest appeal to Americans' minds and imaginations. That side will win over enough people of all colors, races, and religious creeds to put its ideas into effect.

If conservatives equip themselves now for that battle—if they pass along carefully studied and strong arguments to the next generation—then the liberal media will not be able to stop them from changing America for the better. It has never stopped them before.

ACKNOWLEDGMENTS

I would like to thank Daniel Allott, without whose help this book could never have been written, nor would. I would like to thank my wife, who had to live like a single mother for the last few weeks of its assembly. To my Aunt Mel and my cousins, who took my family in for a weekend while I worked—thank you!

Thanks to Stephen Smith at the *Washington Examiner* for his moral support. Thanks also to the entire *Examiner* opinion team, to Mark Tapscott and Tim Carney.

Thanks to Brent Bozell and the good people of the Media Research Center, who follow and catalog media bias year-round. It's never hard for anyone to find examples of it quickly, thanks to your work. And thank you to the entire team at Regnery—especially to Harry Crocker, Maria Ruhl, Marji Ross, and Jeff Carneal.

NOTES

Chapter 1

1. "How Slatesters Voted," *Slate*, November 7, 2000, http://www.slate.com/articles/briefing/articles/2000/11/how_slatesters_voted.html.

2. "Slate Votes: At this magazine, it's Kerry by a landslide!" *Slate*, October 26, 2004, http://www.slate.com/articles/news_and_politics/politics/2004/10/slate_votes.html.

3. "Slate Votes: Obama wins this magazine in a rout," *Slate*, October 28, 2008, http://www.slate.com/articles/news_and_politics/politics/2008/10/slate_votes.4.html.

4. "Slate Votes: Obama wins our staff," *Slate*, November 5, 2012. Available online at http://www.slate.com/articles/news_and_politics/politics/2012/11/slate_votes_2012_why_we_chose_obama_over_romney_stein_and_johnson.single.html.

5. S. Robert Lichter and Stanley Rothman, *The Media Elites*, (Hastings House, 1990). Cited in the Media Research Center report, "Media Bias 101: Twenty Years of Research Showing: What Journalists Think, How Journalists Vote, What the Public Thinks about the Media, What

Journalists Say about Media Bias." Available online at: http://archive.mrc. org/static/uploads/MediaBias101.pdf.

6. Stanley Rothman and Amy E. Black, "Media and business elites: still in conflict?" *The Public Interest*, Spring 2001, 72–86. Available online at the *National Affairs* website: http://www.nationalaffairs.com/doclib/200807 10_20011436mediaandbusinesselitesstillinconflictstanleyrothman.pdf.

7. William Tate, "Putting Money Where Mouths Are: Media Donations Favor Dems 100–1," *Investor's Business Daily*, July 23, 2008.

8. Cited in Tim Groseclose, *Left Turn: How Liberal Media Bias Distorts the American Mind* (St. Martin's Press, 2011), 106.

9. Bernard Goldberg, *Bias: A CBS Insider Exposes How the Media Distort the News* (Regnery, 2001), 122.

10. Stephen Dinan, "Reporters applaud Obama's slam on Romney's wealth," *Washington Times*, October 17, 2012.

11. Noel Sheppard of NewsBusters posted the video and transcript of this exchange on October 16, 2012 at: http://newsbusters.org/blogs/noel-sheppard/2012/10/17/obama-voter-tells-fox-focus-group-presidents-been-bullsh-ting-public.

12. Bernard Goldberg, *A Slobbering Love Affair: The True (and Pathetic) Story of the Torrid Romance between Barack Obama and the Mainstream Media* (Regnery, 2009), 108–9.

13. Michael Dobbs and Howard Kurtz, "Expert Cited by CBS Says He Didn't Authenticate Papers," *Washington Post*, September 14, 2004, http://www. washingtonpost.com/wp-dyn/articles/A18982-2004Sep13.html.

14. Jim Acosta, "Romney aide loses cool, curses at press in Poland," CNN Politics, July 31, 2012, http://politicalticker.blogs.cnn.com/2012/07/31/ romney-aide-loses-cool-curses-at-press-in-poland/.

15. "Low Markes for the 2012 Election: Voters Pessimistic about Partisan Cooperation," Pew Research Center for the People & the Press, November 15, 2012, http://www.people-press.org/2012/11/15/low-marks-for-the-2012-election/.

16. Winning the Media Campaign 2012," Pew Research Center's Project for Excellence in Journalism, November 2, 2012, Journalism.org.

17. Barack Obama, quoted in Saira Anees, "Obama Explains Why Some Small Town Pennsylvanians Are 'Bitter,'" Political Punch, ABC News, April 11, 2008.

18. Margaret Hartmann, "Obama Fund-raiser Sparks 'Total Insanity,' Wine Shortages in West Village," *New York* magazine, June 15, 2012.

Chapter 2

1. Bernard Goldberg, *Bias: A CBS Insider Exposes How the Media Distort the News* (Harper Perennial, 2003), 124.
2. Barack Obama, *The Audacity of Hope*, (Random House, Inc., 2006), 124.
3. John F. Harris, on CNN's *Reliable Sources*, January 13, 2008, transcript available here, http://transcripts.cnn.com/TRANSCRIPTS/0801/13/rs.01.html.
4. Bernard Goldberg, *A Slobbering Love Affair: The True (And Pathetic) Story of the Torrid Romance Between Barack Obama and the Mainstream Media* (Regnery, 2009), 5.
5. Ibid., 8.
6. Mark Morford, "Is Obama an enlightened being? / Spiritual wise ones say: This sure ain't no ordinary politician. You buying it?" *San Francisco Chronicle*, June 6, 2008, http://www.sfgate.com/entertainment/morford/article/Is-Obama-an-enlightened-being-Spiritual-wise-2544395.php. Emphasis in original.
7. "Chris Matthews: 'I Felt This Thrill Going Up My Leg' As Obama Spoke," *Huffington Post*, March 28, 2008; Brad Wilmouth, "Matthews: Obama Speech Caused 'Thrill Going Up My Leg,'" NewsBusters, February 13, 2008.
8. Deborah Howell, "An Obama Tilt in Campaign Coverage," *Washington Post*, November 9, 2008, http://www.washingtonpost.com/wp-dyn/content/article/2008/11/07/AR2008110702895.html.
9. Brent Baker, "Tapper Acknowledges in 2008 the Media 'Tilted on the Scales a Little Bit' for Obama," NewsBusters, January 8, 2012, http://newsbusters.org/blogs/brent-baker/2012/01/08/tapper-acknowledges-2008-media-tilted-scales-little-bit-obama.
10. John Heilemann "Newt's Base," *New York* magazine, January 27, 2012, http://nymag.com/news/politics/powergrid/newt-gingrich-2012-2/.
11. Bernard Goldberg, *A Slobbering Love Affair: The True (And Pathetic) Story of the Torrid Romance Between Barack Obama and the Mainstream Media* (Regnery, 2009), 19.
12. "Winning the Media Campaign 2012," Pew Research Center's Project for Excellence in Journalism, November 2, 2012, http://www.journalism.org/analysis_report/winning_media_campaign_2012.
13. Jeff Jacoby, "Some of Kerry's biggest fans are in the press," *Boston Globe*, August 23, 2004, http://www.boston.com/news/globe/editorial_opinion/oped/articles/2004/08/24/some_of_kerrys_biggest_fans_are_in_the_press/?page=full.
14. Matt Bai, "Working for the Working-Class Vote," *New York Times*, October 15, 2012.
15. Kyle Drennen, "Newsweek's Evan Thomas: Obama Is 'Sort of God,'" NewsBusters, June 5, 2009.

16. "Special Edition: Still Slobbering Over Barack Obama," vol. 25, no. 14, Media Research Center, July 9, 2012, http://www.mrc.org/node/40542.

17. Paul Bedard, "Mainstream scream: Author compares Obama to Jefferson," *Washington Examiner*, November 12, 2012, http://washingtonexaminer.com/mainstream-scream-author-compares-obama-to-jefferson/article/2513256#.UMZa3-TAevg.

18. Matt Hadro, "CNN's Piers Morgan: 'A Lot of Things Are Just Perfect About Barack Obama,'" NewsBusters, December 6, 2011.

19. "Special Edition: Still Slobbering Over Barack Obama," Media Research Center, July 9, 2012.

20. Andrew Sullivan, "Why Are Obama's Critics So Dumb," *Newsweek*, January 23, 2012.

21. "Matthews: Obama Has 'Never Done Anything Wrong,' A 'Perfect Husband,'" Real Clear Politics Video, July 17, 2012., http://www.realclearpolitics.com/video/2012/07/17/chris_matthews_obama_has_never_done_anything_wrong_a_perfect_husband.html

22. Howard Fineman, "Obama Gets Osama: Goodbye Vietnam," *Huffington Post*, May 2, 2011, http://www.huffingtonpost.com/2011/05/02/goodbye-vietnam-finally_n_856416.html.

23. Paul Bedard, "Mainstream scream: NBC Rock Center in 'awe' of Obama," *Washington Examiner*, May 7, 2012, http://washingtonexaminer.com/mainstream-scream-nbc-rock-center-in-awe-of-obama/article/583126#.UMZn—TAevg.

24. Amy Chozick, "Donations by Media Companies Tilt Heavily to Obama," *New York Times*, August 22, 2012, http://mediadecoder.blogs.nytimes.com/2012/08/22/donations-by-media-companies-tilt-heavily-to-obama/.

25. Ibid.

26. Ibid.

27. Jim Rutenberg, "Prominent journalists join Obama team," *New York Times*, February 3, 2009, http://www.nytimes.com/2009/02/03/world/americas/03iht-journalists.1.19890938.html.

28. Ibid.

29. Paul Bedard, "Record 19 reporters, media execs join Team Obama," *Washington Examiner*, February 17, 2012, http://washingtonexaminer.com/record-19-reporters-media-execs-join-team-obama/article/1130971#.UMZuseTAevg.

30. Barack Obama, *The Audacity of Hope* (Random House, Inc., 2006), 10.

31. Ibid., 121.

32. Amy Chozick, "Obama Is an Avid Reader, and Critic, of the News," *New York Times*, August 7, 2012, http://www.nytimes.com/2012/08/08/us/politics/obama-is-an-avid-reader-and-critic-of-news-media-coverage.html?pagewanted=all.

33. Ibid.

34. Jodi Kantor, *The Obamas* (Little, Brown and Company, 2012), 157.

35. Ibid.

36. Byron Tau, "Obama plays media critic: Reporters have 'all got opinions,'" Politico, August 14, 2012, http://www.politico.com/politico44/2012/08/obama-plays-media-critic-reporters-all-have-opinions-132119.html.

37. Chozick, "Obama Is an Avid Reader, and Critic, of the News."

38. Josh Gerstein, "President Obama's muddy transparency record," Politico, March 5, 2012.

39. James Ball, "Obama administration struggles to live up to its own transparency promise, Post analysis shows," *Washington Post*, August 3, 2012.

40. Ibid.

41. Sharon Theimer, "Promises, Promises: A closed meeting on openness," Associated Press, December 6, 2009.

42. Ibid.

43. Ball, "Obama administration struggles to live up to its own transparency promise, Post analysis shows."

44. Gerstein, "President Obama's muddy transparency record."

45. Erik Schatzker, "Mark Pittman, Reporter who Challenged Fed Secrecy, Dies at 52," Bloomberg News, November 30, 2012. Ball, "Obama administration struggles to live up to its own transparency promise, Post analysis shows."

46. Jake Tapper, "Citing Space Constraints, Obama Campaign Kicks Off the Plane Reporters from Newspapers Whose Coverage it Doesn't Like," ABC News, October 31, 2008, http://abcnews.go.com/blogs/politics/2008/10/citing-space-co/.

47. Bernard Goldberg, A *Slobbering Love Affair: The True (And Pathetic) Story of the Torrid Romance Between Barack Obama and the Mainstream Media* (Regnery, 2009), 117–18.

48. Michael Scherer, "Calling 'Em Out: The White House Takes on the Press," *Time*, October 8, 2009, http://www.time.com/time/magazine/article/0,9171,1929220,00.html.

49. Matthew Felling, "Democrats Dismiss Fox News Debate," CBS News, May 31, 2007, http://www.cbsnews.com/8301-500486_162-2870925-500486.html.

50. "Obama: Quit Listening to Rush Limbaugh if You Want to Get Things Done," *New York Post*, January 23, 2009.

51. Mike Allen, "Fox 'not really news,' says Axelrod," Politico, October 18, 2009, http://www.politico.com/news/stories/1009/28417.html.

52. Ibid.

53. "Interview With White House Communications Director; Obama Wins Nobel Peace Prize," CNN, October 11, 2009, transcript available online at http://transcripts.cnn.com/TRANSCRIPTS/0910/11/rs.01.html.

54. Brian Stelter, "Fox's Volley With Obama Intensifying," *New York Times*, October 11, 2009, http://www.nytimes.com/2009/10/12/business/media/12fox.html?pagewanted=all.

55. Mary Katharine Ham, "Escalation: White House Tries to Exclude Fox From Press Pool Interview," *Weekly Standard*, October 22, 2009, http://www.weeklystandard.com/weblogs/TWSFP/2009/10/escalation_white_house_tries_t.asp.

56. Dana Milbank, "Obama's disregard for media reaches new heights at nuclear summit," *Washington Post*, April 14, 2010, http://www.washingtonpost.com/wp-dyn/content/article/2010/04/13/AR2010041303067.html.

57. Daniel Halper, "Mark Halperin: 'The Media Is Very Susceptible to Doing What the Obama Campaign Wants,'" *Weekly Standard*, August 18, 2012, http://www.weeklystandard.com/blogs/mark-halperin-media-very-susceptible-doing-what-obama-campaign-wants_650208.html.

58. Arthur S. Brisbane, "A Hard Look at the President," *New York Times*, April 21, 2012, http://www.nytimes.com/2012/04/22/opinion/sunday/a-hard-look-at-the-president.html.

59. Ibid.

60. Howard Fineman, "Barack Obama Floating Like A Butterfly: Countdown Day 43," *Huffington Post*, September 24, 2012.

61. Ibid.

62. Fred Barnes, "Obama's Boys on the Bus," *Weekly Standard*, vol. 18, no. 5, October 15, 2012.

63. Noreen Malone, "Barack Obama Is Turning the Oval Office Into a Man Cave," *New Republic*, November 30, 2012, http://www.tnr.com/blog/plank/110613/barack-obama-gradually-turning-the-oval-office-man-cave#.

64. Bill Simmons, "B.S. Report Transcript: Barack Obama," ESPN.com, March 1, 2012, http://www.grantland.com/blog/the-triangle/post/_/id/18690/b-s-report-transcript-barack-obama.

65. David Brooks, "The ESPN Man," *New York Times*, May 14, 2012, http://www.nytimes.com/2012/05/15/opinion/brooks-the-espn-man.html?_r=0.

66. "Barack Obama at 'First Four,'" Associated Press, November 30, 2012.

67. Tim Graham, "ESPN Host Oozes Over Obama's 'Smart,' 'Insightful' 'Regular Guy' Sports Talk on Tebow," NewsBusters, August 3, 2012.

68. John Clayton, "5 things to know about NFL ref deal: Despite replacement referee madness, the league will survive," ESPN.com, September 26, 2012, espn.go.com/nfl/story/_/id/8429894/5-things-know-nfl-referee-deal.

69. Michael David Smith, "President Obama weighs in on NFL's referee lockout," NBC Sports, September 25, 2012, http://profootballtalk. nbcsports.com/2012/09/25/president-obama-weighs-in-on-nfls-referee-lockout/.

70. Alex Kantrowitz, "Some Gamers Angered By Obama Ads in Madden," *Forbes*, October 3, 2012, http://www.forbes.com/sites/ alexkantrowitz/2012/10/03/some-gamers-angered-by-obama-ads-in-madden/.

71. Ian Thomsen, "Obama's victory gives basketball another term in the spotlight," *Sports Illustrated*, November 7, 2012, http://sportsillustrated. cnn.com/2012/writers/ian_thomsen/11/07/president-obama-basketball/ index.html.

72. Tim Groseclose, *Left Turn: How Liberal Media Bias Distorts the American Mind* (St. Martin's Griffin, 2011), 109, 118.

73. Ibid., 109.

74. John Tierney, "Finding Biases on the Bus," *New York Times*, August 1, 2004, http://www.nytimes.com/2004/08/01/politics/campaign/01points. html.

75. Jeffrey M. Jones, "In U.S., Nearly Half Identify as Economically Conservative," Gallup, May 25, 2012, http://www.gallup.com/ poll/154889/nearly-half-identify-economically-conservative.aspx.

76. "State of the News Media 2008," Pew Research Center for the People and the Press, Project for Excellence in Journalism.

77. Tim Groseclose, *Left Turn: How Liberal Media Bias Distorts the American Mind* (St. Martin's Griffin, 2011), Preface, ix.

78. Ibid., 1.

79. Ibid.

80. Ibid., 21.

81. Ibid., 2.

82. "51% Expect Most Reporters To Help Obama; 9% Predict Most Will Help Romney," Rasmussen Reports, August, 15, 2012, http://www. rasmussenreports.com/public_content/politics/general_politics/ august_2012/51_expect_most_reporters_to_help_obama_9_predict_ most_will_help_romney.

83. Ibid.

84. "Most Voters Say News Media Wants Obama to Win," Pew Research Center, October 22, 2008, http://www.people-press.org/2008/10/22/most-voters-say-news-media-wants-obama-to-win/.

85. Scott Whitlock, "MSNBC's Chris Jansing: 'Parallels' Between Lincoln and Reelected Obama Are 'Fascinating,'" NewsBusters, November 12, 2012, http://newsbusters.org/blogs/scott-whitlock/2012/11/12/msnbcs-chris-jansing-parallels-between-lincoln-and-reelected-obama-a.

86.   Carrie Budoff Brown and Josh Gerstein, "Hard questions await President Obama at news conference," Politico, November 14, 2012, http://www.politico.com/news/stories/1112/83813.html.

87.   "President Obama's First Re-Election Press Conference (Transcript)," ABC News, November 14, 2012, http://abcnews.go.com/Politics/OTUS/transcript-obama-press-conference/story?id=17719993#.UMdeDOTAevg.

Chapter 3

1.   According to exit polling, only 23 percent blamed Obama for the current economic situation, whereas a combined 65 percent blamed either George W. Bush or "Wall Street bankers."

2.   Henry Blodget, "Here's The Chart That Might Get Obama Fired..." Business Insider, August 9, 2012, http://www.businessinsider.com/chart-obama-unemployment-2012-8-v.

3.   M. J. Lee, "Barack Obama: Clean energy will deliver the 'jobs of the future,'" Politico, May 7, 2011, http://www.politico.com/news/stories/0511/54492.html#ixzz2D74Rl624.

4.   Kendra Marr, "Obama: 'Jobs of the future' in Mich." Politico, July 15, 2010, http://www.politico.com/news/stories/0710/39803.html.

5.   Barack Obama, "Remarks by the President at Town Hall—Elkhart, Indiana," WhiteHouse.gov, February 9, 2009, http://www.whitehouse.gov/the-press-office/remarks-president-town-hall-elkhart-indiana.

6.   M. Alex Johnson, "Obama touts 'New Foundation' for growth," MSNBC.com, April 29, 2009, http://www.msnbc.msn.com/id/30472370/ns/politics-white_house/t/obama-touts-new-foundation-growth/#.UMZ6eYb4Imh.

7.   "The Low-Wage Recovery and Growing Inequality," NELP, August 2012, study is available online at http://www.nelp.org/page/-/Job_Creation/LowWageRecovery2012.pdf?nocdn=1. Note, however, that this study uses a different time frame for the recovery—beginning in January 2010 and running through March 2012.

8.   Bureau of Labor Statistics (BLS.gov) data search, series CES0500000013.

9.   Sentier Research, "Household Income Trends Series," August 2012, http://www.sentierresearch.com/pressreleases/Sentier_Household_Income_Trends_Press_Release_August2012_09_25_12.pdf.

10.   Julie Jargon, Louise Radnofsky, and Alexandra Berzon, "Health-Care Law Spurs a Shift to Part-Time Workers," Wall Street Journal, November 4, 2012, http://online.wsj.com/article/SB10001424052970204707104578094941709047834.html.

11.   Kaiser Family Foundation, "Family Health Premiums Rise 4 Percent to Average $15,745 in 2012, National Benchmark Employer Survey Finds," www.kff.org/insurance/ehbs091112nr.cfm.

12. Fred Lucas, "Three SEIU Locals—Including Chicago Chapter—Waived From Obamacare Requirement," CNSNews, January 24, 2011, cnsnews. com/news/article/three-seiu-locals-including-chicago-chapter-waived-obamacare-requirement.

13. Mary Niederberger, "Health care law brings double dose of trouble for CCAC part-time profs," *Pittsburgh Post-Gazette*, November 19, 2012, http://www.post-gazette.com/stories/local/neighborhoods-city/health-care-law-brings-double-dose-of-trouble-for-ccac-part-time-profs-662697/.

14. Ibid.

15. "Remarks by the President in Holland, Michigan on Investing in Clean Energy," Whitehouse.gov, July 15, 2010, http://www.whitehouse.gov/the-press-office/remarks-president-holland-michigan-investing-clean-energy.

16. Ken Kolker, "Volt no jolt: LG Chem employees idle: Factory has yet to ship out a single battery," WOODTV.com, October 19, 2012, www.woodtv.com/dpp/news/target_8/Volt-no-jolt-LG-Chem-employees-idle.

17. "Remarks of President Barack Obama," Saturday, July 3, 2010 Weekly Address, Washington, DC, http://www.whitehouse.gov/the-press-office/weekly-address-president-obama-touts-nearly-2-billion-new-investments-help-build-a-.

18. Ira Boudway, "The 5 Million Green Jobs That Weren't," *Bloomberg Businessweek*, October 11, 2012, www.businessweek.com/articles/2012-10-11/the-5-million-green-jobs-that-werent.

19. U.S. Department of Labor, Office of Inspector General, Office of Audit: "Recovery Act: Green Jobs Program Reports Limited Success in Meeting Employment and Retention Goals as of June 30, 2012," October 25, 2012, http://www.oig.dol.gov/public/reports/oa/2013/18-13-001-03-390.pdf.

20. "The Department of Energy's Disastrous Management of Loan Guarantee Programs," Staff Report: U.S. House of Representatives, 112th Congress, March 20, 2012, http://oversight.house.gov/wp-content/uploads/2012/03/FINAL-DOE-Loan-Guarantees-Report.pdf.

21. To the extent that the ties were even reported, it was nearly always as a "Republicans claim this" story. See, for example, Jonathan Easley, "RNC hits Obama on ties between top donors, Energy Dept. officials," *The Hill*, July 18, 2012, thehill.com/blogs/e2-wire/e2-wire/238605-rnc-hits-obama-on-ties-between-donors-energy-officials.

22. Ashe Schow, "President Obama's Taxpayer-Backed Green Energy Failures," The Foundry, Heritage Foundation, October 18, 2012, http://blog.heritage.org/2012/10/18/president-obamas-taxpayer-backed-green-energy-failures/.

23. Ronald Bailey, "Obama Calls Opponents of Renewable Energy Subsidies 'Flat Earthers'—What Does That Make Him?" Hit & Run blog, Reason. com, March 22, 2012, http://reason.com/blog/2012/03/22/obama-calls-opponents-of-renewable-energ.

24. Matthew L. Wald, "Solar Firm Aided by Federal Loans Shuts Doors," *New York Times*, August 31, 2011, http://www.nytimes.com/2011/09/01/business/energy-environment/solyndra-solar-firm-aided-by-federal-loans-shuts-doors.html?pagewanted=all.

25. James Pethokoukis, "November Jobs Report: Another nasty, 'new normal' month for US workers," AEI Ideas blog, December 7, 2012.

26. Ibid.

27. Congressional Budget Office, "Social Security Disability Insurance: Participation Trends and Their Fiscal Implications," July 22, 2010, http://www.cbo.gov/sites/default/files/cbofiles/ftpdocs/116xx/doc11673/07-22-ssdisabilityins_brief.pdf.

28. John Merline, "5.4 Million Join Disability Rolls Under Obama," *Investor's Business Daily*, April 20, 2012, http://news.investors.com/business/042012-608418-ssdi-disability-rolls-skyrocket-under-obama.htm?p=full&fromcampaign=1.

29. Calculation based on current payment data from the Social Security Administration and net job creation data from the Bureau of Labor Statistics.

30. U.S. Department of Agriculture, http://www.fns.usda.gov/fns/data.htm.

31. "Quotes from Obama speech to Democratic convention," Associated Press, September 7, 2012, www.boston.com/news/politics/2012/president/candidates/obama/2012/09/07/quotes-from-obama-speech-democratic-convention/iwxHRB3pRmdPtGgDVsYvgN/story.html.

32. Tom Cohen and Alan Silverleib, "Senate Republicans reject Obama call to end 'big oil' tax breaks," CNN, March 29, 2012, http://www.cnn.com/2012/03/29/politics/oil-subsidies/index.html

33. "U.S. Oil Production Up, But On Whose Lands?" Institute for Energy Research, September 24, 2012, http://www.instituteforenergyresearch.org/2012/09/24/u-s-oil-production-up-but-on-whose-lands-2/.

34. Figures available online from EIA at http://www.eia.gov/naturalgas/data.cfm#production.

35. "U.S. Oil Production Up, But On Whose Lands?"

36. "Local Area Unemployment Statistics," U.S. Depart of Labor, Bureau of Labor Statistics, last modified November 20, 2012, http://www.bls.gov/web/laus/laumstrk.htm; see also "North Dakota's Unemployment Rate 2.4% for October, Job Service North Dakota, November 20, 2012, http://jobsnd.com/news/2581.

37. Roberta Rampton, "As unconventional U.S. oil, gas boom, so do jobs: report," Reuters, Octobert 23, 2012, http://www.reuters.com/article/2012/10/23/us-usa-oil-economy-idUSBRE89M05Y20121023.

38. IHS Global, "America's New Energy Future: The Unconventional Oil and Gas Revolution and the US Economy," October 2012.

39. "Our experience with shale gas, our experience with natural gas, shows us that the payoffs on these public investments don't always come right away." Barack Obama, "Remarks by the President in State of the Union Address," WhiteHouse.gov, January 24, 2012, http://www.whitehouse.gov/the-press-office/2012/01/24/remarks-president-state-union-address.

40. For fifty years, the Federal Motor Carrier Safety Administration exempted truckers who haul water and sand to and from drilling sites from certain rules about how many hours they can spend on the job—mostly because they typically spend many hours a day waiting on drilling sites. The Obama administration lifted the exemption in July 2012. For more on the rule change and pushback by Congress, see Jill Dunn, "New oilfield exemption guidance requested," Overdrive online, August 16, 2012, http://www.overdriveonline.com/house-members-rescind-oilfield-exemption-guidance/.

41. Ben Wolfgang, "Fracking industry keeps eye on Obama," *Washington Times*, November 22, 2012, http://www.washingtontimes.com/news/2012/nov/22/fracking-industry-keeps-eye-on-obama/?page=all.

42. Calculation comes to 26.2 percent, based on Bureau of Labor Statistics Current Employment Statistics program data on non-farm employment for all fifty states. Indiana, which became a right-to-work state in 2012, is included among non-right-to-work states in this calculation through February 2012, and as a right-to-work state for the period afterward.

43. Thomas J. Holmes, "The Effect of State Policies on the Location of Manufacturing: Evidence from State Borders," *Journal of Political Economy* (University of Chicago) 106 (1998): 667.

44. James Sherk, "What Unions Do: How Labor Unions Affect Jobs and the Economy," Heritage Foundation Backgrounder, May 21, 2009, www.heritage.org/research/reports/2009/05/what-unions-do-how-labor-unions-affect-jobs-and-the-economy#_ftn24.

45. Eric Pryne, "Boeing to fight NLRB complaint on 787 South Carolina plant," *Seattle Times*, April 20, 2011, http://seattletimes.com/html/businesstechnology/2014824566_charleston21.html.

46. "U.S. port strike ends," Lloyd's Loading List, December 5, 2012, www.lloydsloadinglist.com/freight-directory/news/us-port-strike-ends/20018009440.htm?source=ezine&utm_source=Lloyd's+Loading+List+Daily+News+Bulletin&utm_campaign=9db9e6eaeb-LLL_5_Dec12_5_2012&utm_medium=email#.UMlBfobhd3h.

47.   Shikha Dalmia, "Indiana Leads the Right-to-Work Charge," Reason.com, Feb. 7, 2012, http://www.reason.com/archives/2012/02/07/indiana-leads-the-right-to-work-charge.

48.   For one example of the many stories on foreign automakers setting up plants in the South, see, "In Tough Economy, Toyota Plant Brings Mississippi Jobs," Associated Press, November 7, 2011, http://www.dailyfinance.com/2011/11/07/in-tough-economy-toyota-plant-brings-miss-jobs/.

Chapter 4

1.   Igor Volsky, "O'Reilly Challenges Rick Santorum On Opposition To Birth Control," ThinkProgress, January 5, 2012, http://thinkprogress.org/health/2012/01/05/398191/oreilly-challenges-rick-santorum-on-opposition-to-birth-control/?mobile=nc.

2.   Scott Whitlock, "Chris Matthews: Rick Santorum Wants a 'Theocracy' That Will 'Trump' the Constitution," NewsBusters, January 5, 2012, http://newsbusters.org/blogs/scott-whitlock/2012/01/05/chris-matthews-rick-santorum-wants-theocracy-will-trump-constitution.

3.   Felicia Sonmez, "2012 ABC/Yahoo!/WMUR New Hampshire GOP primary debate (Transcript)," *Washington Post*, January 7, 2012, http://www.washingtonpost.com/blogs/post-politics/post/2012-abcyahoowmur-new-hampshire-gop-primary-debate-transcript/2012/01/07/gIQAk2AAiP_blog.html.

4.   Clarence Page, "Whose reproductive freedom?" *Chicago Tribune*, January 15, 2012.

5.   Anna Holmes, "GOP candidates revive issue of birth control," *Washington Post*, January 13, 2012.

6.   Kyle Drennen, "NBC Keeps Up Drumbeat of GOP 'War Against Women's Health,'" NewsBusters, March 21, 2012, http://newsbusters.org/blogs/kyle-drennen/2012/03/21/nbc-keeps-drumbeat-gop-war-against-womens-health.

7.   Ibid.

8.   Women Members of the House GOP Caucus, "2010: The Year of GOP Women," Politico, December 15, 2010, http://www.politico.com/news/stories/1210/46374.html.

9.   Gallup Daily: "Obama Job Approval," Gallup Politics, http://www.gallup.com/poll/113980/gallup-daily-obama-job-approval.aspx.

10.   Jessica Yellin and Kevin Bohn, "Pelosi: There is a war on women," CNN, April 7, 2011, http://politicalticker.blogs.cnn.com/2011/04/07/pelosi-there-is-a-war-on-women/.

11.   Jeannie DeAngelis, "Loving women to death," *Daily Caller*, May 27, 2011, http://dailycaller.com/2011/05/27/loving-women-to-death/.

12. "The War on Women," *New York Times,* February 25, 2011, http://www.nytimes.com/2011/02/26/opinion/26sat1.html.

13. Ruth Marcus, "Side effects of the GOP's war on family planning," *Washington Post,* February 23, 2011 http://www.washingtonpost.com/wp-dyn/content/article/2011/02/22/AR2011022205350.html.

14. Deirdre Walsh, "House passes bill on abortion funding," CNN, October 13, 2011, http://www.cnn.com/2011/10/13/politics/health-bill-abortion/index.html.

15. Matthew Balan, "MSNBC's Bashir: 'Misogynist' GOP Wants to 'Let Women Die'" NewsBusters, October 13, 2012, http://newsbusters.org/blogs/matthew-balan/2011/10/13/msnbcs-bashir-misogynist-gop-want-let-women-die.

16. Sally Quinn, "Paul Ryan's Abortion Problem," On Faith, *Washington Post,* August 30, 2012, http://www.washingtonpost.com/blogs/on-faith/post/paul-ryans-abortion-problem/2012/08/30/1e1d34b2-f2d0-11e1-adc6-87dfa8eff430_blog.html.

17. Laura Bassett and Amanda Terkel, "House Democrats Walk Out Of One-Sided Hearing On Contraception, Calling It An 'Autocratic Regime,'" *Huffington Post,* February 16, 2012, http://www.huffingtonpost.com/2012/02/16/contraception-hearing-house-democrats-walk-out_n_1281730.html.

18. Ibid.

19. Ibid.

20. Seung Min Kim, "Pelosi blasts dearth of women at contraceptives hearing: 'Duh,'" Politico, February 16, 2012, http://www.politico.com/blogs/on-congress/2012/02/pelosi-blasts-lack-of-women-at-contraceptives-hearing-114712.html.

21. Elizabeth Flock, "Birth control hearing on Capitol Hill had mostly male panel of witnesses (photo)," *Washington Post,* February 16, 2012, http://www.washingtonpost.com/blogs/blogpost/post/birth-control-hearing-on-capitol-hill-had-all-male-panel-of-witnesses/2012/02/16/gIQA6BM5HR_blog.html.

22. Edward Schumacher-Matos, "The Contraception Mandate: Where Are The Women?" National Public Radio, February 17, 2012, http://www.npr.org/blogs/ombudsman/2012/02/17/147060538/the-contraception-mandate-where-are-the-women.

23. Sunlen Miller, "Birth-Control Hearing Was 'Like Stepping Into a Time Machine,'" the Note, ABC News, February 17, 2012, http://abcnews.go.com/blogs/politics/2012/02/birth-control-hearing-was-like-stepping-into-a-time-machine/.

24. Alex Alvarez, "David Axelrod: Maher Doesn't Play Same Role As GOP 'De Facto Boss' Rush Limbaugh," mediaite.com, March 15, 2012, http://www.mediaite.com/tv/david-axelrod-to-erin-burnett-maher-doesnt-play-same-role-as-gop-de-facto-boss-rush-limbaugh/.

25. Matt Hadro, "CNN Rolls Out the Red Carpet for Sandra Fluke," Media Research Center, March 13, 2012, http://www.mrc.org/node/39415.

26. Matt Hadro, "Breaking News? CNN Listens to Sandra Fluke Explain Why She's Voting for Obama," NewsBusters, June 14, 2012, http://newsbusters.org/blogs/matt-hadro/2012/06/14/breaking-news-cnn-listens-sandra-fluke-explain-why-shes-voting-obama.

27. Brent Baker, "CNN to Fluke: Does Limbaugh Calling You a 'Slut' Reflect 'Romney and the Republican Party?'" NewsBusters, September 4, 2012, http://newsbusters.org/blogs/brent-baker/2012/09/04/cnn-fluke-does-limbaugh-calling-you-slut-reflect-romney-and-republican-.

28. Kate Pickert, "Who Should Be TIME's Person of the Year 2012?" *Time*, November 26, 2012, http://www.time.com/time/specials/packages/article/0,28804,2128881_2128882_2129176,00.html.

29. "Nevada newspaper covers Obama surrogate talk attended by 10 people," Foxnews.com, October 22, 2012, http://www.foxnews.com/politics/2012/10/22/obama-surrogate-sandra-fluke-speaks-to-crowd-10-in-nevada/.

30. Frank Newport, "U.S. Voters' Top Election Issues Don't Include Birth Control," Gallup, April 2, 2012, http://www.gallup.com/poll/153689/voters-top-election-issues-don-include-birth-control.aspx.

31. Mary Agnes Carey, "Poll: 42% Of Women Take Action In Response To Contraception Debates," Kaiser Health News, May 31, 2012, http://capsules.kaiserhealthnews.org/index.php/2012/05/poll-42-of-women-take-action-in-response-to-contraception-debates/.

32. "With Voters Focused on Economy, Obama Lead Narrows," Pew Research Center, April, 17, 2012, http://pewresearch.org/pubs/2246/mitt-romney-barack-obama-jobs-swing-voters-gop-primaries-gender-gap.

33. Ibid.

34. Ibid.

35. "Importance of Issues: Economy Continues to Top List of Most Important Issues," Rasmussen Reports, September 21, 2012, http://www.rasmussenreports.com/public_content/politics/mood_of_america/importance_of_issues.

36. John Eligon and Michael Schwirtz, "Senate Candidate Provokes Ire with 'Legitimate Rape' Comment" *New York Times*, August 19, 2012, http://www.nytimes.com/2012/08/20/us/politics/todd-akin-provokes-ire-with-legitimate-rape-comment.html.

37. Eugene Robinson, "Todd Akin's comment brings 'war on women' back to prominence," *Washington Post*, August 20, 2012, http://articles.washingtonpost.com/2012-08-20/opinions/35493942_1_akin-medicaid-funds-end-pregnancies.

38. Ibid.

39. Manu Raju, "Richard Mourdock under fire for rape remarks," Politico, October 23, 2012, http://www.politico.com/blogs/on-congress/2012/10/richard-mourdock-under-fire-for-rape-remarks-139411.html.

40. Emily Friedman, "Romney Hasn't Asked Mourdock to Pull Ad After Rape Comments," ABC News, October 24, 2012.

41. Jonathan Weisman, "Rape Remark Jolts a Senate Race, and the Presidential One, Too," *New York Times*, October 25, 2012.

42. "Akin's comments reignite war on women," NBC News, August 20, 2012, http://video.msnbc.msn.com/jansing-and-co/48725939#48725939.

43. Matt Hadro, "Piers Morgan Says Todd Akin Controversy Supports Narrative That GOP Is 'Anti-Women,'" NewsBusters, August 30, 2012, http://newsbusters.org/blogs/matt-hadro/2012/08/30/piers-morgan-says-todd-akin-controversy-supports-narrative-gop-anti-wome.

44. Brent Baker, "Stephanopoulos Hypes 'Political Hurricane from Todd Akin' While Barbour Scolds Schieffer for His Akin Obsession," NewsBusters, August 26, 2012, http://newsbusters.org/blogs/brent-baker/2012/08/26/stephanopolous-hypes-political-hurricane-todd-akin-while-barbour-scolds.

45. Ibid.

46. Scott Whitlock, "Media Obsession With Akin Hits Overdrive: 96 Minutes in Just Three and a Half Days," NewsBusters, August 23, 2012, http://newsbusters.org/blogs/scott-whitlock/2012/08/23/network-obsession-over-akin-hits-overdrive-96-minutes-just-over-three.

47. Timothy P. Carney, "The 'redefine rape' lie," *Washington Examiner*, September 5, 2012, http://washingtonexaminer.com/the-redefine-rape-lie/article/2507131#.UMe1-uTAevg.

48. Nick Baumann, "Todd Akin, Paul Ryan, and Redefining Rape," *Mother Jones*, August 19, 2012, http://www.motherjones.com/mojo/2012/08/todd-akin-paul-ryan-redefining-rape.

49. Caitlin Dickson, "Republicans Redefine Rape, Outraging Liberals," *Atlantic*, January 28, 2011, http://www.theatlanticwire.com/politics/2011/01/republicans-redefine-rape-outraging-liberals/17879/#.

50. Chris Good, "Todd Akin's Rape Comments May Have Repercussions for Mitt Romney," ABC News, August 20, 2012, http://abcnews.go.com/Politics/OTUS/todd-akins-rape-comments-repercussions-mitt-romney/story?id=17042555#.UMe4nuTAevg.

51. John McCormack, "Democrats Falsely Claim Paul Ryan Tried to 'Redefine Rape,'" *Weekly Standard*, August 22, 2012, http://www.weeklystandard.com/blogs/did-democrat-joe-donnelly-try-redefine-rape_650502.html.

52. Caroline May, "GOP spots immigration, marriage fraud and funding loopholes in Violence Against Women Act," *Daily Caller*, March 17, 2012, http://dailycaller.com/2012/03/17/the-problems-with-the-violence-against-women-act/.

53. Jonathan Weisman, "Senate Votes to Reauthorize Domestic Violence Act," *New York Times*, April 26, 2012.

54. Robert Pear, "House Vote Sets Up Battle on Domestic Violence Bill," *New York Times*, May 16, 2012.

55. Ibid.

56. Ibid.

57. Ibid.

58. Weisman, "Senate Votes to Reauthorize Domestic Violence Act."

59. David Weigel, "The 'War on Women' is Over," *Slate*, April 12, 2012, http://www.slate.com/articles/news_and_politics/politics/2012/04/hilary_rosen_ann_romney_the_birth_adolescence_and_death_of_the_democrats_war_on_women_talking_point_.html.

60. "The War on Women," *New York Times*, February 25, 2011.

61. Ibid.

62. "Super Tuesday," *New York Times*, March 6, 2012.

63. Andrew Rosenthal, "Grand, Old and Anti-Woman," *New York Times*, March 15, 2012.

64. "The Campaign Against Women," *New York Times*, May 19, 2012.

65. "Republicans vs. Women," *New York Times*, July 29, 2012.

66. Katharine Q. Seelye, "Another Senate Race Seizes on Rape Remark," *New York Times*, August 22, 2012.

67. "Mr. Romney's Version of Equal Rights," *New York Times*, October 17, 2012.

68. "If Roe v. Wade Goes," *New York Times*, October 15, 2012.

69. Nicholas Kristof, "How Romney Would Treat Women," *New York Times*, November 3, 2012.

70. Ibid.

71. Ibid.

72. Chris Cillizza, "Rick Santorum doesn't have a (Republican) woman problem," the Fix, *Washington Post*, March 20, 2012, http://www.washingtonpost.com/blogs/the-fix/post/rick-santorum-doesnt-have-a-republican-woman-problem/2012/03/20/gIQAVMtZPS_blog.html.

73. John Cassidy, "Why Republican Women Vote for Santorum," *New Yorker*, March 14, 2012, http://www.newyorker.com/online/blogs/johncassidy/2012/03/why-republican-women-vote-for-santorum.html.

74. Lydia Saad, "In U.S., Nonreligious, Postgrads Are Highly 'Pro-Choice,'" Gallup Politics, May 29, 2012, http://www.gallup.com/poll/154946/non-christians-postgrads-highly-pro-choice.aspx.

75. "Men and Women Hold Similar Views on the Legality of Abortion," Public Agenda, July 2002.

76. Ibid.

77. Joel Roberts, "Poll: Strong Support For Abortion Rights," CBS News, February 11, 2009, http://www.cbsnews.com/2100-500160_162-537570.html.

78. "Second Presidential Debate Full Transcript," ABC News, October 17, 2012, http://abcnews.go.com/Politics/OTUS/2012-presidential-debate-full-transcript-oct-16/story?id=17493848#.UMe_QOTAevg.

79. "Women Still Lag Behind Men in Pay, Report Says," CBS News, March 2, 2011, http://www.cbsnews.com/2100-500202_162-20038250.html.

80. Lynn Sweet, "Women still earn less than men: New Obama White House report on Status of Women," *Chicago Sun-Times*, March 1, 2011, http://blogs.suntimes.com/sweet/2011/03/women_earn.html.

81. Diana Furchtgott-Roth, "White House, Women's Wages, Myths," RealClearMarkets, March 3, 2011, http://www.realclearmarkets.com/articles/2011/03/03/white_house_womens_wages_myths_98895.html.

82. Diana Furchtgott-Roth, "Bogus AAUW study perpetuates wage gap myths," *Washington Examiner*, October 30, 2012, http://washingtonexaminer.com/bogus-aauw-study-perpetuates-wage-gap-myths/article/2512127#.UMfAMuTAevg.

83. Ibid.

84. Ibid.

85. CNN Exit Poll results, http://www.cnn.com/election/2012/results/race/president#exit-polls.

86. "Women's Votes Decisive in 2012 Presidential Race," Center for American Women and Politics at Rutgers University, November 7, 2012.

87. Kathleen Geier, "Democratic women defend Susan Rice, call out her critics' sexism, racism and mediocrity," *Washington Monthly*, November 17, 2012.

88. Dewayne Wickham, "McCain uses Susan Rice to relaunch war on women," *USA Today*, November 19, 2012.

Chapter 5

1. Jay Leno, *Tonight Show*, NBC, November 15, 2012.

2. Cnn.com, Election Results, Exit Polls, http://www.cnn.com/ELECTION/2004/pages/results/states/US/P/00/epolls.0.html.

3. *Washington Post*, "Exit polls 2012: How the vote has shifted."

4. Chris Cillizza and Jon Cohen, "President Obama and the white vote? No problem," *Washington Post*, November 8, 2012.

5. "Young voters supported Obama less, but may have mattered more," Pew Research Center, November 26, 2012.

6. Sean Trende, "Case of the Missing White Voters," RealClearPolitics, November 8, 2012.

7. "Chris Mathews: My Job Is To Make Obama Presidency Successful," YouTube, November 7, 2012.

8. Peter Wehner, "Chris Matthews Hero Worships Obama," *Commentary*, May 2, 2012.

9. Scott Whitlock, "Chris Matthews Swoons Again: 'Everything' Obama's Done 'Has Been Good for This Country,'" NewsBusters, March 4, 2011.

10. Ibid.

11. "Matthews: 'Racial Hatred' For Obama Makes Right Want To Get Rid Of Obama," YouTube, October 23, 2012.

12. Rusty Weiss, "Chris Matthews and MSNBC Now Claim the Word 'Chicago' Is Racist," NewsBusters, August 29, 2012.

13. Ibid.

14. Noel Shepherd, "Now Chris Matthews Thinks The Word 'Urban' Is Racist," NewsBusters, November 14, 2012.

15. "President Exit Polls," Election 2012, *New York Times*, http://elections.nytimes.com/2012/results/president/exit-polls.

16. Shepherd, "Now Chris Matthews Thinks The Word 'Urban' Is Racist."

17. Scott Whitlock and Dan Gainer, "MSNBC's Richard Wolffe smears John McCain as a racist," Fox News, November 20, 2012.

18. Ibid.

19. Ibid.

20. Glenn Kessler, "Barack Obama: the 'food-stamp president'?" *Washington Post*, December 8, 2011.

21. Peter Kasperoqicz, "Dem accuses Gingrich of racism with 'food stamp president' comment," *The Hill*, January 23, 2012.

22. "Sheila Jackson-Lee: Newt's Food Stamp Talk Has 'Underlying' Message," RealClearPolitics video, January 18, 2012.

23. Alan Bjerga and Jennifer Oldham, "Gingrich Calling Obama 'Food-Stamp President' Draws Critics," Bloomberg News, January 25, 2012.

24. Kathy Lohr, "Can Expanding Food Stamps Jolt the Economy?" NPR, July 7, 2009.

25. Ibid.

26. "Obama Ag Secretary Vilsack: Food Stamps Are A 'Stimulus,'" RealClearPolitics August 16, 2011, video available herehttp://www.realclearpolitics.com/video/2011/08/16/obama_ag_secretary_vilsack_food_stamps_are_a_stimulus.html.

27. Geoffrey Dickens, "Newt Takes it to Chris Matthews on His 'Racist Thinking,'" NewsBusters, August 27, 2012.

28. Scott Whitlock, "Martin Bashir: Stop Newt Gingrich's Food Stamp Talk Before Someone Gets Killed," NewsBusters, January 6, 2012.

29. Rich Noyes, "Ex-CNN Reporter Slams 'Hateful' Appeals to 'Extreme White Wing' of GOP," MRCTV, January 6, 2012.

30. Jacob Weisberg, "If Obama Loses," *Slate*, August 23, 2008, http://www.slate.com/articles/news_and_politics/the_big_idea/2008/08/if_obama_loses.html.

31. Jonathan Freedland, "The world's verdict will be harsh if the US rejects the man it yearns for," *The Guardian*, September 9, 2008, http://www.guardian.co.uk/commentisfree/2008/sep/10/uselections2008.barackobama.

32. Peter Beinert, "Erasing The Race Factor," *Washington Post*, August 13, 2008, http://www.washingtonpost.com/wp-dyn/content/article/2008/08/12/AR2008081202827.html.

33. Bob Herbert, "Running While Black," *New York Times*, August 2, 2008.

34. Jeffrey Meyer, "ABC's Barbara Walters to Michelle Obama: 'Will Racism be a Part of This Campaign?'" NewsBusters, May 29, 2012, http://newsbusters.org/blogs/jeffrey-meyer/2012/05/29/abcs-barbara-walters-michelle-obama-will-racism-be-part-campaign.

35. Andrew Rosenthal, "Nobody Likes to Talk About It, but It's There," *New York Times*, January 3, 2012.

36. Ibid.

37. Jeffrey Scott Shapiro, "The Treatment of Bush Has Been a Disgrace;" *Wall Street Journal*, November 5, 2008, http://online.wsj.com/article/SB122584386627599251.

38. 911Truth.org, "911 Truth Statement," October 26, 2004, http://www.911truth.org/article.php?story=20041026093059633.

39. Jonathan Chait, "The Real Reason 'You didn't build that' works," *New York* magazine, July 27, 2012, http://nymag.com/daily/intelligencer/2012/07/real-reason-you-didnt-build-that-works.html.

40. "MSNBC's Toure: Mitt Romney Engaged In 'Niggerization' Of Obama," RealClearPolitics Video, August 16, 2012, http://www.realclearpolitics.com/video/2012/08/16/msnbcs_toure_mitt_romney_engaging_in_niggerization_of_obama.html.

41. Ibid.

42. "MSNBC Apologizes To Romney Over KKK Comparison, Says It Was 'Appalling' (VIDEO)," *Huffington Post*, December 15, 2011, http://www.huffingtonpost.com/2011/12/15/msnbc-romney-kkk_n_1150597.html.

43. Kevin Baker, "The Man Who Would Be Ex-President," *Harper's*, October 4, 2012, http://harpers.org/blog/2012/10/the-man-who-would-be-ex-president/.

44. David Jackson, "Obama: Congress should be more like my kids," *USA Today*, June 29, 2011, http://content.usatoday.com/communities/theoval/post/2011/06/obama-congress-should-be-more-like-my-kids/1#.UMjK7OTAevg.

45. Mark Knoller, "President Obama plays 100th round of golf, draws fire from critics," CBS News, June 17, 2012, http://www.cbsnews.com/8301-503544_162-57454890-503544/president-obama-plays-100th-round-of-golf-draws-fire-from-critics/.

46. Nick Gillespie, "MSNBC's Lawrence O'Donnell: Mocking Obama's Golfing is an Attempt to Portray Him as an Oversexed Black Man," *Reason*, August 30, 2012, http://reason.com/blog/2012/08/30/msnbcs-lawrence-odonnell-mocking-obamas.

47. Colbert I. King, "Mitt Romney could be the next Andrew Johnson," *Washington Post*, November 2, 2012, http://articles.washingtonpost.com/2012-11-02/opinions/35503852_1_southern-states-mitt-romney-civil-rights-act.

48. Ethan Magoc, "Many states' voter-ID laws, including Pennsylvania's, appear to have tie to same U.S. group," *Philadelphia Inquirer*, August 14, 2012.

49. National Council of State Legislatures, "Voter Identification Requirements," http://www.ncsl.org/legislatures-elections/elections/voter-id.aspx.

50. Forrest Wickman, "Why Do Many Minorities Lack ID?" *Slate*, August 21, 2012, http://www.slate.com/articles/news_and_politics/explainer/2012/08/voter_id_laws_why_do_minorities_lack_id_to_show_at_the_polls_.html.

51. Rachel Weiner, "Eric Holder calls photo ID laws 'poll taxes,'" *Washington Post*, July 10, 2012, http://www.washingtonpost.com/blogs/the-fix/post/eric-holder-calls-photo-id-laws-poll-taxes/2012/07/10/gJQA9JyPbW_blog.html.

52. "Voter Identification Laws—Washington Post Poll July 7–19, 2012," *Washington Post*, http://www.washingtonpost.com/page/2010-2019/WashingtonPost/2012/08/12/National-Politics/Polling/question_6226.xml?uuid=Nd4PSOTWEeGXOe75nF-yhQ.

53. Noah Rothman, "MSNBC Broadcasts 19 Segments On Voter I.D. This Week, Ignores Poll Showing 74% Support For I.D. Laws," Mediaite.com, August 16, 2012, http://www.mediaite.com/online/msnbc-broadcasts-19-segments-on-voter-i-d-this-week-ignores-poll-showing-74-support-for-i-d-laws/.

54. Jeffrey Meyer, "MSNBC Brings On Democrat John Lewis To Whine That Voter ID Laws Are Racist," NewsBusters, September 18, 2012, http://newsbusters.org/blogs/jeffrey-meyer/2012/09/18/msnbc-brings-democrat-john-lewis-whine-voter-id-laws-are-racist.

55. Todd Huston, "Once Again CNN Fans Flames of Racism in Election Coverage," wizbangblog.com, August 9, 2012.

56. Noah Rothman, "MSNBC Anchor Irresponsibly Frames Question On Voter ID As GOP Advancing A 'Poll Tax,'" Mediaite.com, September 4, 2012.

57. Colleen Jenkins, "Insight: Scant evidence of voter suppression, fraud in states with ID laws," Reuters, November 2, 2012, http://www.reuters.com/article/2012/11/02/us-usa-campaign-voterid-idUSBRE8A10UJ20121102.

58. Government Accountability Office, "Welfare Reform: HHS Should exercise oversight to help ensure TANF work participation is measured consistently across states," August 2005, www.gao.gov/new.items/d05821.pdf.

59. Robert Rector, "Obama Ends Welfare Reform as We Know It, Calls for $12.7 Trillion in New Welfare Spending," The Foundry, Heritage Foundation, July 17, 2012.

60. Ron Fournier, "Why (and How) Romney is Playing the Race Card," National Journal, September 1, 2012, http://www.nationaljournal.com/2012-election/why-and-how-romney-is-playing-the-race-card-20120829.

61. Jeff Zeleny and Jim Rutenberg, "Romney Adopts Harder Message for Last Stretch," New York Times, August 25, 2012.

62. Jack Coleman, "Maddow's Kneejerk Response to Romney's Welfare Reform Ad: It Is 'Dog-Whistle Racism,'" NewsBusters, August 10, 2012, http://newsbusters.org/blogs/jack-coleman/2012/08/10/maddows-kneejerk-response-romneys-welfare-reform-ad-it-dog-whistle-rac.

63. Touré, "How To Read Political Racial Code," Time, September 6, 2012, http://ideas.time.com/2012/09/06/how-to-read-political-racial-code/.

64. Ibid.

65. Ibid.

66. Some parts of this section are a paraphrase of the same editorial I wrote, quoted from directly below: "Obama's defenders cry wolf on racism," Washington Examiner, August 19, 2012.

67. "Obama's defenders cry wolf on racism," Washington Examiner, August 19, 2012.

68. David A. Love, "GOP attacks on Susan Rice make for bad racial optics," The Grio, November 21, 2012.

69. Dan Gainor, "MSNBC Anchor Touré makes shameful attack on McCain," Fox News, November 27, 2012.

70. "The GOP's bizarre attack on Susan Rice," *Washington Post*, November 22, 2012.

71. Ibid.

72. Matt Hadro, "Soledad O'Brien Tees Up Clyburn to Identify Racial Code In GOP Opposition to Susan Rice," NewsBusters, November 20, 2012.

73. Ibid.

74. Brian Montopoli, "Obama Tells Letterman: I Was Black Before the Election,"CBS News, September 21, 2009, http://www.cbsnews.com/8301-503544_162-5327972-503544.html.

Chapter 6

1. Catholic Bishop William Lori made this case in his "Parable of the Kosher Deli," *National Catholic Register*, February 16, 2012, http://www.ncregister.com/daily-news/the-parable-of-the-kosher-deli.

2. "A statement by U.S. Department of Health and Human Services Secretary Kathleen Sebelius," HHS.gov, January 20, 2012, http://www.hhs.gov/news/press/2012pres/01/20120120a.html.

3. "U.S. Bishops Vow to Fight HHS Edict," USCCB website, January 20, 2012, http://www.usccb.org/news/2012/12-012.cfm.

4. Laurie Goodstein, "Obama Shift on Contraception Splits Catholics," *New York Times*, February 14, 2012.

5. "FACT SHEET: Women's Preventive Services and Religious Institutions," whitehouse.gov, February 10, 2012, http://www.whitehouse.gov/the-press-office/2012/02/10/fact-sheet-women-s-preventive-services-and-religious-institutions.

6. Rich Noyes, "How Network News Has Twisted Obama's War on Religion Into a Conservative War Against Women," NewsBusters, February 28, 2012, http://newsbusters.org/blogs/rich-noyes/2012/02/28/how-network-news-has-twisted-obama-s-war-religion-conservative-war-again.

7. Ibid.

8. Louise Radnofsky, "Catholic Bishops Oppose Compromise on Birth-Control Insurance," *Wall Street Journal*, February 12, 2012, http://online.wsj.com/article/SB10001424052970203646004577217181415407806.html.

9. Matthew Balan, "Study: Media Go to Bat for Abortion Giant, Ignore Catholics vs. Obama Controversy," NewsBusters, February 6, 2012, http://newsbusters.org/blogs/matthew-balan/2012/02/06/study-media-go-bat-abortion-giant-ignore-catholics-vs-obama-controver.

10. "Fury Spreads: Catholic Leaders Join MRC Outrage Over Network Silence on Catholics vs. Obama Lawsuit," NewsBusters, May 23, 2012, http://

newsbusters.org/blogs/nb-staff/2012/05/23/fury-spreads-catholic-leaders-join-mrc-outrage-over-network-silence-cathol.

11. "Brent Bozell, "Shameless Bias by Omission," Townhall.com, May 23, 2012, http://townhall.com/columnists/brentbozell/2012/05/23/shameless_bias_by_omission/page/full/.

12. Balan, "Study: Media Go to Bat for Abortion Giant, Ignore Catholics vs. Obama Controversy."

13. Erik Eckholm, "Poll Finds Wide Support for Birth Control Coverage," *New York Times*, March 1, 2012.

14. S.Rept. 4389, 58th Cong., 3d Sess. 2 (1905); 39 Cong. Rec. 3823-24 (1905). Cited in Congressional Research Service, "Recess Appointments: A legal overview."

15. Joel Gehrke, "Obama's DOJ says 'recess' appointment illegal," *Washington Examiner* Beltway Confidential blog, January 4, 2012, http://washingtonexaminer.com/obamas-doj-says-recess-appointment-illegal/article/1042181#.ULp5BIb4Imh.

16. Virginia A. Seitz, "Lawfulness of Recess Appointments During a Recess of the Senate Notwithstanding Periodic Pro Forma Sessions," Memorandum Opinion for the Counsel to the President, January 6, 2012, http://www.justice.gov/olc/2012/pro-forma-sessions-opinion.pdf.

17. "Courts begin hearing legal challenges to Obama recess appointments," Associated Press, November 29, 2012, available on the Washington Post website, http://www.washingtonpost.com/politics/courts-begin-hearing-legal-challenges-to-obamas-recess-appointments/2012/11/29/ec4ff2b0-3a4d-11e2-9258-ac7c78d5c680_story.html.

18. "Obama's justifiable 'power grab' on recess appointments," *Washington Post*, January 5, 2012, http://www.washingtonpost.com/opinions/obamas-justifiable-power-grab-on-recess-appointments/2012/01/05/gIQAColidP_story.html.

19. "Obama's recess appointment challenge," *Los Angeles Times*, January 6, 2012, http://articles.latimes.com/2012/jan/06/opinion/la-ed-recess-20120106.

20. Andrew Rosenthal, "Richard Cordray's Appointment: Was It Justified?" *New York Times*, January 5, 2012, http://takingnote.blogs.nytimes.com/2012/01/05/richard-cordrays-appointment-was-it-justified/.

21. Byron York, "White House recess-appointed Berwick after questions about $49M nonprofit group," *Washington Examiner*, July 6, 2010, http://www.sfexaminer.com/blogs/beltway-confidential/white-house-recess-appointed-berwick-after-questions-about-49m-nonprofit-g.

22. The Federalist, No. 69, "The Real Character of the Executive," *New York Packet*, March 14, 1788. Available online courtesy of the Constitution Society at http://www.constitution.org/fed/federa69.htm#1.

23. James Madison, Letter to Thomas Jefferson, April 2, 1798. (For the sake of clarity, I have taken the liberty of spelling out Madison's original abbreviations.) Available online from the University of Chicago at http://press-pubs.uchicago.edu/founders/documents/a1_8_11s8.html.

24. Terence P. Jeffrey, "Obama's 'Writ' Unleashed War Criminals," CNSNews.com, October 3, 2012, http://cnsnews.com/blog/terence-p-jeffrey/obamas-writ-unleashed-war-criminals.

25. Brian Williams, "Ten minutes to cover the world," *The Daily Nightly*, NBC, http://dailynightly.nbcnews.com/_news/2011/03/29/6370385-ten-minutes-to-cover-the-world.

26. Brent Baker, "In Libya Interview, Sawyer Asks Obama About Praying Like Lincoln and 'How Much Do You Think Kentucky Will Win By?" NewsBusters, March 30, 2011, http://newsbusters.org/blogs/brent-baker/2011/03/30/libya-interview-sawyer-asks-obama-about-praying-lincoln-and-how-much-do.

27. Charlie Savage and Thom Shanker, "At Deadline, U.S. Seeks to Continue War in Libya," *New York Times*, May 12, 2011, http://www.nytimes.com/2011/05/13/world/africa/13powers.html.

28. "Libya and the War Powers Act," *New York Times*, June 16, 2011, http://www.nytimes.com/2011/06/17/opinion/17fri1.html

29. Natasha Lennard, "The Obama/Gitmo Timeline," *Salon*, April 25, 2011, http://www.salon.com/2011/04/25/obama_guantanamo_rhetoric/.

30. "In party platform, Democrats soften on Obama's 2007 promise to close Gitmo," *Daily Caller*, September 4, 2012, http://dailycaller.com/2012/09/04/in-party-platform-democrats-soften-on-obamas-2007-promise-to-close-gitmo/#ixzz2Dx8HR8Q2.

31. "Creating a 'Gitmo North' an Alarming Step, Says ACLU," American Civil Liberties Union, December 15, 2009, http://www.aclu.org/national-security/creating-gitmo-north-alarming-step-says-aclu.

32. Glenn Greenwald, "The Obama GITMO myth," Salon.com, July 23, 2012, http://www.salon.com/2012/07/23/the_obama_gitmo_myth/

33. See, for example, "Lawmakers Spar Over Decision to Transfer Gitmo Detainees to Illinois Prison," Fox News Online, www.foxnews.com/politics/2009/12/14/illinois-prison-house-gitmo-detainees/.

34. Although the original May 22, 2009, letter on Feingold's site was pulled after he lost for reelection and left office in 2011, Greenwald links to a copy published by *The Progressive*, "Feingold to Obama: Preventing Detention 'Likely Unconstitutional,'" May 22, 2009, available at http://www.progressive.org/fein052309.html.

35. "Executive Order 13567—Periodic Review of Individuals Detained at Guantánamo Bay Naval Station Pursuant to the Authorization for Use of Military Force," Whitehouse.gov, March 7, 2011, http://www.whitehouse.

gov/the-press-office/2011/03/07/executive-order-periodic-review-individuals-detained-guant-namo-bay-nava.

36. Steve Coll, "Kill or Capture," *New Yorker*, August 2, 2012, http://www.newyorker.com/online/blogs/comment/2012/08/kill-or-capture.html#ixzz2Dg1vDKVs.

37. Ibid.

38. Jo Becker and Scott Shane, "Secret 'Kill List' Proves a Test of Obama's Principles and Will," *New York Times*, May 29, 2012, http://www.nytimes.com/2012/05/29/world/obamas-leadership-in-war-on-al-qaeda.html?_r=1&pagewanted=all.

39. Ibid.

40. See, for example, Katie Pavlich, *Fast and Furious: Barack Obama's Bloodiest Scandal and Its Shameless Cover-Up* (Regnery, 2012).

41. "Holder Suggests 'Fast and Furious' Guns Will Be Used in Crimes for 'Years to Come,'"Fox News, December 8, 2011, http://www.foxnews.com/politics/2011/12/08/holder-suggests-fast-and-furious-guns-will-be-used-in-crimes-for-years-to-come/.

42. Kim Murphy and Ken Ellingwood, "Mexico demands answers on guns," *Los Angeles Times*, March 11, 2011, http://articles.latimes.com/2011/mar/11/nation/la-naw-mexico-guns-20110311.

43. "Leahy: Bush not involved in attorney firings," Associated Press, November 29, 2007, available online at MSNBC, www.msnbc.msn.com/id/22025702/ns/politics-capitol_hill/t/leahy-bush-not-involved-attorney-firings/.

44. Katie Pavlich, "Fast and Furious: DOJ Wants Executive Privilege Lawsuit Dropped," Townhall.com Tipsheet blog, http://townhall.com/tipsheet/katiepavlich/2012/10/16/fast_and_furious_doj_wants_executive_privilege_lawsuit_dropped.

45. Sharyl Attkisson, "Heads roll after Fast and Furious Investigation," CBS News Online, www.cbsnews.com/8301-201_162-57557358/heads-roll-after-fast-and-furious-investigation/.

Chapter 7

1. Charles Blow, MSNBC's *The Last Word*, July 17 2012, transcript available on MSNBC website, http://www.msnbc.msn.com/id/48224789/ns/msnbc/t/last-word-lawrence-odonnell-tuesday-july/#.UMjhzOTAevg.

2. Brad Wilmouth, "MSNBC's Alter: 'A Lot of People Will Die' If Romney Is Elected," NewsBusters, August 10, 2012, http://newsbusters.org/blogs/brad-wilmouth/2012/08/10/msnbcs-alter-lot-people-will-die-if-romney-elected.

3. Michael Tomasky, "Romney: The Wimp Factor; Is He Just Too Insecure To Be President?" *Newsweek*, July 29, 2012.

4. Brent Baker, "Bob Schieffer Cues Up DNC Chairwoman: 'Is Mitt Romney a Wimp?'" NewsBusters, July 29, 2012, http://newsbusters.org/blogs/brent-baker/2012/07/29/face-nation-showcases-newsweek-s-romney-wimp-cover-cues-wasserman-schul.

5. Ibid.

6. Halimah Abdullah, "Romney debate challenge: High stakes, lowered expectations," CNN, September 28, 2012, http://www.cnn.com/2012/09/28/politics/romney-debate/index.html.

7. "Public has low expectations for Romney in debate," McClatchy, October 2, 2012, http://blogs.mcclatchydc.com/washington/2012/10/public-has-low-expectations-for-romney-in-debate.html.

8. Charles M. Blow, "Don't Mess With Big Bird," New York Times, October 5, 2012, http://www.nytimes.com/2012/10/06/opinion/blow-dont-mess-with-big-bird.html.

9. Alice Hines, "Mitt Romney's Big Bird Attack Threatens Thousands of U.S. Jobs," Huffington Post, October 4, 2012, http://www.huffingtonpost.com/2012/10/04/romney-big-bird-attack-us-jobs_n_1939766.html.

10. Amy Bingham, The Presidential Debate's Biggest Loser: Big Bird." ABC News, October 4, 2012, http://abcnews.go.com/blogs/politics/2012/10/the-presidential-debates-biggest-loser-big-bird/.

11. "Winning the Media Campaign 2012," Pew Research Center's Project for Excellence in Journalism, November 2, 2012, http://www.journalism.org/analysis_report/winning_media_campaign_2012.

12. "The Final Days of the Media Campaign 2012," Pew Research Center's Project for Excellence in Journalism, November 19, 2012, http://www.journalism.org/analysis_report/final_days_media_campaign_2012.

13. "What They Said, Before and After the Attack in Libya," New York Times, September 12, 2012, http://www.nytimes.com/interactive/2012/09/12/us/politics/libya-statements.html.

14. Ibid.

15. "Romney's opportunism," Los Angeles Times, September 13, 2012, http://articles.latimes.com/2012/sep/13/opinion/la-ed-libya-20120913.

16. Philip Klein, "How the media turned Obama's foreign policy bungle into a Romney gaffe," Washington Examiner, September 12, 2012, http://washingtonexaminer.com/how-the-media-turned-obamas-foreign-policy-bungle-into-a-romney-gaffe/article/2507779.

17. "CBS transcript: Obama wouldn't call Benghazi terrorism'" USA Today, www.usatoday.com/story/news/world/2012/11/05/benghazi-attack/1684503/.

18. Jennifer Rubin, "Obama still wrong on Libya; Crowley blows it," Washington Post: Right Turn blog, October 17, 2012.

19. Matt Negrin, "In Memoriam: The Old Obama, Who Wanted to Bring People Together," ABC News, May 23, 2012, http://abcnews.go.com/Politics/OTUS/memoriam-obama-wanted-bring-people/story?id=16407876#.UMjoCOTAevg.

20. Jason McLure, "Romney says he is 'in sync' with Tea Party," Reuters, August 17, 2011, http://www.reuters.com/article/2011/08/17/us-usa-campaign-romney-idUSTRE77E64720110817.

21. Jay Cost, "Morning Jay: Bain Capital and Media Bias," Weekly Standard, July 16, 2012, http://www.weeklystandard.com/blogs/morning-jay-subtle-exercise-media-bias_648608.html.

22. Ibid.

23. Mark Maremont, "Romney at Bain: Big Gains, Some Busts," Wall Street Journal, January 9, 2012, http://online.wsj.com/article/SB10001424052970204331304577140850713493694.html.

24. Andy Sullivan and Greg Roumeliotis, "Special Report: Romney's Steel Skeleton in the Bain Closet," Reuters, January 6, 2012.

25. William D. Cohan, "Bain's 'Creative Destruction' Destroys Lives," Bloomberg News, August 12, 2012.

26. Callum Borchers and Brian MacQuarrie, "Account of Romney's Bain departure has evolved," Boston Globe, July 14, 2012, http://www.bostonglobe.com/metro/2012/07/13/evidence-mounts-mitt-romney-continuing-ties-bain-after/w9vGMpkCKg1GaYdaU8l8GL/story.html.

27. Glenn Kessler, "Mitt Romney and his departure from Bain," Washington Post, July 12, 2012, http://www.washingtonpost.com/blogs/fact-checker/post/mitt-romney-and-his-departure-from-bain/2012/07/12/gJQAASzUfW_blog.html.

28. Dylan Byers, "FactCheck.org: 'Little new' in Globe story," Politico, July 12, 2012, http://www.politico.com/blogs/media/2012/07/factcheckorg-little-new-in-globe-story-128751.html.

29. Dylan Byers, "Globe: 'Evidence mounts' of Bain ties," Politico, July 14, 2012, http://www.politico.com/blogs/media/2012/07/globe-evidence-mounts-of-bain-ties-128939.html.

30. Transcript of The Situation Room, CNN, August, 23, 2012, http://transcripts.cnn.com/TRANSCRIPTS/1208/23/sitroom.01.html.

31. Eugene Robinson, "Romney tour '12—gaffepalooza," Washington Post, July 30, 2012, http://articles.washingtonpost.com/2012-07-30/opinions/35489936_1_romney-tour-mitt-dressage-horse.

32. Hélène Mulholland, "Mitt Romney gets cold reception from UK media after Olympic gaffe," The Guardian, July 27, 2012, http://www.guardian.co.uk/world/blog/2012/jul/27/mitt-romney-uk-media-olympic.

33. Bruce Crumley, "After Gaffe-Filled Foreign Tour, Europe Asks: 'Is Mitt Romney a Loser?'" *Time*, July 31, 2012, http://world.time.com/2012/07/31/after-gaffe-filled-foreign-tour-europe-asks-is-mitt-romney-a-loser/.

34. Julie Hirschfield Davis "Romney's Gaffe Joins Quayle's Potatoe on Gore's Internet,"Bloomberg, July 28, 2012, http://www.bloomberg.com/news/2012-07-27/romney-s-gaffe-joins-quayle-s-potatoe-on-gore-s-internet.html.

35. Jon Swaine and Christopher Hope, "Mitt Romney's Olympics gaffe overshadows visit to London," *The Telegraph*, July 26, 2012, http://www.telegraph.co.uk/news/worldnews/mitt-romney/9431064/Mitt-Romneys-Olympics-gaffe-overshadows-visit-to-London.html.

36. "G4S Olympic failure prompts ministers to 'think again' over outsourcing," BBC News, August 14, 2012, http://www.bbc.co.uk/news/uk-19251772.

37. Erik Wemple, "Media should consider mentioning that Romney was right about Olympic preps," *Washington Post*, July 27, 2012.

38. Scott Whitlock, "Networks That Fawned Over Obama's World Tour Mock Romney's International 'Blunders,'" NewsBusters, August 2, 2012, http://newsbusters.org/blogs/scott-whitlock/2012/08/02/networks-fawned-over-obamas-world-tour-mock-romneys-international-bl.

39. Bill Schneider, "Why Europe Loves Barack Obama," CNN, July 4, 2008, http://www.cnn.com/2008/POLITICS/07/04/obama.europe/.

40. Jonathan Freedland, "US elections: Obama wows Berlin crowd with historic speech," *The Guardian*, July 24, 2008, http://www.guardian.co.uk/global/2008/jul/24/barackobama.uselections2008.

41. Devin Dwyer, "Does Walesa Embrace of Romney Mean Poland Dislikes Obama?" ABC News, June 30, 2012, http://abcnews.go.com/blogs/politics/2012/07/does-walesa-embrace-of-romney-mean-poland-dislikes-obama/.

42. Ibid.

43. Dylan Byers, "Three Counties in Kentucky," Politico, December 4, 2012, http://www.politico.com/blogs/media/2012/12/three-counties-in-kentucky-151076.html.

44. Geoffrey Dickens, "ABC, CBS, NBC Hype Romney Hidden Camera Tape, Bury Obama's 'Redistribution' Clip," NewsBusters, September 21, 2012, http://newsbusters.org/blogs/geoffrey-dickens/2012/09/21/abc-cbs-nbc-hype-romney-hidden-camera-tape-bury-obamas-redistribut.

45. Josh Barro, "Today, Mitt Romney Lost the Election," Bloomberg News, September 17, 2012, http://www.bloomberg.com/news/2012-09-17/today-mitt-romney-lost-the-election.html.

46. "Romney's 47 Percent Bigger than Eastwooding," Visible Measures Blog, September 18, 2012, http://corp.visiblemeasures.com/news-and-events/blog/bid/89715/Romney-s-47-Percent-Bigger-than-Eastwooding.

47. Ben Smith, "Obama on small-town Pa.: Clinging to religion, guns, xenophobia," Politico, April 11, 2008, http://www.politico.com/blogs/bensmith/0408/Obama_on_smalltown_PA_Clinging_religion_guns_xenophobia.html.

48. "Romney's '47 percent' Comments Criticized, But Many Also Say Overcovered," Pew Research Center, October 1, 2012, http://www.people-press.org/2012/10/01/romneys-47-comments-criticized-but-many-also-say-overcovered/.

49. Michael Tomasky. "Convention: Lies and Dog Whistles: Gop: a party dedicated to five ideas, all reprehensible," *Daily Beast*, August 27, 2012, http://www.thedailybeast.com/articles/2012/08/27/convention.html.

50. Kyle Drennen," NBC's Lauer Frets: Is 'Conservative' GOP Convention Reaching Moderates and Women?" NewsBusters, August 30, 2012, http://newsbusters.org/blogs/kyle-drennen/2012/08/30/nbcs-lauer-frets-conservative-gop-convention-reaching-moderates-and-wo.

51. Mark Finkelstein, "Barnicle Blathers: 'What Percentage Of GOP Convention Delegates Are Total Nutcases?'" NewsBusters, August 22, 2011, http://newsbusters.org/blogs/mark-finkelstein/2011/08/22/barnicle-blathers-what-percentage-gop-convention-delegates-are-tot.

52. Clay Waters, "GOP Convention 'Colossal Hoax,' Party 'Trades in Human Horridness,' New York Times Columnists Say," NewsBusters, September 3, 2012, http://newsbusters.org/blogs/clay-waters/2012/09/03/gop-convention-colossal-hoax-party-trades-human-horridness-new-york-tim.

53. Maureen Dowd, "When Cruelty is Cute," *New York Times*, August 14, 2012, http://www.nytimes.com/2012/08/15/opinion/dowd-when-cruelty-is-cute.html.

54. "NBC Anchor Rips GOP Budget: 'Where Is the Empathy?'" Media Research Center, April 16, 2012, http://www.mrc.org/sites/default/files/documents/April162012.pdf.

55. Randy Hall, "The Top 10 Most Outrageous Media Attacks Against Paul Ryan," NewsBusters, August 12, 2012, http://newsbusters.org/blogs/randy-hall/2012/08/12/liberal-journalists-hate-paul-ryan-look-their-top-10-most-outrageous-att.

56. Charles P. Pierce, "Paul Ryan: Murderer of Opportunity, Political Coward, Candidate for Vice President of the United States," *Esquire*, August 11, 2012, http://www.esquire.com/blogs/politics/paul-ryan-romney-vp-pick-11562917.

57. Tim Graham, "Thom Hartmann Calls Rep. Paul Ryan a 'Sociopath,'" NewsBusters, December 19, 2011, http://newsbusters.org/blogs/tim-graham/2011/12/19/thom-hartmann-calls-rep-paul-ryan-sociopath.

58. Philip Rucker, "Mitt Romney's dog-on-the-car-roof story still proves to be his critics' best friend," *Washington Post*, March 14, 2012, http://articles.washingtonpost.com/2012-03-14/news/35450454_1_tagg-romney-romney-first-romney-supporter.

59. Ibid.

60. Sam Stein, "Mitt Romney: I Wouldn't Put Dog On The Roof Again," *Huffington Post*, April 16, 2012, http://www.huffingtonpost.com/2012/04/16/mitt-romney-seamus_n_1429925.html.

61. Rucker, "Mitt Romney's dog-on-the-car-roof story still proves to be his critics' best friend."

62. "First Lady beloved, Seamus a problem for Romney?" Public Policy Polling, March 20, 2012, http://www.publicpolicypolling.com/main/2012/03/first-lady-beloved-seamus-a-problem-for-romney.html.

63. Jason Horowitz, "Mitt Romney's prep school classmates recall pranks, but also troubling incidents," *Washington Post*, May 10, 2012, http://articles.washingtonpost.com/2012-05-10/news/35456919_1_school-with-bleached-blond-hair-mitt-romney-george-romney.

64. Diane Sawyer, ABC's *World News*, May 10.

65. Amy Davidson, "Mitt Romney, Bully," *New Yorker*, May 10, 2012, http://www.newyorker.com/online/blogs/closeread/2012/05/mitt-romney-bully.html.

66. Ashley Parker and Jodi Kantor, "Bullying Story Spurs Apology From Romney" *New York Times*, May 10, 2012, http://www.nytimes.com/2012/05/11/us/politics/years-later-a-prep-school-bullying-case-snares-romney.html.

67. Lydia Saad, "In U.S., 22% Are Hesitant to Support a Mormon in 2012," Gallup, June 20, 2011, http://www.gallup.com/poll/148100/hesitant-support-mormon-2012.aspx.

68. Will Saleton, "Latter-Day Sins," *Slate*, October 20, 2012, http://www.slate.com/articles/news_and_politics/frame_game/2011/10/mitt_romney_s_mormon_cult_controversy_anti_mormonism_is_the_prej.html.

69. "Washington Post-Pew Research Center Poll," October 16, 2011, available on the *Washington Post* website, http://www.washingtonpost.com/wp-srv/politics/polls/postpewpoll_101611.html.

70. Joe Coscarelli, "Charles Blow Is Sorry for Mentioning Mitt Romney's 'Magic Underwear,'" *New York* magazine, February 24, 2012, http://nymag.com/daily/intelligencer/2012/02/charles-blow-mitt-romney-mormon-underwear-twitter.html.

71. "Lawrence O'Donnell: Mormonism Is An 'Invented Religion,'" RealClearPolitics Video, April 4, 2012, http://www.realclearpolitics.com/video/2012/04/04/lawrence_odonnell_mormonism_is_an_invented_religion.html.

72.   "2012 Fox News Exit Polls," Fox News, http://www.foxnews.com/politics/elections/2012-exit-poll.

73.   Gary Langer, "A Draw on the Economy, a Win on Empathy—and the Face of a Changing Nation," ABC News, November 7, 2012, http://abcnews.go.com/blogs/politics/2012/11/a-draw-on-the- economy-a-win-on-empathy-and-the-face-of-a-changing-nation/.

Chapter 8

1.   The 2012 exit polls, like those of elections before them, confirm that a college degree has an almost imperceptible effect on party voting patterns, and in fact makes one just ever so slightly more likely to vote Republican.

2.   "Chris Matthews Unloads On Protester Who Carried Gun To Obama Event," YouTube, August 11, 2009, http://www.youtube.com/watch?v=AYUmCj4yud4.

3.   "Shooting victim is tied to Occupy Oakland," *Los Angeles Times* LA NOW blog, November 13, 2011, latimesblogs.latimes.com/lanow/2011/11/shooting-victim-tied-to-occupy-oakland.html. An accessory to this murder was convicted in November 2012, and the shooter, Norris Terrell, was awaiting trial. Henry K. Lee, "Felon convicted in Occupy Oakland case," *San Francisco Chronicle*, November 30, 2012, http://www.sfgate.com/crime/article/Felon-convicted-in-Occupy-Oakland-case-4082040.php.

4.   John Caniglia, "Would-be bridge bombing suspect Anthony Hayne sentenced to 6 years in prison," *The (Cleveland) Plain Dealer*, November 30, 2012, www.cleveland.com/metro/index.ssf/2012/11/would-be_bridge_bombing_suspec.html.

5.   The video is available online at http://www.youtube.com/watch?feature=player_embedded&v=86XhCwHhwn8 Accessed Dec. 12, 2012.

6.   This ugly incident was reported by the local CBS affiliate, and, from I can tell, barely made it beyond the conservative blogosphere. New York CBS Local, "OWS Protesters Chant 'Follow Those Kids!' As Small Children Try To Go To School On Wall Street," http://newyork.cbslocal.com/2011/11/17/ows-protesters-chant-follow-those-kids-as-small-children-try-to-go-to-school-on-wall-street/.

7.   Peter Hermann, "'Occupy' memo could discourage victims from reporting assaults," *Baltimore Sun*, October 18, 2011, http://articles.baltimoresun.com/2011-10-19/news/bs-md-ci-occupy-baltimore-rape-20111019_1_sexual-assaults-sexual-abuse-report-crimes.

8.   Amber Southerland and Bob Fredericks, "Occupiers terrorize us: eatery," *New York Post*, November 8, 2011, www.nypost.com/p/news/local/manhattan/occupiers_terrorize_us_eatery_o4dKzxi3n03WyJWAJu4AhO?CMP=OTC-rss&FEEDNAME=.

9.   PBS NewsHour For October 26, 2011, transcript "Does U.S. Economic Inequality Have a Good Side?" available on the PBS website, http://www.pbs.org/newshour/bb/business/july-dec11/makingsense_10-26.html.

10.   "The Ed Show for Tuesday, December 6, 2011," transcript on MSNBC website, http://www.msnbc.msn.com/id/45582331/ns/msnbc-the_ed_show/t/ed-show-tuesday-december/.

11.   Eduardo Porter, "Wall Street Protesters Hit the Bull's-Eye," *New York Times*, October 29, 2011, http://www.nytimes.com/2011/10/30/opinion/sunday/wall-street-protesters-hit-the-bulls-eye.html?scp=2&sq=eduardo%20porter&st=cse.

12.   *Morning Joe*, MSNBC, December 2, 2011.

13.   "Your Money," CNN, October 9, 2011.

14.   Alan Reynolds, "Inequality and Taxes," Cato Policy Report, September/October 2008, http://www.cato.org/pubs/policy_report/v30n5/cpr30n5.pdf.

15.   "The Distribution of Household Incomes and Federal Taxes, 2008 and 2009," Congressional Budget Office, July 10, 2012, http://www.cbo.gov/publication/43373.

16.   This is for others to explore, but it would coincide roughly with the sales and price peaks in existing single-family home sales. Sales broke 5.5 million in 2003 and stayed there through 2007, with the peak above 7 million in 2005. The median sale price peaked in 2006 and fell by less than 2 percent in 2007. Data available from the U.S. Census online, "Table 977. Existing One-Family Homes Sold and Prices by Region: 1990 to 2010," and "Table 978. Median Sales Price of Existing One-Family Homes by Selected Metropolitan Area: 2005 and 2010," at http://www.census.gov/compendia/statab/2012/tables/12s0977.pdf.

17.   "Income Mobility in the U.S. from 1996 to 2005," report of the Department of the Treasury, November 13, 2007, typographical revisions—March 2008, http://www.treasury.gov/resource-center/tax-policy/Documents/incomemobilitystudy03-08revise.pdf.

18.   Although the raw numbers show much greater mobility during the Reagan era—a fact that some conservatives have gleefully pointed out—the report puts these numbers in perspective: "The high degree of mobility reported by this (1992) study resulted from several features of the analysis, most importantly the inclusion of taxpayers under age 25, the lack of data on Social Security benefits for older taxpayers, and comparison to the full taxpayer population. When the sample was limited to taxpayers age 25 to 64 and compared to taxpayers in the panel, rather than to all taxpayers aged 25 to 64, the Treasury study showed that 50 percent of the lowest income quintile had moved to a higher quintile after 10 years (between 1979 and 1988)."

19. *Slate*'s Timothy Noah, who wrote a ten-part series on income inequality in 2010 (it was republished in 2011 to honor Occupy) was one of the very few reporters even to acknowledge that immigration and income inequality might have a connection. Of course, his series also concluded that income inequality is basically Republicans' fault, but at least he thought to ask some real questions about the topic. "Did Immigration Create the Great Divergence?" Slate.com, September 7, 2010, http://www.slate.com/articles/news_and_politics/the_great_divergence/features/2010/the_united_states_of_inequality/did_immigration_create_the_great_divergence.html.

20. Elizabeth McNichol, Douglas Hall, David Cooper, and Vincent Palacios, "Pulling Apart: A State-by-State Analysis of Income Trends," Center on Budget and Policy Priorities, November 15, 2012, http://www.cbpp.org/cms/index.cfm?fa=view&id=3860.

21. Michael Hoefer, Nancy Rytina, and Bryan Baker, "Estimates of the Unauthorized Immigrant Population Residing in the United States: January 2011," Population Estimates March 2012, Office of Immigration Statistics Policy Directorate, http://www.dhs.gov/xlibrary/assets/statistics/publications/ois_ill_pe_2011.pdf.

22. "District Crime Data at a Glance," Metropolitan Police Department, the District of Columbia website, http://mpdc.dc.gov/page/district-crime-data-glance.

23. Lydia Saad, "'Pro-Choice' Americans at Record-Low 41%," Gallup, May 23, 2012, http://www.gallup.com/poll/154838/pro-choice-americans-record-low.aspx.

24. Karen Pazol, et al., "Abortion Surveillance—United States, 2009," Surveillance Summaries, November 23, 2012, Centers for Disease Control and Prevention, http://www.cdc.gov/mmwr/preview/mmwrhtml/ss6108a1.htm?s_cid=ss6108a1_w.

25. Frank Newport, "Mississippi Most Conservative State, D.C. Most Liberal," Gallup, February 3, 2012, http://www.gallup.com/poll/152459/mississippi-conservative-state-liberal.aspx.

26. I wrote about this in greater detail in "Looking at charter schools, apples to apples," *Washington Examiner*, November 26, 2012, http://washingtonexaminer.com/looking-at-charter-schools-apples-to-apples/article/2513811.

INDEX